Strategies for Engaging

Young Adult Readers:

A Social Themes Approach

Strategies for Engaging

Young Adult Readers:

A Social Themes Approach

Jacqueline N. Glasgow, Ph.D.

Copyright

Contents
· · · · · · · · · · ·

CD ROM Table of Contents

List of Tables

• • • • • • • • • • • • • •

List of Figures
• • • • • • • • • • • • • •

Overview
• • • • • • • • • • •

Jacqueline N. Glasgow

On January 8, 2002, President George W. Bush signed into law the *No Child Left Behind Act of 2001* (NCLB). This new law represents his education reform plan and contains the most sweeping changes to the Elementary and Secondary Education Act (ESEA) since it was enacted in 1965. It changes the federal role in education by asking America's schools to describe their success in terms of what each student accomplishes. The Act contains the president's four basic education reform principles for public schools: stronger accountability for results, local control and flexibility, expanded options for parents, and an emphasis on effective and proven teaching methods. In summary, this law—in partnership with parents, communities, school leadership, and classroom teachers—is intended to ensure that every child in America receives a good education and that "no child is left behind."

The child most left behind in the English/Language Arts classroom is the one who *chooses not to read*. Interest in reading declines in the middle grades and continues its descent through the high school years. According to Thomas & Moorman (1983), "The student who *can* read but chooses *not to* is probably the most crucial concern confronting our educational institutions today. It is not illiteracy we are combating, but *aliteracy*" (p. 137). Because time spent reading is correlated with competence in reading, students who do not read often lose ground academically even if they were not initially struggling readers (Mullis, Campbell, & Farstrup, 1993). Traditionally, the struggling reader has been viewed as a low achiever. Low-achieving students are said to be "at risk" of school failure (Slavin, 1989). Their school lives are characterized by poor attendance, retention in grade, high dropout rates, and behavior problems. These unsuccessful readers can often be found "hiding out" in classrooms. That is to say, they develop a complex set of coping strategies to avoid reading or being held accountable for reading (Brozo, 1990). These coping behaviors include avoiding eye contact with the teacher, engaging in disruptive classroom behavior, forgetting to bring books to class, and seeking help from friends. Poor self-image also contributes to a sense of helplessness and lack of motivation to make any effort to read. Students who are at-risk in text-related learning situations do not feel competent as readers and display little confidence in their ability to make meaning with texts. They avoid reading at all costs because they believe (rightly or wrongly) that they can't learn with texts successfully (Vacca & Vacca, 1999). Hiding out perpetuates a cycle of failure, ensuring that the unsuccessful reader will remain passive and helpless in text-related learning situations, failing to learn the reading strategies we associate with successful readers. In the end, students who won't read become indistinguishable from those who can't in the English/Language Arts classroom.

In addition to lower cognitive competence and lack of motivation, struggling readers feel socially marginalized (Anderman, 1999). They are often placed in lower-level classes, where they are demoralized and separated from their friends. They feel disrespected and uncomfortable in the school environment. These struggling readers are less eager to form positive relationships in school and are less concerned with close friendships and peer acceptance than higher-achieving students (Anderman, 1999). All of these qualitites point to reader disengagement in text-related learning situations.

As several investigators have shown (see Guthrie & Wigfield, 2000, for a review), these qualities of cognitive competence, motivation, and social interaction are dynamically interrelated. Combined, they refer to *engagement*. Students who are weak in these qualities are disengaged from literacy. Guthrie & Davis (2003) define struggling readers as those who are disengaged from school reading activities. For these students, empowerment only begins as they become engaged in literacy activities. Therefore, the purpose of this book is to provide reading materials and teaching methods that will motivate those students who are disengaged from reading. Of course, students who are already engaged will benefit from these activities as well, since they embody good teaching using research-based reading strategies.

Engagement Model of Instruction for Middle School and High School Reading

While elementary teachers actively teach reading in their Language Arts programs, secondary teachers may mistakenly assume basic reading levels and prefer to focus on teaching literature. They don't always see the teaching of reading as part of their mission or job description. However, we know that struggling middle and high school students are often left behind in the traditional classrooms, without strategies to approach the text successfully. Normally, during the middle grades young adolescents build the foundation for lifelong reading habits. They develop their own reading interests and learn to read different kinds of texts—informational articles and books, poetry and plays, as well as stories and novels. They increase their vocabularies by reading widely and begin to use reading to help answer important questions about themselves and the world. How can we engage students in reading, so that they benefit from instruction and get the practice they need to become competent readers? How can we motivate struggling readers to succeed? In order to create a classroom that fosters reading engagement, Guthrie & Davis (2003) have identified six characteristics of a classroom environment that lead to reading competence: "1) knowledge goals, 2) real-world interactions, 3) an abundance of interesting texts, 4) support for student choice and self-determination, 5) direct strategy instruction, and 6) collaboration support" (pp. 71–72). These practices provide the framework for an engagement model of instruction for middle and high school reading, as shown in Table 0:1. Each practice is briefly described, according to Guthrie & Davis (2003) suggestions.

Table 0:1 Engagement Model of Instruction for Middle School and High School Reading

Instructional Practices	Examples: Teaching/Learning Activities
Knowledge goals	Teaching with thematic units; Student questions as learning goals; Big ideas and supporting concepts; Staying concept-oriented in reading.
Real-world interactions	Hands-on activities; Inquiry science connections to reading; Historical enactments as basis of reading and writing instruction; Selecting personally relevant texts.
Interesting texts	Using trade books for reading instruction; Linking trade books and multimedia; Merging texts, illustrations, and animations in learning; Connecting themes from popular genre and classical literature; Using cultural responsive texts addressing adolescent characters, issues, and social crises; Diversity of text difficulty in the classroom.
Autonomy support	Student choices of specific texts for learning about a required topic; Student input into instructional decisions or tasks; Student construction of rubrics for evaluation of work.
Strategy instruction	Direct modeling, scaffolding, and guided practice for reading comprehension strategies such as: questioning, searching, summarizing, using graphic organizers, comprehension monitoring, and critical evaluation.
Collaboration support	Teams work toward attaining multifaceted conceptual goals; Positive interdependence (students need each other to reach a shared goal); Use individual expertise to learn and share with group; Build norms for interaction and evaluate these regularly; Require full participation in teams.

Knowledge Goals

Written for English/Language Arts educators, this book offers research-based reading strategies in the context of thematic units based on social issues. To some degree, the choice of social issues as a thematic unit is somewhat arbitrary; other topics could be chosen that would also engage the readers. Social issues, however, may work better because they address more directly the transition of child to adult. In Gary Salvner's (2001) address to the ALAN Workshop, November, 2000, he said: "Modern society, it seems, is obsessed with keeping the young in an illusory bubble of protective insulation—in other words, with pretending that we can keep our young innocent" (p. 9). He went on to point out that, in doing so, what is overlooked is the powerful lesson that Lois Lowry (1993) offers in *The Giver*, about the personal and cultural price of such presumed safety. Sitting with the baby Gabriel one night after learning the cost of his society's "sameness," Jonas ponders, "Things could change, Gabe. Things could be different. I don't know how, but there might be some way for things to be different. There could be colors . . . and grandparents . . . and everybody could have the memories." And then leaning over the sleeping baby, Jonas whispers, "There could be love" (pp. 128–129).

Each chapter in this book presents a thematic unit based on award-winning Young Adult novels that have been recognized by the Young Adult Library Services Association (YALSA) of the American Library Association (ALA). These novels allow students to identify and assimilate different world views. Since the topics developed through literature transcend traditional content-area boundaries, they lend themselves to an integrated curriculum that explores issues beyond the typical English/Language Arts curriculum. The topics were chosen by a collaboration among students, teachers, administrators, and community members who stepped out of the comfortable Language Arts curriculum and dared to undertake controversial topics that deal with the realities of our democratic society. Our approach to planning a unit was not necessarily to generate a predetermined teacher-created plan, but rather to include an overall structure that would stimulate students' thinking and engagement in the topic. Of the many options given, teachers, with students, may choose some or all of the strategies presented. The idea was to use literacy as a tool to explore the complex issues of a democracy, with a critical stance toward active involvement in making a difference. If our goal is to create an informed citizenry, then we must show students the ways they might participate and take responsibility in creating justice. Like Short & Burke (1991), the goal was to design units that fostered student engagement in a variety of reading, writing, listening, viewing, and talking activities that immersed them in the topic from a variety of perspectives over a long stretch of time.

While many of the students in these teachers' classes came from privileged middle-class backgrounds, others had been marginalized by their family's circumstances. For some students, these topics were only hearsay—out there—but for many students the topics reflected the difficulties of their personal lives. This Young Adult literature (fiction and nonfiction), along with other primary sources and interviews required by social inquiry, created in students empathy for other people—but also provided an opportunity for them to reflect on the pain and hurt in their own situations. Within the context of the social issue selected by teachers and students for exploration, students were encouraged to inquire into their own lives as well as understand the perspectives of others—classmates, characters, and community members. Personal and social knowing is at the heart of this curriculum (Short & Harste (with Burke), 1996). For additional readings on social issues and education, see the bibliography at the end of the overview.

The first part of this book, "Youth in Search of the American Dream," includes thematic units about topics, such as homelessness, poverty, immigration, and internment. The second part, "Youth Living in Crisis," includes thematic units about adolescents who are misfits, suicidal, grieving the loss of a classmate, violent, helpless, or victimized. In reading about these themes, adolescents may either identify with the protagonist or empathize with youth that are marginalized and suffering in our culture.

Real-World Interactions

Bill Clinton, in his President's Summit for America's Future, in April 1997, highlighted service and volunteerism as one of the five key "promises" that Americans must keep in order to ensure the survival of our democracy. In response to this commission, service-learning projects have proliferated in public schools and have been endorsed as valuable experiences for students and teachers. Since we are considering social issues in our English/Language Arts classrooms, a natural extension project might be some type of community action project that promotes literacy. Of course, some social issues are more amenable to service learning than others. For instance, in the unit on homelessness, almost every community has an outreach project, while for units based in past historical periods students might find little to do in their community. In urban communities, students could volunteer to read to children in schools, day care, and community centers. In rural communities, students could volunteer to read and tutor children in schools and churches. Where Internet services are provided, students could communicate with other students reading books together online as cyber buddies. (For more information, see Glasgow's *Cyber Journaling for Justice*, 2002).

On a cautionary note, Clark (2003) suggests that "learning must accompany service if we are to avoid positioning others as helpless or needy against their own constructions of self" (p. 295). In other words, many public school students are sent out to complete community service work in order to meet graduation requirements, but they are not required to reflect on their experiences in a classroom context. Clark says that students "need opportunities to be both supported and challenged as they reflect on their service work" (p. 295). This discussion and reflection might take place in a Reflective Journal, assigned readings, and ongoing class discussions, so that students "begin to challenge the taken-for-granted stereotypes" (p. 295) that they brought into the situation from their prior experiences.

To ensure that no child is left behind in the English classroom, pedagogy must move from the traditional lecturing to facilitating students' active learning. Thematic instruction serves as a vehicle for providing students with meaningful substance, applications to their lives in their real world, and cooperative learning experiences. This book provides a wealth of instructional strategies for the teaching of reading that provide students with choices which allow for their unique ways of learning and responding to literature, both independently and collaboratively. Students are empowered by activities which ask them to utilize both cognitive and affective components of the mind to make meaning of their reading experiences. Reader-response activities, which originate in the work of Louise Rosenblatt, personally engage students in the story and provide opportunities for them to articulate their feelings, opinions, and thinking about the books they read. Rosenblatt (1995) posits that "once the work has been aesthetically evoked, it can then become the object of reflection and analysis, according to the various critical and scholarly approaches" (*Literature as Exploration*, p. 293). This book provides teachers and students with a plethora of ideas for evoking the aesthetic stance toward reading and responding to literature, and at the same time, making connections with the self and the real world that students live in—school, friends, home, and community.

Interesting Texts

In developing this curriculum for inquiry into social issues, we didn't want to generate a predetermined, teacher-created instructional unit that might stifle student inquiry, but we did intend to provide strategies that would support the students' reading competence and development. While secondary English teachers tend to organize curriculum according to literary time periods of genres of literature and struggle to motivate readers, this book offers student-centered approaches to English/Language Arts which organize the curriculum by units based on social issues in award-winning Young Adult literature. Young Adult literature appeals to the interests of adolescents in that the main characters—also teenagers—must solve real-life dilemmas, often using "teen" or "street" language. Young Adult literature works so well, in part, because it focuses on the tension between being a dependent child and an independent adult. Contemporary Young Adult literature reflects the complexities, insecurities, and realities of modern society, which, of course, include social issues. The topics represented in the novels are meaningful and relevant to the young adults of today and lend themselves readily to the development of thematic units as a context for the teaching of reading strategies.

Using multiple texts in a single unit not only helps to accommodate a wide range of reading and interest levels, but also introduces students to multiple perspectives on a topic, rather than being limited to a single view presented in any one text. The discussion of social issues in this book is taken from a wide range of materials: informational picture and chapter books, biographies, and photographic essays, as well as Internet, newspaper, and magazine articles. The use of multiple texts can help students become part of a larger community of readers. Including multiple interpretations of events provides students with the information they need to discuss the social, political, and economic issues raised in the unit. They sharpen their critical thinking skills as they learn to synthesize the ideas raised in the various texts. According to Robb (2002), "Multiple texts enable teachers to offer students books they can read, improve students' application of reading-thinking strategies, build confidence, and develop motivation to learn" (p. 32). By using multiple texts, students can contribute meaningful ideas in discussions and deepen their knowledge of social issues that effect their lives.

Autonomy Support

Students are empowered when they have voice and choice in decisions concerning curriculum, instruction, and assessment. Giving students choice is asking them to make decisions about their interests, what they already know about a task, and what they would like to know in the future. Since we know that when students choose their books, topic, or response, they expend more effort on these activities, the thematic units in this book not only provide a core novel for the social issue, but also provide a bibliography of related Young Adult literature. Students may choose from fiction and nonfiction titles for reading in book clubs, Literature Circles, and/or for their inquiry projects. Students perceive these choice activities as providing useful competence information because they can learn both about themselves and the task (Turner, 1997). Thus, giving students voice and choice in curricular decisions helps them develop a sense of competence and increases motivation and engagement (Turner, 1997). Teachers can easily provide choice activities within the context of social issues presented in this text.

In traditional assessments, where students *select a response* (multiple-choice, true-false, matching), responses can be scored using a key or a scantron machine. But when students are asked to *construct a response*, scoring must be based on high-quality performance criteria to avoid a subjective evaluation and make visible the standards we expect learners to meet. The best scoring tool for authentic, performance-based assessments is the *rubric*. A rubric is a scoring tool "containing criteria and a performance scale that allows us to define and describe the most important components that comprise *complex* performances and products" (Arter & McTighe, 2001, p. 8). It is a formative type of assessment because the assessment rubric is available to students at the beginning of instruction, serving as a learning tool. As such, the assessment rubric serves to drive instruction. It sets the criteria that teachers will teach and the criteria that students will strive to meet.

As students work toward meeting the performance criteria specified in the rubric, it becomes an ongoing part of the whole teaching and learning process. Students themselves can be involved in the assessment process using the rubric for both peer and self-assessment. As students become familiar with rubrics, they can assist in the rubric-design process. This involvement empowers the students and, as a result, their learning becomes more focused and self-directed. This book provides assessment rubrics for some of the major projects required in the thematic units.

Strategy Instruction

When students enter middle school, they often encounter new texts that challenge vocabulary, text structure, genre, and content. These texts require a variety of reading strategies for students to make meaning of their reading. As Wilhelm, Baker, & Dube (2001) contend, "the best way to teach students these new and necessary strategies is by carefully guiding them through actual readings in a context where they have a personal and social need to understand and then act on their growing understanding" (p. xv). In this book, we provide many techniques for modeling, scaffolding, and guiding students to internalize the strategies that will engage them in reading and support their literacy development. Each chapter is set up to engage students in reading according to the Structured Reading Lesson that includes strategies for before, during, and after reading. See the section that follows for a detailed discussion of the Structured Reading Lesson.

Collaboration Support

Though we have the physical ability to exist individually and alone, we are also social animals who thrive and grow when involved with others. This ability to interact with others, understand them, and interpret their behavior is known as interpersonal intelligence. According to Howard Gardner's theory of multiple intelligences (1983, 1993), interpersonal intelligence is seen in how we "notice distinction among others; in particular, contrasts in their moods, temperaments, motivations, and intentions" (p. 239). When students collaborate with others in a meaningful pursuit toward understanding a social issue, they are more likely to engage in reading, discussion, and inquiry.

What the Russian psychologist Vygotsky (1978) tells us about the social construction of language helps us to see how language is unlocked in a social situation. When students work together in collaborative tasks, their talk can be used to produce a confidence and a fluency in their reading and writing that they do not possess when working alone. Dale's (1994) research shows that collaborative writing groups become better than other student groups at taking conversational turns because they learn together, are better focused on the task at hand, and are better able to handle productive disagreement. In his later research, Dale (1997) describes the collaborative process as coauthoring, when students are asked to write in groups. Activities such as writing letters to congressmen, editorials, and brochures require group members to think for themselves, talk about their differences of opinion, analyze the problem or phenomenon together, and compose a forceful position statement that has a real and well-defined audience. Dale says that the advantage of the topics and procedures is their strong appeal to students. They deal with contemporary issues that fully engage adolescents' political and social interests.

Collaborative learning, whether in teams or in small groups such as Literature Circles, draws heavily on a well-developed field of study called *group dynamics*. According to Schmuck & Schmuck (2000), there are six ingredients in the development of mature, interdependent, productive groups:

- clear expectations
- mutually developed norms
- shared leadership and responsibility
- open channels of communication
- diverse friendship patterns
- conflict-resolution mechanisms

Therefore, if we want to have effective classroom group work, we must ensure that each of these factors is provided for in the task at hand. Students need the opportunity to engage in collaborative learning, where they are expected to set and meet certain goals, share leadership responsibility, balance and negotiate conflicting interpretations of text, develop social skills, and resolve disagreements. McClure (1990, p. 66) concludes that collaborative learning "is the most direct means of initiating [students] into participation in the active shaping of knowledge and meaning for themselves." Activities in this book challenge students to work collaboratively in such a manner in Literature Circles, Socratic seminars, inquiry projects, problem-based learning groups, and debates of the social issues they are studying. We believe in this sort of learning—authentic, problem solving, collaborative—as enumerated in the foundational work of John Dewey (1916).

The Structured Reading Lesson

In order to implement the Guthrie & Davis Engagement Model of Instruction (2003) in the English/Language Arts classroom, we turn to the Structured Reading Lesson. Although we've been exposed to a host of frameworks for creating daily lesson plans in which students are expected to complete transactions with the text as in reading, writing, listening, speaking, and viewing, the Structured Reading Lesson serves as an appropriate model for a transactional approach to reading. As Ryder & Graves (2003) suggest, "proficient readers employ a number of strategies before, during, and after reading" (p. 108). These three components of the Structured Reading Lesson are outlined in Table 0:2, as adapted from Ryder & Graves (p. 110).

Table 0:2 Components of the Structured Reading Lesson

Before Reading	During Reading	After Reading
• Establish purpose for reading • Draw on students' prior knowledge • Present vocabulary that may be unfamiliar to students • Motivate students to want to read the selection	• Focus attention on the purpose • Stimulate discussion • Relate students' experiences to the text • Apply monitoring strategies	• Reflect upon the meaning of the text • Engage students in higher order thinking • Engage students in written and oral summaries of what was learned • Extend concepts in the reading selection
Lesson Objectives **Ongoing Assessment**		

The Structured Reading Lesson provides a continuity of various instructional activities and how each element contributes to students' learning and the lesson objectives, as well as ongoing assessment of the reading process. Each of the chapters in this book are organized according to this plan, giving the reader many strategies for before, during, and after reading for each social issues topic.

Traditionally, English/Language Arts teachers have focused on *after reading* activities. The typical procedure would be to give a reading assignment, expect the students to read it silently in class or out of class, hand out a worksheet, and then begin the discussion and information giving about the author and topic. More often than not, only a few students respond to this approach, while others remain apathetic and disinterested. In this scenario, much of the teaching time is spent reexplaining, rereading, retelling, resummarizing, or whatever it takes to "pour" knowledge into their empty heads. This approach to teaching does not acknowledge what we now know about the critical importance of what happens *before* and *during* reading. In the early days, we didn't help the students enter the text, make connections with their personal lives, construct meaning of their reading, understand the organization of the text, learn strategies needed to deal with the text, or realize the purpose for reading in the first place. With the adoption of the Structured Reading Lesson, we found that the *after* reading went much more smoothly.

Before Reading Strategies

Using Rosenblatt's transactional approach to reading, students must be actively engaged in understanding the purpose for reading a text. According to Wilhelm, Baker, & Dube (2001), *frontloading* is the use of any prereading strategy that prepares students for successful reading (p. 92). These authors posit that the most powerful time to support reading is before the students begin to read. Frontloading includes activating students' prior knowledge, preparing them for the challenge ahead with appropriate strategies, and helping them monitor their own performance. Students also need a sense of purpose and motivation. There needs to be a knowledge of content to build on what is already known, and a knowledge of necessary processes that the text requires of readers. Frontloading is a technique used by teachers to help readers better comprehend and approach a new text or kind of task that might include such strategies as making predictions, brainstorming ideas, role playing, and using the K-W-L Chart.

Here are some questions that Wilhelm et al. (2001, pp. 102–103) recommend to guide our thinking about frontloading in general:

1. How might I organize this reading experience to make it personally and socially relevant? How might this text lend itself to exploration of a contact zone, or lead to social action (something that mattered)?

2. What do my students probably already know about the text that we will read? (If you do not have any idea how to answer this question, you may want to use the "quick write" strategy to find out.)

3. What background information do my students need to know prior to their reading of this text? How can I help them "get" this stuff?

4. What procedural knowledge should they have to help them in this reading? How can I alert them to the importance of this skill and begin to help them develop it?

5. What knowledge of skills is most "generative?" That is, what will have the most transfer value and be most useful as a touchstone to return to throughout our unit and beyond?

By addressing these questions, teachers can generate appropriate prereading strategies for the unit.

During Reading Strategies

The purpose of *during reading* strategies is to help the students read constructively, use a range of transactions appropriate to the task, and capture personal responses to the text. A recent National Assessment of Educational Progress (NAEP) review (see Campbell, Voekl, & Donahue, 1998, for a review) shows that high school students are very adept at decoding words and ascertaining literal-level meanings of text. However, they do very poorly on more sophisticated tasks, such as making inferences and drawing conclusions about text. In fact, only a very small percentage of students in the 12th grade can identify and support an author's generalization—a thematic statement or point—from a piece of writing. This means that even though students have the ability to decode text, they do not have the ability to infer, critique, make meaning, converse with authors, or think with or about the text they have read. This certainly points to the lack of support students receive as readers once they enter the upper grades, and demonstrates the need to provide students with instruction that leads to deeper understanding and critical reading of the more sophisticated kinds of literary texts they encounter in secondary schools.

The during reading strategies in this book help students construct meaning individually and collaboratively during their reading. Students might be asked to discuss key points on electronic message boards, keep journals, interpret photographs of social issues, answer essential questions, identify significant passages, or create sound tracks for their novels. These strategies invite students to participate in dialogue, role play, music, art, and creative writing to develop critical thinking skills as they engage in the novels of social issues.

After Reading Strategies

After finishing a good book, especially one that focuses on social issues, real readers find someone to talk to, to share favorite parts, to question the ideas, and/or to savor the beautiful language. Reflecting on a book after completing it invites readers to reexperience favorite parts, to think about a story's meanings, and to relate its themes to their lives. *After reading* strategies encourage reflection and lead readers deeper into the book, allowing them to probe and clarify ideas. When readers become better acquainted with the characters, plot, and details of a story, they can use events in the text to explore implied meanings and make connections to other books, as well as to their community. Students may be asked to interpret literature with art, dance, music, and drama. Through these interpretations, students learn new things about the stories they read, as well as about themselves.

The culminating projects in this book usually require students to use what Smagorinsky (2002) calls *multimedia composing*. Multimedia composing requires students to represent their understanding of literature and social issues through unconventional types of compositions, such as multigenre research papers, zines, dramatizations, and video productions. Our rationale for emphasizing multiple forms of compositions was that students became, almost without exception, highly engaged in the projects they would undertake—often far more so when evaluated exclusively through writing. In particular, low-achieving students were often among the most enthusiastic and productive workers on these projects. In addition to being engaged, students clearly demonstrated an understanding of literature in ways not always accessible through writing. Students learned to delve into deeper explorations of meaning, to take risks as they experimented with multiple meanings and perspectives, to transact with the text to draw inferences, and to share with others. Culminating projects give students the opportunity to discuss, perform, and share their readings in a social setting. (See examples of student projects on the accompanying CD-ROM.)

Additional Readings for Social Issues and Education

Adams, M., Bell, L. A., & Griffin, P. (Eds.). (1997). *Teaching for diversity and social justice: A sourcebook*. New York: Routledge.

Ayers, W., Hunt, J. A., & Quinn, T. (Eds.). (1998). *Teaching for social justice: A democracy and education reader*. New York: Teachers College Press.

Busching, B., & Slesinger, B. A. (2002). *"It's our world too": Socially responsive learners in middle school language arts*. Urbana, IL: National Council of Teachers of English.

Carey-Webb, A. (2001). *Literature and lives: A response-based, cultural studies approach to teaching English*. Urbana, IL: National Council of Teachers of English.

Danks, C., & Rabinsky, L. (Eds.). (1999). *Teaching for a tolerant world: Grades 9–12: Essays and resources*. Urbana, IL: National Council of Teachers of English.

Edelsky, C. (Ed.). (1999). *Making justice our project: Teachers working toward critical whole language practice*. Urbana, IL: National Council of Teachers of English.

Rochman, H. (1993). *Against borders: Promoting books for a multicultural world*. Chicago: American Library Association.

References

Anderman, L. H. (1999). Classroom goal orientation, school belonging, and social goals as predictors of students' positive and negative affect following the transition to middle school. *Journal of Research and Development in Education, 32*, 89–103.

Arter, J. & McTighe, J. (2001). *Scoring rubrics in the classroom: Using performance criteria for assessing and improving student performance*. Thousand Oaks, CA: Corwin Press, Inc.

Brozo, W. G. (1990). Learning how at-risk readers learn best: A case for interactive assessment. *Journal of Reading, 33*, 522–527.

Campbell, J., Voekl, K., & Donahue, P. (1998). *NAEP 1996 trends in academic progress. Achievement of U.S. students in science, 1969–1996; mathematics, 1973–1996; reading, 1971–1996; writing, 1984–1996.* (NCES Report No. 97-985). Washington DC: U.S. Department of Education.

Clark, C. T. (2002, December/2003, January). Unfolding narratives of service learning: Reflections on teaching, literacy, and positioning in service relationships. *Journal of Adolescent and Adult Literacy, 46*(4), 288–297.

Dale, H. (1994). Collaborative writing interactions in one ninth-grade classroom. *Journal of Educational Research, 87*(6), 334–344.

Dale, H. (1997). *Coauthoring in the classroom.* Urbana, IL: National Council of Teachers of English.

U.S. Department of Education. (1965). Elementary and Secondary Education Act (Public law 89-10). Washington, DC: U.S. Government Printing Office.

Dewey, J. (1916/1944). *Democracy and education.* New York: Free Press.

Gardner, H. (1983). *Frames of mind: The theory of multiple intelligences.* New York: Basic Books.

Glasgow, J. (2002). Cyber journaling for justice. In *Standards-based activities with scoring rubrics for middle and high school English. Vol. 1: Performance-based portfolios.* Larchmont, NY: Eye on Education.

Guthrie, J. T., & Davis, M. H. (2003). Motivating struggling readers in middle school through an engagement model of classroom practice. *Reading & Writing Quarterly, 19,* 59–85.

Guthrie, J. T., & Wigfield, A. (2000). Engagement and motivation in reading. In: M. Kamil, R. Barr, P. L. Mosentah, & P. D. Pearson (Eds.), *Handbook of reading research* (Vol. 3, pp. 403–425). New York: Longman.

Lowry, L. (1993). *The giver.* New York: Bantam Doubleday Dell.

McClure, M. F. (1990). Collaborative learning: Teacher's game or students' game? *English Journal, 79*(2), 66–68.

Mullis, I., Campbell, J., & Farstrup, A. (1993). *NAEP 1992 reading report card for the nations and the states.* Washington, DC: National Center for Education Statistics.

U.S. Department of Education. (2001). No child left behind (Public Law 107-110). Washington, DC: U.S. Government Printing Office.

Robb, L. (2002, May). Multiple texts: Multiple opportunities for teaching and learning. *Voices in the Middle, 9*(4), 28–32.

Rosenblatt, L. M. (1995). *Literature as exploration* (5th ed.). New York: Modern Language Association.

Ryder, R. J., & Graves, M. F. (2003). *Reading and learning in content areas* (3rd ed.). Hoboken, NJ: John Wiley & Sons.

Salvner, G. M. (2001). Lessons and lives: Why young adult literature matters. *The ALAN Review, 28*(3), p. 9.

Schmuck, R., & Schmuck, P. (2000). *Group processes in the classroom* (8th ed.). Dubuque, IA: William C. Brown.

Short, K. G. & Burke, C. (1991). *Creating curriculum: Teachers and students as community of learners.* Portsmouth, NH: Heinemann.

Short, K. G., & Harste, J. C. (with Burke, C.). (1996). *Creating classrooms for authors and inquirers* (2nd ed.). Portsmouth, NH: Heinemann.

Slavin, R. E. (1989). Students at risk of school failure: The problem and its dimensions. In R. E. Slavin, N. L. Karweit, & N. A. Madden (Eds.), *Effective programs for students at risk.* Needham Heights, MA: Allyn & Bacon.

Smagorinsky, P. (2002). *Teaching English through principled practice.* Upper Saddle River, NJ: Merrill/Prentice Hall.

Thomas, K., & Moorman, G. (1983). *Designing reading programs.* Dubuque, IA: Kendall Hunt.

Turner, T. N. (1997). Engaging social studies book reports. *Social Studies and the Young Learner, 9*, 5–7.

Vacca, R., & Vacca, J. (1999). *Content area reading: Literacy and learning across the curriculum* (6th ed.). New York: Longman.

Vygotsky, L. (1978). *Mind in society: The development of higher psychological processes.* Cambridge, MA: Harvard University Press.

Wilhelm, J., Baker, T., & Dube, J. (2001). *Strategic reading: Guiding students to lifelong literacy, 6–12.* Portsmouth, NH: Heinemann Boynton/Cook.

Chapter One

Japanese-American Relocation Experiences During World War II

Jacqueline N. Glasgow

Three months after the Japanese attack on Pearl Harbor on December 7, 1941, the U.S. Government ordered a mass evacuation of all people of Japanese ancestry from the three West Coast states. It was the largest forced evacuation in American history. Two thirds of these people were American citizens who had to leave their homes, their schools, and their friends and live in relocation camps created by the U.S. Army. Why do we not know the names of the camps, Heart Mountain, Manzanar, Minidoka, and Poston, as well as we know the names of Auchwitz, Terezin, and Dachau? On the one hand, the government censored and controlled the dissemination of information in media and film and sought to represent life in the internment camps as a benevolent exercise in civil obedience. Cameras were confiscated from the Japanese-Americans, so the only photos we have from this period were taken by government photographers, such as Dorothea Lange and Ansel Adams. Furthermore, this limited cultural representation of the camps was compounded by the protracted silence of many of the former internees, due to their sense of humiliation and shame.

As students inquire into life in a Japanese Relocation Camp in Young Adult literature, they will acquire understanding of this dark period of our history, as well as improve their reading and writing strategies. For this unit, students will read autobiographical fiction, such as *Journey to Topaz* by Yoshiko Uchida, *The Moon Bridge* by Marcia Savin, *Farewell to Manzanar* by Jeanne Wakatsuki Houston, *Nisei Daughter* by Monica Sone, and *Under the Blood-Red Sun* by Graham Salisbury. They will read information books, such as *Remembering Manzanar* by Michael Cooper, *The Children of Topaz* by Michael Tunnell and George Chilcoat, and *I Am American* by Jerry Stanley. Older students will benefit from reading Inada's *Only What We Could Carry*, which students will read as a Readers' Theater. At the end of this unit, students will participate in a simulation of the Japanese-American Relocation experience. The culminating project for the students' inquiry and research will be a multigenre research paper on some aspect of the relocation experience or the Japanese culture. See Table 1:1 for Reading and Writing Skills Addressed in the Japanese Relocation Camp Unit.

Table 1:1 Reading Skills Addressed in this Unit

Strategy	Set Purpose	Activate Prior Knowledge	Make Predictions	Critical Thinking	Asking Questions	Visualizing the Text	Making Connections	Main Idea	Monitor Reading	Cause Effect	Compare Contrast	Making Inferences
KWL Strategy	•	•	•	•		•	•	•				
Film Clip	•	•	•	•		•	•	•		•	•	•
Listen to Picture Book	•	•	•	•		•	•	•	•	•	•	
Word Sort	•	•	•	•			•	•		•	•	•
Japanese Vocab		•		•		•					•	
One-Minute Vocab Report	•	•	•	•		•	•	•		•	•	•
Literature Circles	•	•		•	•	•	•	•	•	•	•	•
Timeline of Citizenship	•	•	•	•	•		•	•	•	•	•	•
Tanka Poetry	•	•	•	•		•	•	•		•	•	•
Image Freewrite	•	•	•	•	•	•	•	•	•	•	•	•
Photo Essay	•	•		•		•	•	•	•	•	•	
Shape/Color	•	•	•	•		•	•	•		•	•	•
Cause and Effect	•	•	•	•	•	•	•	•		•	•	•
Simulation of Japanese American Internment	•	•	•	•	•	•	•	•	•	•	•	•
Readers' Theater				•		•	•	•	•	•	•	•
Multigenre Research Paper	•	•		•	•	•	•	•	•	•	•	•

Frontloading: Building Background Knowledge for Japanese Relocation Camps

According to Wilhelm, Baker, & Dube (2001), *frontloading* is a way "to prepare, protect, and support students into the acquisition of new content and new ways of doing things. It is the use of any prereading strategy that prepares students for success" (p. 92). Frontloading is important in activating or building content (we can only learn about something we already know something about) prior to reading activities. It is essential to providing a sense of purpose and motivation. Frontloading helps to familiarize the reader with material and concepts that might otherwise be foreign. There are many strategies to accomplish this purpose, but the following ones are appropriate for this unit of study.

The K-W-L Strategy (What Do You Know? What Do You Want to Know? What Did You Learn?)

K-W-L is a meaning-making strategy that engages students in active text learning. The strategy creates an instructional framework that begins with what students *know* about the topic to be studied, moves to what the students *want to know* as they generate questions about the topic, and leads to a record of what students *learn* as a result of their engagement in the K-W-L strategy. Before assigning a text, explain the strategy. Donna Ogle (1992), the originator of the strategy, suggests that dialogue begin with the teacher asking students questions: "What do you already know about the Japanese-American Relocation camps?" "When did this happen?" "Why did it happen?" "Who was in charge?" "How many people were evacuated?" Record student responses on chart paper, and display in the room to serve as a focus for the unit. If your students are like my students, they will know very little about the whole situation. Once having established their background knowledge, ask them, "What would you like to know?" Record the results of their brainstorming to guide their inquiry throughout the unit, making sure they explore the issues of most concern to them. At the end of the unit, complete the chart by asking students to list "What have you learned during this unit?" and "What do you still need to learn?"

Film Clip

Since most of our students have very little background knowledge about the Japanese-American Relocation, begin this unit with a film clip of the Japanese-American Relocation from *The Shadow of Hate: A History of Intolerance in America*, produced by Charles Guggenheim, 1995 Teaching Tolerance, Montgomery, Alabama. This seven-minute clip will serve to introduce students to the realities of the relocation experience from the official government notice to evacuate their homes, to packing up and selling their possessions, to arrival at the assembly centers, to deportment to the relocation camps. At this point, students may have more questions that they would like to know about to add to the above K-W-L Chart.

Children's Picture Book

To add to students background knowledge of the Japanese Relocation experience, read aloud *So Far From the Sea* by Eve Bunting. This is a tender story about a young girl, Laura Iwasaki, and her family, who make the pilgrimage to the National Historic Site where the Manzanar War Relocation Camp once stood. Laura wants to say goodbye to her grandfather, who died there while he and his family were interned at the camp. Manzanar, in eastern California, was the first of 10 War Relocation Centers that had a population of approximately 10,000. Elicit student responses, or ask them to write a journal entry or one-minute paper response.

Word Sort

According to Vacca & Vacca (1996), "Teaching words well means giving students multiple opportunities to learn how words are conceptually related to one another in the material they are studying" (p. 133). They go on to say that word sorts are one such activity that require students to understand conceptual relationships, as they classify words into categories based on their prior knowledge. For this strategy, the teacher selects the key words from the unit and invites students to sort them into logical arrangements of two or more. Individually or collaboratively in small groups, students literally sort out technical terms that are written on cards or listed on an exercise sheet. The object of word sorting is to group words into different categories by looking for shared features among their meanings. According to Gillet & Kita (1979), a word sort gives students the opportunity "to teach and learn from each other while discussing and examining words together" (pp. 541–542). In the closed sort, students know in advance of sorting what the main categories are. The closed sort reinforces and extends the ability to classify words. Open sorts, on the other hand, prompt divergent and inductive reasoning. No category, or criterion for grouping, is known in advance of the sorting. Students must search for meanings and discover relationships among the terms without the benefit of any structure. Students must group the words into categories and be able to justify the reason or reasons for each arrangement. A word sort used as a before reading activity serves to help learners make predictive connections among the words. See Table 1:2 for Word Sort for Japanese-American Relocation.

Table 1:2 Word Sort for Japanese-American Relocation

Arrange the following words into categories. Be able to justify the reason or reasons for each arrangement.		
Disloyals	Poston War Relocation Camp	Voluntary evacuation
Day of Infamy	Walter-McCarran Immigration	Manzanar War Relocation Camp
Rohwer War	and Nationality Act	Issei
Relocation Camp	Jerome War Relocation Camp	December 7, 1941
Civil Liberties Act of 1988	sabotage	Resettlement Camp
Evacuee	Loyalty Questionnaire	Nisei
Executive Order 9066	Purple Heart Battalion	Curfew
Topaz War	Lt. General DeWitt	War Relocation Authority
Relocation Camp	Tule Lake War Relocation Camp	Granada War Relocation Camp
Secretary of War Stimson	Resident alien	Japanese American Evacuation
Internment	Heart Mountain War Relocation	Claims Act
Tanforan	Camp	Pearl Harbor
Sansei	Assembly Center	Chan
President Roosevelt	Agitator	Declaration of War
San	Yonsei	Hostages
	contraband	*Go* Board

Besides the prison camp category, students typically identify government officials and actions, Japanese vocabulary, terms of oppression, and acts of patriotism. From these categories, ask students to predict the influences, causes, and reactions of the Japanese to the relocation process. Since all groups undoubtedly have a "War Relocation Camp" category, another prereading strategy is to locate the Assembly Centers and Internment Camps on a map of the United States. There is a good map of the United States with the Assembly Centers and Internment Camps in Inada's *Only What We Could Carry* (2000, p. 418) and at the National Archives Web site, http://www.archives.gov/education/cc/relocate.html.

One-Minute Vocabulary Reports

To learn more about these concepts, ask students to prepare a one-minute report for a term of their choice, or one that the teacher assigns. As described by Glasgow (2002), One-Minute Vocabulary Reports provide background knowledge of the time period, phrases, places, and names that students will find in their novels. These reports are even more effective if students are required to prepare a visual for the report. The visual reports can be displayed around the room for easy reference during the unit. Information and photos for these reports are accessible in the following information books, plus others mentioned in the bibliography: *Only What We Could Carry: The Japanese-American Internment Experience* edited by Lawson Fusao Inada, The *Children of Topaz: The Story of a Japanese-American Internment Camp* by Michael Tunnell and George Chilcoat, *I am American: A True Story of Japanese Internment* by Jerry Stanley, and *Re-*

membering Manzanar: Life in a Japanese Relocation Camp by Michael L. Cooper. More information can be found at the National Archives Web site, http://www.archives.gov/education/cc/relocate.html. See Table 1:3 for Kathleen's One-Minute Vocabulary Report for Manzanar Relocation Camp.

Table 1:3 One-Minute Vocabulary Report for Voluntary Evacuation

In February 1941, General DeWitt designated the coastline of California Restricted Area Number One. He sternly suggested that persons of Japanese ancestry voluntarily migrate inland. But when some 4,000 tried to move, they were met with hostility. If the Japanese were a threat to California, then they were a threat to them also. The plan failed. DeWitt ordered the Japanese-Americans to stay in California until war hysteria, hate, and rumors of sabotage mounted to the point he justified their removal as "military necessity."

—taken from Stanley's (1994) *I Am An American.*

Photo from National Archives Web site

Japanese Vocabulary Lesson

With the list of Japanese vocabulary generated in the word sort, discuss the meanings of the Japanese words that students will encounter in their reading of the novels. Begin with learning the sounds of Japanese vowels, so words can be sounded out phonetically:

a = ah as in awesome   i = ee as in feet

u = oo as in hoot   e = eh as in egg

o = oh as in coat

Japanese vocabulary:

Issei = The first generation of a Japanese family to immigrate to the United States, mostly between 1890 and 1915.

Nisei = The second generation, children of the Issei; American citizens by birth, most of which were born before World War II.

Sansei = The third generation of Americans with Japanese ancestry, mostly born during or after World War II.

Yonsei = The fourth generation of Japanese-American ancestry, born after World War II.

chan = when attached to the end of a name, it is a sign of endearment

san = shows respect when added to the end of an adult's name

Go = means five in Japanese; a board game in which the object is to get five discs of the same color in a row

Literature Circles to Gain Multiple Perspectives

This unit maybe be approached in the traditional manner in which everyone in the class reads the same book, or in Literature Circles, in which each group of four or five students reads a different book related to the Japanese-American Relocation. *Literature Circles* is a teaching strategy originally developed by Harvey Daniels (2002) that allows students to become critical thinkers as they engage in ongoing dialogue with a book. In small groups, students read, discuss, and respond to the book through discussion, as well as extended written and artistic responses. The key aspect of this strategy is the structured use of role sheets, as the students learn to discuss and contribute to the group. The role sheets typically include: Discussion Director, Summarizer, Illustrator, Connector, Researcher, and Word Wizard. These sheets, found in Daniels' book, can also be used as evaluation tools for assessing both individual and group process.

If using Literature Circles, select members for the discussion groups based on student interest and selection of the books suggested on the booklist at the end of this chapter. The booklist contains books of various genres, such as autobiography, historical fiction, post-war fiction, or nonfiction (information books) for this unit. Assign roles for the member of each circle. Assign reading to be completed by the circles inside or outside of class. Select circle meeting dates, and help students prepare for their roles in their circle. The teacher acts as a facilitator for the circles. Begin reading the selected novels.

During Reading Strategies to Deepen Understanding of the Japanese Relocation Camps

Timeline of Citizenship Eligibility

It doesn't take much reading to discover that the Sakane's, Wakatsuki's, and other Issei had been denied American citizenship, whereas the young protagonists born in the United States became citizens at birth. Students should begin the timeline in 1869, when the first Japanese settled in the United States mainland at Gold Hill, near Sacramento, California. Other important dates should include 1870, when the U.S. Congress granted naturalization rights to free Whites and people of African descent, but omitted mention of Oriental races. In 1913, the Alien Land Bill prevented Japanese aliens from owning land in California. Continue with important events, such as the bombing of Pearl Harbor, Roosevelt's Executive Order 9066 to relocate those of Japanese ancestry, to August 14, 1945, when Japan surrendered, to 1952, when the Walter-McCarran Act was passed, and Japanese aliens were granted the right to become naturalized U.S. citizens. Public Law 100-383 was passed in 1988, offering redress of $20,000 cash payment to each person who was interned. More information can be found at the National Archives Web site, http://www.archives.gov/education/cc/relocate.html.

Ask students to discuss what qualifications would be appropriate for eligibility for citizenship in a democratic society. Then compare their suggestions to the actual requirements for naturalization. Go to the U.S.A. Immigration Services Web site for information: http://www.usais.org. At this site, students can take the Citizen Eligibility Quiz, find information on the Green Card Lottery Requirements, and/or take the Immigration Tutorial. You may want to discuss reasons why the persons of Japanese ancestry living in Hawaii were treated differently, as found in *Under the Blood-Red Sun* by Graham Salisbury.

Tanka—An Ancient Style of Poetry that Speaks to the Modern Soul

Tanka is the modern name of a form of Japanese verse that dates back over 12 centuries. Older than haiku, tanka differs from haiku in both its form (divided into five lines of 5-7-5-7-7 syllables) and its style of expression. In Japan, tanka has long been considered the most important form of Japanese poetry. In recent decades, not only have Western readers begun to discover Japanese-language tanka through originals and translations, but Western poets have begun to explore the power of the tanka form in their own languages. It is probably not an exaggeration to say that when many people first discover tanka, they experience a revelation about the power of poetry in their lives, as if they at last understand the transformative emotional significance both of reading others' words and of writing one's own poetry. Around the world, tanka poetry is making poets out of people who never would have thought of writing a poem before.

Ask students to bring in a photograph, calendar picture, or computer graphic that shows a poignant image in nature, preferably from the Japanese Relocation period. From these images, ask students to write a tanka poem. Some students may prefer to write the poem first, and then illustrate it. The poem should convey emotions or feelings in an understanding of nature. The first three lines make a statement for which the last two lines comment. See Table 1:4 for Erin's Tanka of Manzanar Relocation Camp.

Table 1:4 Tanka of Manzanar Relocation Camp

A flag floats in blue

Above the dirty dust floor

Barrack rows await.

Sun, wind, and cloth—the sentries:

Forgotten desert exile.

Photo from National Archives Web site
by Dorothea Lange

Photo Essays

Download photographs from the Internet that portray the Japanese-American Relocation experiences. There are 278 images in Yoshiko Uchida's photograph collection, found at http://findaid.oac.cdlib.org/findaid/ark:/13030/ft6k4007pc. There are many more images found at http://www.oz.net/~cyu/internment/main.html and at http://www.archives.gov/education/cc/relocate.html. Students can also find provocative images in the information books provided at the end of the chapter. Students should choose a photograph that attracts their attention. Ask students to write as though they were inside the photo. Ask them to enter the scene and become one of the persons in the photo. Ask them to write about the situation. What's going on? What is the person thinking? What emotion is the person expressing? What questions are they asking? What is the story that they want to tell? Write that story. See Table 1:5 for Inada's model for a photo essay taken from his book of poems, *Drawing the Line* (1997, pp. 1–2).

Table 1:5 Inada's Photo Essay

Here is a picture of an Issei woman. What do you suppose she is thinking and feeling? Obviously, she is thinking about her grandson, and feeling joy and love. She is also feeling her labors on the farm.

She can look back at her life with pride and satisfaction. Born and raised in a Japanese village, she came to America in 1901, joining her husband who had labored there since 1896. They became sharecroppers, moving from farm to farm with other pioneer families, making history and communities along the way.

Hers was a grueling, fulfilling life, full of struggle, sacrifice, celebration, and wonder. She served as fieldhand, healer, community counselor, always counted on to hold things together. She could make soup from rain, beauty from scrap; she made everything feel special with her appreciation and grace. The land was beautiful, the harvests plentiful. What more to ask?

Thus, today, she feels happy, blessed. Within a year, she would be dead and her grandson, Lawson, in a concentration camp.

Baseball Saved Us

Ask students to brainstorm ways to entertain children in the internment camps. What activities have students found in their reading? What could one do out there in the middle of the desert, surrounded by guards and barbed-wire fences. Read aloud *Baseball Saved Us* (1993) by Ken Mochizuki. Since Mochizuki's family was sent to the Minidoka Camp, this story was likely set in Idaho. The story portrays the bleakness of the area from which the Japanese-American community worked together to create a baseball field, make uniforms, and acquire equipment to play ball beneath the guard towers. Baseball gave them a purpose and inspired them to endure the injustice and humiliation of the internment camp. The baseball skills this boy acquired at camp helped him overcome the prejudice against the Japanese, once he returned home after the war.

Image Freewrite

As described in Glasgow (2002), the purpose of the image freewrite is to encourage students to infer meaning from a given statement and create a visual expression of the idea. Ask students to find their favorite passage and select a quotation that is meaningful to them. Then, ask them to create a visual picture that, in some way, illustrates the words in the quotation. After they create their pictures, ask them to freewrite about their thoughts on the words and images they created. See the CD-ROM for Kiesha's image freewrite after reading *Remembering Manzanar: Life in a Japanese Relocation Camp* (2003).

Shape/Color Interpretation

This strategy, taken from Stephanie Kight's presentation at the SOCTE Conference, in Athens, Ohio, on April 29, 2000, is excellent for helping students understand the main ideas/themes in the novel and representing them visually. Students must analyze the character development and determine the relationships among them. As students are nearly finished with the novel, ask them to decide on a shape and a color for at least three of the characters; the colors and shapes should indicate something about the characters' attitudes, personalities, and behavior. Ask them to arrange the shapes in such a way that they express the relationships of the characters to one another. Then ask students to write a brief explanation of the finished product, clarifying the meaning of the abstract representation. If you like, have the students explain their finished project to the class as a brief oral presentation. These pictures, with attached essays, make a colorful bulletin board. See Table 1:6 for Shape/Color for Alan Parkers's *Come See The Paradise* by Amy Spencer.

Table 1:6 Shape/Color for Come See the Paradise

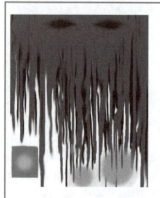

In the bottom right corner are Lily and her daughter, Mini, represented by the two floating golden suns (Japan = Nihon = "origin of the sun"). The black and grey, ruinous mass that is melting and spreading over the picture is a mixed "character." It is both the racist law against the Japanese-American citizens and the prejudice of the White American citizens. The staring eyes are pitiless and self-righteous. With its oppressive nature, the hatred stings, envelopes, and consumes everything around it. It has begun devouring Lily and Mini, and although they are in anguish from this injustice, they are *not* consumed, due to the stronger spirits within. Jack, Lily's husband, is the red, solid square to the bottom left. The red symbolizes his great love towards his wife and child, while the small sun *within* his shape is a direct sign of his loyalty towards all of the Japanese-Americans. He is not so much harmed by the law or the people, but rather looked

cont.

down upon for his nonconformity. A physical barrier is placed between him and his family on the other side. Having to join the army to avoid being jailed for his parole violation, he is constantly watched by the over-shadowing, maleficent eyes. However, because of his enlistment, he is finally able to visit his family within the confines of the camp until they are eventually released. Amy Spencer

Cause and Effect Relationships

Since understanding cause and effect relationships is one of the critical skills necessary to pass proficiency tests in most of the United States, this strategy will help students strengthen their skills. In Table 1:7 are many of the emotions that Japanese-Americans experienced in the relocation process. Describe a situation or event from the novel you read that caused it to happen. This strategy was based on the one in Nakajima's *A Guide for Using Journey to Topaz in the Classroom* (1993).

Table 1:7 Cause and Effect Relationships

EFFECT (Emotion)	CAUSE (Event in story)
fear	
anger	
bitterness	
disenchantment	
sorrow	
embarrassment	
befuddlement	
irritability	
disappointment	
hopefulness	
courage	
love	
relief	
loneliness	
helplessness	
happiness	

After Reading Strategies to Extend Meaning of the Japanese Internment Experience

Simulation of the Japanese Internment Experience

For this simulation of the Japanese Internment experience, divide the class into Japanese-American families of four or five students, according to the books they read. Arrange the desks in sets of four or five to represent a family setting.

Each student should assume a role of a family member in the book. One student should assume the role of U.S. Army Lieutenant General J. L. DeWitt. Another two or three students may act as FBI agents. One person will need to manage the police station. You will need someone to be manager of the Civil Control Station. See Table 1:8 for family arrangements if students have read the books in their Literature Circles.

Table 1:8 Family Configurations for Role Play

The Invisible Thread by Uchida	*The Moon Bridge* by Savin	*Farewell to Manzanar* by Houston	*Under the Blood-Red Sun* by Salisbury	*Nisei Daughter* by Sone
Uchida's Business Manager	**Fugimoto's** Grocery Store Owners	**Wakatsuki's** Fisherman, Terminal Island	**Nakaji's** Fisherman, Hawaii	**Sone's** Hotel Owners
Papa	Uncle Joe	Papa	Grampa	Papa
Mama	Papa	Mama	Papa	Mama
Keiko	Mama	Bill	Mama	Kazuko Monica
Yoshiko	Mitzie	Woody	Tomikazu	Ken
	Sab	Jeanne	Kimi	Henry
	Friend, Ruthie		Friend, Billy	Sumiko

In preparation for the simulation, you will need to secure a copy of the Civilian Exclusion Order No. 82. (A copy of this order can be found in Inada's *Only What We Could Carry*, 2000, pp. 8–9, or the National Archives Web site.) Make copies of what evacuees must carry with them on departure for the Assembly Center as determined in the instructions: bedding and linens for each member of the family; toilet articles for each member of the family; extra clothing for each member of the family; and essential personal effects for each member of the family (Inada, p.8). Also, make evacuation tags that each family member will be required to wear around their necks. You can decide how long they should wear them and bear the humiliation. See Table 1:9 for Sample Evacuation Tag, replicated from Inada (p. 57), also available on the National Archives Web site.

Table 1:9 Sample Evacuation Tag

Name:	
Family Lot 13664 TO BE RETAINED BY PERSON TO WHOM ISSUED	YOU ARE INSTRUCTED TO REPORT READY TO TRAVEL ON: Thursday, April 20 at 8:00 a.m.

- The simulation begins with the FBI agents knocking at the door of each family and abruptly taking away the father to an unknown detention center. Families can then discuss the consequences of this action. What will this mean for each of them? Ask each family to share their thoughts. After the discussion settles, family members are called to attention by a radio announcement.

- Everyone listens to Lt. General DeWitt as he reads the Civilian Exclusion Order No. 82, which details the evacuation procedures. Each family should have time to think about their reactions to the edict. Will they be docile in its acceptance, or angry and hostile toward the implications of the order? Ask students to discuss the practical aspects of getting families organized for the move, as well as their feelings of being removed from their homes and workplaces. What about their constitutional rights? Was there a purpose for the sacrifices they were being asked to make? Did it preserve their liberty in the long run?

- Each family should send one member (preferably the head of the family, or the person in whose name most of the property is held) to the Civil Control Station to register and receive further instructions.

- At the Civil Control Station, the manager will hand out the instructions for evacuees to carry with them on departure for the Assembly Center and identification tags for each member of the family.

- Send one member of the family to the police station to turn in radios, cameras, and any other article considered to be contraband.

- Once everyone has returned to their family, show a movie clip from the VHS version of *Come See The Paradise*, produced by Alan Parker (1990). The scene is near the beginning, when Lily Kawamura returns home to her family and her mother is in the bedroom burning all the family photos, grade cards, and so on. Watch as they pack up their household and head for the train. Stop the film as the train departs the station, dividing Lily and her child from her American husband, Jack McGurn.

- Ask each family to itemize what they will need to sell, what they will give away, what they will ask trusted friends to keep for them, and what they will carry with them. In addition to the items mentioned in the instructions, each member can take only what they can carry. Members must provide a rationale for their choices. All items must be securely packaged, tied, and plainly labeled.

- Since no pets of any kind will be permitted, decide how you will dispense with your pets.

- Close the simulation by saying goodbye to friends and neighbors. How will you bring closure to your life on the West Coast? How do you feel about leaving? Is there any way to show your loyalty?

Readers' Theater

Readers' Theater is an excellent strategy to engage students in presenting literature to other students. McCaslin (1990) defines Readers' Theater as the oral presentation of drama, prose, or poetry by two or more readers. Readers' Theater differs from orally reading a selection in that several readers take the parts of the characters in the story or play. Instead of memorizing or improvising their parts as in other types of theater productions, the players read them, which to many students is much less intimidating. Since the emphasis is on what the audience hears rather than sees, selection of the literature is very important. Readers' Theater scripts generally contain a great deal of dialogue and are paraphrased or adapted from a piece of literature. The scripts can be student generated or teacher generated, and a limited number are available commercially. The following Readers' Theater is an adaptation of an article originally printed in the *Topaz Times* New Year's Edition, and is found in Inada's *Only What We Could Carry* (2000). Perform it with eight different speakers from a script and a Microsoft PowerPoint presentation found on the accompanying CD-ROM. During the reading of the script, *Adagio for Strings*, Opus 11, by Samuel Barber can serve as background music.

Multigenre Research Paper

The multigenre research paper is a student-centered approach to research and learning. In this unit, it is designed to be the culminating experience for the unit. Students are given a choice of topic and choice of creative formats for representing their findings. This research requires that students make interdisciplinary connections and use high-level thinking skills to gather information, conduct interviews, collect information about historical events, and then report the information in nontraditional formats. Instead of a traditional research paper format, students report their research in a series of creative pieces that tell a story. These creative pieces are connected together with repetends (graphics, quotes, memos, etc.) that students have written themselves or documented from other sources. In this way, students develop personal voices to express the multiple perspectives they are representing. Students provide a notes page describing the inspiration for their creative pieces and a works cited page to document their resources. Students are required to prepare a presentation to the class to share their research findings. For more information about this type of research paper, see Romano's (2000) *Blending Genre, Altering Style: Writing Multigenre Papers.*

Instructions for Students to Get Started on the Multigenre Research Paper

1. Choose a topic related to the Japanese Relocation experience or the Japanese culture (art, cuisine, drama, festivals, history, etc.). Prepare a prospectus that states your topic, interest, purpose, audience, and materials you will use for information.

2. As you find information for your topic, keep a one- to two-page journal entry of your findings and your reactions to what you are reading. You should find information using at least three different types of sources (Internet, magazines, newspapers, interviews, etc.) These journal entries will be helpful in drafting your genres.

3. Begin drafting genres for the final paper. A genre is a form of writing, such as short stories, diary entries, news articles, letters, memos, etc. Your paper should include at least four different genres.

4. The best papers are cohesive; there is some structure that holds the creative pieces together. Look for images, quotes, photos, statistics, or other devices that would be appropriate as repetends or connectors of your pieces.

5. See Table 1:10 for Multigenre Reserch Paper Requirements.

Table 1:10 Multigenre Research Paper Requirements

Minimum Requirements for the Multigenre Paper	Due Date
• Prospectus • Table of Contents • Prologue (provides a context for the reader; tells the reader how to read the paper) • Five creative pieces (representing four different genres) • Repetends (to connect the creative pieces) • Notespage (reflective in nature; describes the inspiration for each of the pieces and repetends in the project) • Works Cited (traditional MLA or APA format) • Plan for a five-minute presentation to the class (must include a visual)	

Choose a day for presentations to begin. Provide a sign-up sheet so that students can prepare for the event. Invite parents, guardians, and administrators to join in the celebration. These papers are often the students' best work of the year. They take great pride in their accomplishments. For an assessment rubric for the Multigenre Research Paper, See Table 1:11. See the CD-ROM for a Multigenre Research Paper written by Erin Rogers.

Table 1:11 Assessment Rubric for the Multigenre Research Paper

	Exemplary (5points)	Admirable (4 points)	Adequate (3 points)	Minimal (2 points)	Score
Front Matter: Cover, Title Page, Table of Contents	Organizes material in a creative, clear, appropriate and precise manner	Organizes the material in an effective manner that is appropriate and precise	Organizes the material in an appropriate manner, but may lack some clarity or consistency	Little evidence of a cohesive plan. Little or no description or detail.	___ x 1 =
Prospectus	Includes a creative plan detailing the topic, theme, purpose for the research	Includes a plan detailing the topic, theme, and purpose for the research	Little evidence of a plan detailing the topic, theme, and purpose for the research	No plan provided for stating the topic, theme, and purpose for the research	___ x 1 =
Prologue	Creatively situates the reader with information they need to know before reading or listening to the paper	Situates the reader with important information for understanding the research paper	Does not give the reader enough information to understand the research paper	Does not acknowledge that the reader needs certain information to make the most of the research	___ x 1 =
Multigenre Writing Section	Unified, focused compositions; topic or ideas consistently clear; details varied and vivid	Generally well organized; topics or ideas generally clear; details generally varied and vivid	Topics, ideas, or plans may not be clear; minimal use of supportive detail	Topic may be clear but no overall organizational plans; little development of ideas	___ x 5 =
Research	Research evident from a variety of media, reference, and technological sources	Research evident from Internet and print material	Research from only one source	No research evident	___ x 4 =
Conventions	Correct grammar, punctuation, and spelling	Mostly correct grammar, punctuation, and spelling	Frequent errors in grammar, punctuation, and spelling	Numerous problems with grammar, punctuation, and spelling	___ x 1 =
Unity	A unique repetend or structure unites the piece	A repetend or structure unites the piece	A repetend or structure unites the piece but it may seem contrived or trite	Pieces may seem disjointed	___ x 2 =
Notes page	Includes a notes page which reflects on the actual event and the liberties taken within each genre and the writing process	Includes a notes page which reflects on the actual event and the liberties taken within each genre	Includes a notes page which mentions the actual event and the liberties taken within each genre	Notes page only shallowly acknowledges source of information	___ x 1 =

Japanese-American Young Adult Literature: World War II

Japanese-American Children's Literature

Bunting, E. (1998). *So far from the sea*. Illustrated by C. K. Soenpiet. New York: Clarion Books.

Coerr, E. (1977). *Sadako and the thousand paper cranes*. Illustrated by Ronald Himler. New York: Dell Yearling.

Kodama, T. (1992). *Shin's tricycle*. Illustrations by Noriyuki Ando. New York: Walker and Company.

Maruki, T. (1982). *Hiroshima no pika*. Boston: Lothrup.

Mochizuki, K. (1993). *Baseball saved us*. Illustrated by Dom Lee. New York: Lee and Low Books, Inc.

Shigekawa, M. (1993). *Blue jay in the desert*. Illustrated by Isao Kikuchi. Chicago: Polychrome Publishing Corporation.

Uchida, Y. (1976, 1993). *The bracelet*. New York: The Putnam & Grosset Group.

Japanese-American Autobiography

Houston, J. W., & Houston, J. D. (1990). *Farewell to Manzanar*. New York: Bantam.

Savin, M. (1992). *The moon bridge*. New York: Scholastic.

Sone, M. (1979). *Nisei daughter*. Seattle, WA: University of Washington Press.

Takashima, S. (1974). *A child in prison camp*. New York: William Morrow and Company.

Uchida, Y. (1984). *Desert exile: The uprooting of a Japanese-American family*. Seattle, WA: University of Washington Press.

Uchida, Y. (1991). *The invisible thread*. Surrey, England: Beech Tree.

Japanese-American Historical Fiction

Guterson, D. (1994). *Snow falling on cedars*. San Diego, CA: Harcourt Brace.

Salisbury, G. (1994). *Under the blood-red sun*. New York: Delacorte.

Tajiri, V. (Ed.). (1990). *Through innocent eyes*. Los Angeles: Keiro Services Press.

Uchida, Y. (1978). *Journey home*. New York: Atheneum.

Uchida, Y. (1971). *Journey to Topaz*. New York: Charles Scribner's Sons.

Uchida, Y. (1987). *Picture bride*. Flagstaff, AZ: Northland Press.

Yep, L. (1995). *Hiroshima*. New York: Scholastic.

Japanese-American Information Books

Armor, J., & Wright, P. (1988). *Manzanar*. New York: Times Books.

Banim, L. (1993). *American dreams*. London: Silver Moon Press.

Cooper, M. L. (2000). *Fighting for honor: Japanese-Americans and World War II*. New York: Houghton Mifflin Company.

Cooper, M. L. (2003). *Remembering Manzanar: Life in a Japanese relocation camp*. New York: Clarion Books.

Daniel, R. (1993). *Prisoners without trial: Japanese-Americans in World War II*. New York: Hill & Wang.

Davis, D. (1982). *Behind barbed wire: The imprisonment of Japanese-Americans during World War II*. New York: E. P. Dutton, Inc.

Drinnon, R. (1987). *Keeper of concentration camps: Dillon S. Myer and American racism*. Berkeley, CA: University of California Press.

Hamanaka, S. (1990). *Journey: Japanese-Americans, racism, and renewal*. London: Orchard Books/Franklin Watts.

Inada, L. F. (Ed.). (2000). *Only what we could carry: The Japanese-American internment experience*. Berkeley, CA: Heyday Books.

Inada, L. F. (1997). *Drawing the line*. Minneapolis, MN: Coffee House Press.

Kessler, L. (1994). *Stubborn twig: Three generations in the life of a Japanese-American family*. New York: Plume.

Levine, E. (1995). *A fence away from freedom: Japanese-Americans and World War II*. New York: Putnam's Sons.

Masaoka, M. (1987). *They call me Moses Masaoka*. New York: William Morrow and Company.

Means, F. C. (1992). *The moved-outers*. New York: Walker and Company.

Smith, P. (1995). *Democracy on trial: The Japanese-American evacuation and relocation in World War II*. New York: Simon & Schuster.

Stanley, J. (1994). *I am an American: A true story of Japanese internment*. New York: Crown Publishers.

Tunnell, M., & Chilcoat, G. (1996). *The children of Topaz: The story of a Japanese-American internment camp*. New York: Holiday House.

Japanese-American War Poetry

Inada, L. F. (1997). *Drawing the line*. Minneapolis, MN: Coffee House Press.

Nakano, J., & Kay N. (Eds.). (1983). *Poets behind barbed wire*. Honolulu: Bamboo Ridge Press.

Japanese-American Young Adult Literature Post War: Struggle with Prejudice and Search for Identity

Glenn, M. (2000). *Split-images: A story in poems*. New York: HarperCollins.

Guterson, D. (1994). *Snow falling on cedars*. San Diego, CA: Harcourt Brace.

Irwin, H. (1987). *Kim/Kimi*. New York: M.K. McElderry Books.

Miklowitz, G. (1985). *The war between the classes*. New York: Delacorte.

Namioka, L. (1994). *April and the dragon lady*. San Diego, CA: Harcourt Brace.

Wolff, V. E. (1998). *Bat 6: A novel*. New York: Scholastic.

Japanese-American Video and Film

Hicks, S. (2000). *Snow falling on cedars*. Hollywood, CA: Universal Studios.

Ina, S. (1999). *Children of the camps: The documentary*. Alexandria, VA: Public

Broadcasting Service.

Parker, A. (1990). *Come see the paradise*. Los Angeles: Twentieth Century Fox.

Tajiri, R. (1995). *History and memory*. New York: Electronic Arts Intermix.

References

Barber, S. (1990, October 25). *Adagio for strings, opus 11*. Leonard Slatkin, Conductor. Angel Classics.

Daniels, H. (2002). *Literature Circles: Voice and choice in book clubs & reading groups* (2nd ed.). York, ME: Stenhouse Publishers.

Gillet, J., & Kita, M. J. (1979). Words, kids, and categories. *The Reading Teacher, 32*, 538–542.

Glasgow, J. (2002). *Using young adult literature: Thematic activities based on Gardner's multiple intelligences*. Norwood, MA: Christopher-Gordon Publishers, Inc.

Kight, S. (2000, April 29). *World literature: Opening the door to a 'world' of assessments*. Athens, OH: Southeast Ohio Council of Teachers of English.

McCaslin, N. (1990). *Creative drama in the classroom* (5th ed.). White Plains, NY: Longman.

Nakajima, C. (1993). *A guide for using Journey to Topaz in the classroom*. Westminster, CA: Teacher Created Materials.

Ogle, D. M. (1992). KWL in action: Secondary teachers find applications that work. In E. K. Dishner, T. W. Bean, J. E. Readence, & D. W. Moore (Eds.), *Reading in the content areas: Improving classroom instruction* (3rd ed.). Dubuque, IA: Kendall Hunt.

Romano, T. (2000). *Blending genre, altering style: Writing multigenre papers*. Portsmouth, NH: Heinemann Boynton/Cook.

Vacca, R. & Vacca, J. (1996). *Content area reading* (5th ed.). New York: HarperCollins.

Wilhelm, J., Baker, T., & Dube, J. (2001). *Strategic reading: Guiding students to lifelong literacy, 6–12*. Portsmouth, NH: Heinemann Boyton/Cook.

Chapter Two

The Long Walk Home:
Equity in Alabama

Linda J. Rice

"Watching this [film] was shocking, seeing the way [Blacks] were treated. I mean, I knew this happened and all, but actually seeing it, although in a movie, was just horrifying." —Faith, age 18

Nearly 50 years ago, a Black woman refused to give up her seat to a White passenger on a bus in Montgomery, Alabama, the heart of the segregated South. In her book, *Quiet Strength* (2000), this courageous woman, Rosa Parks, explained why. She said:

> "Our mistreatment was just not right, and I was tired of it. I kept thinking about my mother and my grandparents, and how strong they were. I knew there was a possibility of being mistreated, but an opportunity was being given to me to do what I had asked of others."

The result of Parks' actions has become an integral part of American history. Parks was arrested and tried, convicted and fined. Yet more importantly, her principled decision inspired others to make sacrifices, challenge the constitutionality of segregation, and press on toward the goal of racial equality.

While to many adults the impact of this struggle and the sacrifices endured by those fighting for necessary change are heartfelt and real, to many adolescents the Civil Rights Movement is a mere event objectified by pages in a history text, often no closer to their experience than World Wars I and II, Korea, and Vietnam. Today's teens were toddlers during Dessert Storm; the time in which they have been cognizant of history-in-the-making includes Columbine, the Clinton impeachment, the Enron scandal, the September 11th attack, the tragedy of space shuttle *Columbia*, and the War on Terror. In these events, students have seen sacrifices of teachers, firemen, soldiers, spouses, and scientists. Yet, as flags have been unfurled from houses and magneted to automobiles in the spirit of national unity, our students must not dismiss the Civil Rights Movement as something passé and over—some wrong that has been righted and that, therefore, may be forgotten. Yet, how do we, as teachers, bring to life the real struggles of a citizenry, of individual people working for the common good? How do we help students to "experience" the injustices and question: What would I really do in the face of injustice? Would I really be willing to "do the right thing?" Or, would I fall into my world of comfort and let the status quo be?

Understanding the past struggles of a nation—a nation made up of individual people with rights and choices—is tantamount to living responsibly in a democracy, for we do not know what the next struggle may be, the next challenge to personhood, the next affront to freedom. We cannot be sure that our faith or family or friend will not one day be the target of discrimination, marginalization, or persecution.

Situated in the context of the Montgomery Bus Boycott of 1955, *The Long Walk Home*, starring Whoopi Goldberg and Sissy Spacek, offers teachers a powerful instructional tool for bringing history to life, prompting students to examine racial issues and tensions past and present, identify with characters, and consider the extent to which they would sacrifice their own comfort and security to promote necessary change. The film unit includes one-minute vocabulary reports, reflective writing and discussion, a parallel poem, and a culminating project using students' multiple intelligences. After viewing the film, teachers may extend the unit by having students form Literature Circles, where each group reads a different book related to the Montgomery Bus Boycott or Civil Rights Movement at large. In their Literature Circles, students will discuss their reading in order to deepen their understanding of the era, compose and present an analytical/reflective paper to the class, write a Readers' Theater, and make a scrapbook. Recommended books for the Literature Circles are: *Free at Last: A History of the Civil Rights Movement and Those Who Died in the Struggle* (1994) by Sara Bullard; *Just Like Martin* (1995) by Ossie Davis; Margaret Davidson's *I Have a Dream: The Story of Martin Luther King* (1999); *The Watsons Go to Birmingham—1963: A Novel* (1997) by Christopher Curtis; *Bayard Rustin: Behind the Scenes of the Civil Rights Movement* (1997) by James Haskins; *Spite Fences* (1994) by Trudy Krisher; and *Freedom's Children: Young Civil Rights Activists Tell Their Own Stories* (2000) by Ellen Levine.

A Word About the Film

What is particularly noteworthy about *The Long Walk Home* is the way that it highlights the divide among the White citizens of Montgomery. While many, such as the "Citizens' Council," perpetuated stereotypes and devised schemes of intimidation to oppress the African-Americans, some looked beyond their own comfort and risked their personal safety, family harmony, and "social respectability" to support necessary change. This film, therefore, may be particularly useful in schools with predominantly Caucasian student populations, where it is easy for students to assume, as beneficiaries of those who brought our nation through the Civil Rights Movement, a superior moral mindset that quickly concludes: "I would have done the right thing." The violence and racist language of *The Long Walk Home* (rated PG), while disturbing to view and hear, help to convey the truth of what Blacks endured; the film plunges the viewer into the world of injustice and suffering that, without such a film, may be in students' eyes just "so many words about the past," realities gone by that no longer resonate feeling, hurt, and lived history. As the film shows the courageous actions of the Black community, it also poignantly portrays the social mores and dialogue of segregation imbedded in the South, thus conveying the dilemma of Whites who wanted to help with the car pool.

While Odessa Cotter, the Thompson's maid, played by Whoopi Goldberg, supports the boycott by walking miles to work each day, leaving her tired and with sore, swollen, bleeding feet, Miriam Thompson, against her husband's will, supports the boycott by secretly participating in the car pool, picking up Black workers and dropping them off at their places of employment. When Miriam's husband Norman discovers she has defied him, he demands that she stop driving Odessa and others or leave him altogether. Heightening the impact of Miriam's choice to fight for racial equality or maintain harmony at home is the presence of Mary Catherine, the Thompson's 7-year-old daughter. The narration of *The Long Walk Home* is seen through her eyes and told in the voice-overs of Michelle Pfeiffer.

The film comes to a close in a powerfully threatening, yet simultaneously inspiring scene, in which Miriam is caught and confronted by her husband, Norman, and brother-in-law Tucker, in the car pool lot and told that 150 men would be coming in a matter of minutes to shut down the lot. On instinct, Miriam seeks to shepherd Odessa and Mary Catherine to her car and drive them to safety, but is told by another member of the "Citizens Council," "You're not taking your nigger maid out of here." Again, Miriam must decide whether to stay or go. As the mob of angry men descend on the lot, they back the Blacks up against a wall and then make a narrow gauntlet, pointing for the Blacks to walk through and shouting: "Walk, nigger, walk. Walk, nigger, walk." Mary Catherine, at her mother's side, looks on in fear, and one woman steps forward toward the roars of chanting men and begins to sing a Negro spiritual. Another woman joins her, hand and voice, and another, and another, until a line of Black women face the crowd with voices raised in confident faith. Odessa, toward the end of the line, tears streaming down her face, looks to Miriam standing at the edge of the lot with her husband on one side, the principle she believes in on the other, and Mary Catherine leaning in to her. The woman at the end of the line opens her hand to Miriam, and Miriam joins the line. Met only with peaceful song, the once-raging mob dissipates, and the closing voice-over—the words of Mary Catherine—begin:

> "It would take years to learn what standing in that line meant to my mom—and later to me. Fifty thousand boycotted the buses in Montgomery. I knew one of them. Her name was Odessa Cotter."

Before-Viewing Strategies to Understand the Civil Rights Era

One-Minute Vocabulary Reports

As a way to introduce students to the important organizations, events, legislation, slogans, artistic renderings, and people influential in the Civil Rights era, the teacher will give each student a "topic" to investigate. Once students have been assigned their topics—or they may simply draw from a stack of 3 in x 5 in note cards—it is advisable to spend a class period in the library or media center, where the teacher will be available to assist students with their research. Students are to find enough information on their topic to deliver a one-minute report in front of the class (Glasgow, 2002). Students also find or create a visual aid to accompany their brief presentation. The visual aid may be from a book, magazine, or Web site; it might also be a student-created drawing or collage. Some students even manage to find artifacts, such as a 15-cent stamp honoring Martin Luther King, Jr., sheet music for "We Shall Overcome," or Ruby Bridges' autobiographical book, *Through My Eyes* (1999). The "reports" and visuals may be posted on a bulletin board for review throughout the unit. As students listen to the reports of their peers, they should take notes, as some of the organizations, events, legislation, slogans, and people are referenced in the film, and the notes will provide a quick review.

See Table 2:1 for 25 "terms" that work well to introduce the Civil Rights era.

Table 2:1 Terms for One-Minute Vocabulary Reports

1.	Ralph Bunche
2.	Governor Orvel Faubus
3.	Little Rock Nine
4.	Rosa Parks
5.	Malcolm X
6.	Martin Luther King, Jr.
7.	Chief Justice Earl Warren
8.	Joseph McNeill
9.	James Meredith
10.	Ralph Abernathy
11.	March from Selma to Montgomery
12.	"Letter from Birmingham Jail"
13.	Sit-ins
14.	Freedom Riders
15.	SCLC
16.	CORE
17.	Watts Riots
18.	March on Washington
19.	Voting Rights Act of 1964
20.	NAACP
21.	Brown vs. Board of Education
22.	Bloody Sunday, 1965
23.	Ruby Bridges
24.	"The Problem We All Live With" (Norman Rockwell)
25.	"We Shall Overcome"

Table 2:2 One-Minute Vocabulary Report for "The Problem We All Live With"

Visual Aid

From www.normanrockwellmuseum.com (Store)

Written Report "The Problem We All Live With" is a 1964 illustration by Norman Rockwell depicting 6-year-old Ruby Bridges surrounded by federal marshals as she became the first Black student to attend the all-White William Frantz Public School in New Orleans, Louisiana, on November 14, 1960. This effort to desegregate the school happened four years after the "Little Rock Nine" were the first Black students to integrate Central High School, an all-White school known for its excellent academic program. President Eisenhower ordered U.S. Marshals to escort the students. Notice the word "Nigger" spray-painted on the wall, and the tomato that has hit just behind Ruby's head. Brave young people like Ruby had to have great courage to help the cause for equality.

Information from:

Norman Rockwell: A Classic Treasury by Robin Langley Sommer
and www.amazon.com (Ruby Bridges)

Inventory of Experiences Through Reflective Writing and Discussion

After students have shared their one-minute vocabulary reports, they draw on background knowledge by responding in writing to several prompts. These prompts (see Table 2:3) are designed to help situate students' readiness to view the film as a purposeful, relevant endeavor. As students take inventory of their own experiences, the film becomes more applicable to their own lives.

Table 2:3 Before-Viewing Questions

- What have your experiences been with books and movies about minorities and civil rights? For this, you might consider films in which issues of race, religion, ethnicity, and/or gender are key issues. You might even consider the Holocaust, and the failure of citizens to speak out against injustice and persecution.
- In recent times, where have you seen civil rights abuses? Prejudicial practices?
- To what degree are race and prejudice "issues" in our school? Our community? Our nation? Explain.

The students should be given at least 30 minutes to respond to the prompts. Because some students may know very little about the Civil Rights Movement, including issues of religion, gender, and the Holocaust provides them with more opportunities for responding. Likewise, because some students have had limited exposure to multicultural literature, especially that in which the impact of minority status is a central issue, including films helps students to generate more ideas. The key here is for students to take inventory of what they know about injustice and the treatment of minorities—to promote thinking before viewing that fosters a sense of readiness to see the film not as Hollywood entertainment or a flat documentary but as a narrative to be vicariously lived by the viewer. By drawing on students' own experiences, we seek to situate them with a readiness to view, realizing that the film is, in a sense, about "something they already know and understand."

After students have responded to the prompts in writing, the class may "circle up" to facilitate sharing and discussion of the topic. When all students are expected to share, and when the teacher encourages spontaneous responses to build a dialogue as ideas are presented, the discussion can easily last 45–60 minutes and may need two class periods on a traditional (not block) schedule. If it appears that students are failing to identify with the plight of minorities as victims of prejudice, the teacher may introduce the issue of stereotyping (in particular, "stereotype by dress") into the discussion. Many students will be able to relate to being "tagged" or "labeled" because of the clothes they wear, and some students will offer specific examples of where they have been "wrongly judged" because of their appearance. For instance, students who dress in "alternative" or "gothic" styles or have pierced eyebrows, lips, and/or noses commonly report being followed around as presumed shoplifters when they enter stores. They report being "looked at like criminals." Teachers will consider the unique characteristics of their students in posing questions that help students to identify with what it feels like to be treated unfairly, to be the victim of prejudice.

Once there has been sufficient time for the class to take inventory and share their knowledge of and experience with civil rights abuses and prejudicial practices, it is time to begin viewing *The Long Walk Home*.

During-Viewing Strategies to Encourage Discussion and Reflection

Although students could view the film beginning to end in two class periods, taking time out at the beginning, or end, of each class for writing and discussion deepens students' critical engagement with its issues and characters. Therefore, the teacher may elect to show 20–40 minutes of the film at a time and extend the viewing over a period of three to four days (with discussion and parallel-poem activity interspersed) to encourage ongoing reflection. This deliberate approach helps students to part from the "movie as entertainment" or "day off from English class" view to the "movie as instruction" and "I'm expected to learn something" view.

Critical Viewing and Initial Response

As the film begins and students are introduced to characters, they should take note of names and relationships. Students should also be encouraged to take notes on the plot and setting; they may even elect to record specific lines (quotes) that provide examples of building tensions within, and between, characters. Using these informal notes, students should be given the last 10 minutes of class to reflect on their first day of viewing the film. The prompt may be broad, as follows:

- Reflections after day 1 of video (make sure your response demonstrates your emerging understanding of race issues and tensions—for Blacks and Whites—in the film).

Students' responses to the prompt may be shared at the end of class, if there is time, or at the beginning of the next class. Either way, a time for sharing and discussion is crucial to help deepen the students' critical viewing of the film's issues. If the discussion takes place at the beginning of the second day of viewing, it will provide a review of what happened; if it takes place at the end of the first day, the teacher may want to reiterate several of the key issues before starting the tape on day 2.

Personal Identification and Meaning Construction

To help students develop a personal understanding of the film and its key issues and consider these in light of human experience, students respond to the following prompts after the second day of viewing:

- What character do you most identify with in the film? Explain.
- Identify what you perceive to be the central causes and effects of the growing tensions in the film.
- What does this film say to you about humanity?

Students may begin their responses to these three prompts in class at the end of the second day of viewing; however, they should continue—so as to give more thought and consideration—their responses as homework. A class period (50 minutes) could easily be dedicated to discussing students' responses. While some students, female and male, will identify with Odessa and Miriam for their willingness to stand up for what is right, others will identify strongly with Theodore, who defends his sister—even though it means being severely beaten by three White teens. In the event that students are quick to identify with Miriam (the heroine of sorts), the teacher should make sure to emphasize the characteristics of the segregated South, a region where many White citizens maintained positions of power and privilege and benefited economically and socially by opposing racial equality. Encourage students to carefully examine the personal risks that Miriam faced in participating in the car pool against her husband's wishes. Emphasize that "in light of where we stand today, knowing that as a nation we have made great strides in racial equality, it's easy to say, 'I would have done the same,'" but that given the time and circumstance, Miriam's decision was one that may have been very difficult, was certainly unpopular, and wrought judgment from her husband, in-laws, and friends. Bridging this emphasis with the idea that "we don't know who might be the next victim of prejudice, marginalization, or discrimination" is the key—helping students to reflexively press the question: "To what degree am I willing to give up my personal comfort, social standing, and safety in order to do what is right for someone else?"

Parallel Poem in Response to "Across the Lines," a Song by Tracy Chapman

Writing a parallel poem is an effective way to begin class on a day students will be discussing the film (particularly between days 2 and 3 of viewing). The activity is free-flowing and fun for students and tends to generate writing for sharing. In a two column handout, the teacher gives students the lyrics for "Across the Lines," a song by Tracy Chapman (Electra, 1988). The song tells to story of a young African American girl who is assaulted without provocation. Though her name is unknown, the tragedy is reported in the newspapers, causing racial tensions, hatred, and violence to flare up. In corresponding riots and fighting, two African American boys are murdered, and one Caucasian boy loses his sight.

With the lyrics printed on the left side of the page, the right side of the page is open for students to write, making connections and free-associations with the lyrics and instrumentation that tell the story of how the nameless young African American girl has become the scapegoat for the anger that erupted in the community. Combining poetry (lyrics) with music helps writers, both novice and expert, articulate impressions and construct meaning.

The song's subtle but beating instrumentation is built around a single acoustic guitar and Chapman's voice—that of the seemingly casual questioner in verse one, asking who would be brave enough to cross the metaphorical lines separating while and black communities. Chapman's voice intensifies as the song's story unfolds, and its narrator appears caught in the vortex of one raging against the driving rhythms of injustice and one who has resigned, feeling powerless to rage against "humanity's" senseless actions toward a nameless victim.

After explaining the task of writing a parallel poem or story, using "Across the Lines" as the impetus for writing, the teacher should play the song twice—first at regular volume, then lowered, as a kind of background inspiration and reminder of ideas generated. Instructions to the students are as follows:

- As you listen to the song by Tracy Chapman, write a parallel poem—you may borrow words or phrases from the song. Try to have a sense of rhythm to what you write. Make free associations, and just let your creativity flow. There's no "right" or "wrong" way to do this, so long as you write in line (rather than sentence) form, so as to be lyrical or poetic . . . and so long as you are connecting with (or extending from) the song.

Table 2:4 includes two student responses. While the example on the left is a direct response to Chapman's song, the one on the right has made parallels between "Across the Lines" and *The Long Walk Home*.

Table 2:4 Student Examples of Parallel Poems in Response to "Across the Lines"

Tonya's Parallel Poem	E'lise's Parallel Poem
Across the Lines	When will we be able
Where we need to go	To go where they are
On the other side of the tracks	When will we be able
Force us to understand and know	As we're driving in our car
Refuse to choose sides	Does there have to be a wall
Learn to embrace life	Between our sons and daughters
Today acceptance begins	That separates us all
When we refuse racism with strife	Because of our mothers and fathers
Children play together	Listen to our words and actions
The lines are now blurred	The way we treat each other
Dreams of America are restored	How our skin color clashes
When the colors become stirred	Against the different colors
Black and white turns to grey	There are hurt and angry people
In this utopian America	That don't know who to blame
	Let's look a little deeper
	We're all a lot the same

After playing the song twice, the teacher should ask students to continue working for 5 to 10 minutes with the notes and ideas generated as they listened. During this time, students are to revise and craft the parallel poem. While students may elect to take their writing home for further revision and language play, this activity is intended primarily as an in-class expressive writing exercise and discussion prompter. As students volunteer to share their writing, the teacher should facilitate a discussion, drawing out major ideas and connections between past and present, the film and the song. For instance, Katie's parallel poem (see Table 2:5) introduced interracial dating, a topic which promotes dialogue among students.

Table 2:5 Katie's Parallel Poem

Mom says I can look at them
Brush by them
Maybe even talk to them
But don't ever date them

They can't keep you happy
Why can't I see
She says I'm making a mistake
But that's a risk I'm willing to take

Why not a White boy she disappointingly asks
Why are these boundaries I want to pass
Why would I take this taboo to chance
Why would I allow him to lead me in this dance

She looks at me with angered shame
Asking why I want to play in the color game
She says what I'm doing is a horrible sin
But then why should I listen to her—
She's no better than him.

Gabriel's response focused on looking beyond skin color. He wrote: "We can't see through skin/to the real issue within/It must be learned like an art/that to judge someone, you look to the heart/ If there weren't all this hate/There'd be no debate/That your true color shines from within." Gabriel's poem ends with a call to keep working for positive change. He writes: "The wait may be long/But you have to stay strong/As we wait for the healing to begin." Following the students' ideas as expressed in writing, the teacher can deepen the dialogue about prejudice and healing. Oftentimes, one or two lines from a student's writing introduce a powerful concept, such as these from Danielle's poem: "Little Black girl beaten/Picture yourself in her shoes." Here arise concepts of empathy and reflexivity—stepping into the perspective of another long enough to understand and potentially bring change to one's own view. Engaging in reflective writing and discussion, including the parallel-poem activity, helps students to view the film constructively, capitalizing on students related prior knowledge and personal responses.

After-Viewing Strategies to Capture the Teachable Moment

Initial Response

Because the final scene of *The Long Walk Home* is so powerful and effective in eliciting emotional responses where students strongly identify with one or more characters, having students respond in writing immediately after the film ends tends to produce fluid, expressive writing. The writing time also ensures that students develop independent responses first rather than sharing verbally immediately after the film, a practice which is more likely to limit the range and variety of free response. This activity works best if the teacher gives the instructions before showing the end of the film. This way, when the film ends, no voice interrupts; students simply begin writing. Instructions to the students are as follows:

- Immediately after the film ends, freewrite about the conclusion for approximately 15 minutes. Let your thoughts, impressions, responses, reactions, feelings, emotions, and associations just flow. There is no "right" or "wrong" way to approach this, so long as you keep writing, connecting, extending, and responding to the film.

Tables 2:6 and 2:7 include two responses that demonstrate how different students identified with the conclusion of the film and used it as a venue for considering what they would have done. Gabriel is an African-American student in a predominantly White school; Heather is Caucasian.

Table 2:6 Gabriel's Initial Response to the Conclusion of *The Long Walk Home*

Wow! I wonder if anyone saw the tear that rolled down my face at the end. I hope someone did. I wish everyone had. So they can know how I feel. This movie, however years before I was born, is a part of me. I felt Odessa's pain. The end was the one clear-cut separation of the two races in Montgomery. All the Negroes wanted to do was live, and live better. For Norman to say that we would never be like "them" pissed me off sumthin fierce. But you know, I hope he's right. I don't want my people to become so filled with hatred that they are blinded by it, and as a result have no abandonment in their actions. Why did the human race have to start like it did? I wanted to sing along with the women at the end, because they basically said, "I will not be intimidated!" Neither will I (unless I'm asked to read my words in front of the class). Would Odessa be justified in having a "Killing Rage*"? It hurts to know what we once were, as a country.

*"Killing Rage" is a reference to an essay the class had read by bel hooks.

Table 2:7 Heather's Initial Response to the Conclusion of *The Long Walk Home*

I felt the ending of this movie was very powerful. It was really sad, but for a good reason. I'm really glad that Miriam Thompson stood in the line with Odessa and the other Blacks. This act by Miriam showed a lot of strength. It makes me wonder if I would be able to stand with the Blacks and not hide. I really like the way Miriam fought for what she believed in. She stood up not only for herself and the Blacks, but to show her husband just how strong she is. It's amazing how someone could be that strong. Risking her life to fight for something she felt right. Risking her relationship with her husband and not to mention her place as a White woman in her community. It made me so very proud and happy that Odessa was the first to come forward. That would not be a very easy thing to do. I really enjoyed this movie, and I feel that it was a great way to show acts of civil rights and prejudices. Having Miriam Thompson stand up for the Blacks made it more realistic and better to understand how hard it was for the Blacks, but the Whites who fought with them and risked their lives in the fight for equality. The movie was very strong and powerful. The feelings were intense. I do wonder what happened to Miriam and her husband.

After students have had 10 to 15 minutes to write a response to the film's conclusion, the class will benefit from a time of sharing. Having students write responses first tends to facilitate sharing from students who otherwise might not volunteer, because students may simply read a portion of what they have written. This informal discussion provides a review of the film, its characters and central issues, and allows students the opportunity to engage in higher levels of thinking, and reflect on the meaning of the text (film) in ways that have personal relevance. For instance, Anna said:

> It is amazing the strength the Black women had. I couldn't imagine what it would be like to be bombarded with the wall of hate the White men created. The faith they had as well was even more incredible. Their singing was all they needed to combat the hatred of the crowd. It must have been very difficult for Miriam to step up into that line, but she knew she made the right decision. She was not only taking a stand against her husband for Black people, but also for women. It would be interesting to see what happened to their marriage. I know I could not live with someone after I found out how fundamentally different he was.

Shelly considered Norman Thompson's perspective, saying:

> Deep down I thought Mr. Thompson wanted to help the Black community, but he felt, as a citizen, that he couldn't because he knew the terror that would be brought on him and his family . . . In 1955 my mother would have been 6 years old which is about the same age as Mary Catherine. I always wonder what type of experiences my mother had living during these times. I wonder if she knew what was going on.

After the class has discussed the conclusion, assign the following question for homework:

- In what ways has the film expanded your understanding of the struggles that existed during the Civil Rights era?

This question causes students to rethink what they know and consider how a text (film) changes or confirms that understanding (Claggett, 1996). Sarah's example (see Table 2:8) models this kind of rethinking, change, and confirmation.

Table 2:8 Sarah's Response to How the Film Expanded Her Understanding

The film made me realize many things about the struggles that existed during the Civil Rights era. I knew that times were hard and that Blacks were discriminated against, but I never fully understood the extent of the horrible treatment of Blacks and what they went through. I learned about the bus boycott before, but I never really thought about all of the Black people walking to work and how far they had to walk. I guess I just imagined them driving to work. I don't know if I could have done what Odessa did in the film. She walked that far in shoes that didn't even fit her. I was extremely impressed with the Black race's attitude through all of their persecution. I know that their faith in God played a major role in their lives, but I was amazed that their faith stayed so strong through everything. The film showed all of the people standing outside of the church because there was not even standing room left inside. The White race didn't seem to have such a

cont.

strong belief in God. The film also made me realize what a strong sense of pride the Blacks had. They were willing to walk for miles day in and day out because they didn't want the White people to have the satisfaction of degrading the Blacks once more. Also, whenever I pictured the buses that everyone rode back then, I would picture them as being extremely full with hardly any room. But the film showed the buses being full in the "Black section" but the front of the bus, where the White people sat, was almost empty. Now that I think about it, it makes sense because the White people had the money to drive cars so they didn't need to ride the buses. This makes me even more mad about the buses being separated into sections anyways because there weren't even that many White people that rode the buses. During the boycott, the buses would ride around practically empty. I'm glad the Black people stayed strong and won most of their struggles.

Final Artistic and Written Response Options

As a culminating project for *The Long Walk Home*, students choose from the options that follow and create a response to share in class. Students should be given at least two nights to prepare their work.

OPTION 1: Draw, paint, or use another media to convey something important about the film, its issues, or characters. Then, write a descriptive paper telling about your creative/artistic rendering. Use plenty of detail to show the importance and explain symbolism, if applicable, in your creation. Anna's response (see Table 2:9 or the CD-ROM to see the painting in color) provides an example of this option.

Table 2:9 Anna's Artistic Response to Option 1 (Painting)

Anna's Artistic Response to Option 1 (Painting)

Anna's Written Response to Option 1

My creative response is an ink drawing with a watercolor wash of White hands washing a Black foot. The film showed the strong faith of the Black community, and it brought to mind the Biblical symbolism of washing feet. In the Bible, roles were changed when Jesus washed the feet of his apostles. In the Civil Rights era roles of Blacks and Whites were also challenged and changed. Odessa was Miriam's maid, but soon Miriam was serving Odessa and other Black people by driving them to work. Another part of the movie that brought to mind washing feet was when Miriam caught a glimpse of Odessa's bleeding, sore feet. In a way, Miriam was "washing the blood off" of Odessa's feet by driving her to work. She didn't want Odessa to suffer from the blisters on her feet anymore. Washing feet is a way of showing respect for someone else. When Miriam saw Odessa's feet, she realized how seriously committed the Black people were to the bus boycott, and that made her respect her maid. Another symbol I used in my piece was the red washcloth. The color symbolizes the blood shed by the Black people during their struggle for civil rights. Many, like Theodore, did not fight back when attacked by hateful White people. They experienced much violence even though their protest was peaceful.

OPTION 2: Collect at least 10 "artifacts," and bring them to class, showing how each reveals something important about the film, its issues, or characters. Arrange your written response as a list. In the order in which you intend to present the items in class, list the item followed by its significance. Use plenty of detail to show the importance and explain the symbolism, if applicable, for each artifact. E'lise brought in a bag full of artifacts; her written explanation of each appears on Table 2:10.

Table 2:10 E'lise's Response to Option 2 (Collection of Artifacts)

1. **Makeup**—The makeup represents the "cover up" that Miriam had to do when she was helping Odessa by driving her to work, and her eventual participation in the car pool. Not only did Miriam have to "cover up" her actions from her husband, she also had to avoid being confronted by other White townspeople who might see her driving Odessa and become angry.

2. **Tissue**—The tissue represents the tears that were wept during the Civil Rights transformation. I know I cried in the scene when Theodore Cotter got beat up by the White boys from the bus because he was trying to protect his sister. The Blacks had it rough during those times, and many tears were shed due to the discrimination toward them and the oppression they faced.

3. **Tape**—The tape represents the adhesiveness that was present throughout the Black community. Even when things did not look promising, the Blacks kept their faith and stuck together, while continuing to encourage one another.

4. **Rubber Band**—The rubber band represents how Miriam felt during the Civil Rights Movement. She was being pulled in two different directions because on one hand, she knew it was right to help Odessa and the rest of the Black community, but on the other hand, she knew that she could not disrespect her husband. By participating in the car pool, Miriam let her heart pull her towards what she knew was right.

5. **Clay**—The clay represents the women during the time. They were molded into what society needed them to be and what their husbands wanted them to be. This prevented women from being able to think and act independently.

6. **Glove**—The glove represents the hand that Miriam, and other White community members, held out to the Black community in their time of oppression, despite the ridicule they faced from the rest of the White community for it. Those people cared enough to risk their own social standing to help those who needed it most.

7. **Band-Aid**—The band-aid represents the pain that the Blacks went through when they refused to ride the bus to further their advancement in society. Like Odessa, hundreds of Blacks in Montgomery sacrificed their own comfort so that one day they would be treated as equals by the Whites.

8. **Matches**—The matches represent the "fire" that drove the Blacks in Montgomery to take action against their oppressors. They were relentless in their quest for equality, and the fire of years of mistreatment burned inside of them.

9. **Camera**—The camera represents the different views that the members of Montgomery possessed. For instance, Miriam and Norman Thompson had very different views of the Black community and how they should be treated. Also, the Whites viewed themselves differently than the way that Blacks viewed them.

10. **Paper Doll Chain**—The paper doll chain represents the unity that the Blacks were trying to achieve between themselves and the Whites of Montgomery. It also represents the people in the car pool scene in the film. When the Blacks were pushed up against the wall, being yelled at by the men of the Citizen's Council, they united and began to sing and hold hands. Then, as the ultimate act of support for their cause, Miriam takes Odessa's hand along with Mary Catherine.

OPTION 3: Compose a letter (minimum 200 words) to a character in the film, expressing something you really want to say; the letter may be of a critical or supportive nature.

The examples that follow (see Table 2:11) demonstrate the contrasts that emerge in the letter-writing option. Philip's letter to Odessa not only shows admiration, but also the desire to know more about the character, as though she could actually respond to his questions. John N's letter shows a kind of psychological awareness and understanding of Norman—building on the inference that he is left alone at the end of the film—by reaching out to him to help in a "time of emotional struggle," but ultimately urges Mr. Thompson to consider his actions.

Table 2:11 Examples of Option 3 (Letter to Character)

Dear Odessa,	Dear Norman:
I would like to compliment you on your courageous ability to handle everything that is going on around you. After viewing what you did every day and every night, I now realize what the Civil Rights era is all about. Your courage and attitude toward life is unbelievable.	I am writing you to try and help you through your time of emotional struggle. I believe that you are very distraught inside, and I may be able to offer some advice. First of all you are too firmly set in your beliefs of women's inferiority to men. Your wife is college educated and can offer you much in the way of counsel; you would be wise to listen to her. If she wants to drive people around on her own time then she should be free to do so.
If you wouldn't mind, I have a few questions I would like to ask you. How did you get up every morning and walk to work and walk home? After seeing you do this, I began to realize your heart has to be as big as a house. During the Christmas dinner at the Thompson's, how did you hold back from not saying anything to Mrs. Thompson's mother-in-law? I found this remarkable. There is no way I would have been able to just continue cooking and passing out food. I would have packed up and walked home.	I realize that you fear society, you fear for your wife, your child, and for the safety of your family unit as a whole in the rough days to come. You do not, however, realize that there are probably many people like your wife, who wish to help the Blacks in any way they can. All it would take is a firm White leader and a small group of White followers to turn Montgomery around. There are few people like your brother Tucker, radicals that are stubbornly holding on to the past when a united future holds the way to greatness. Norman, if you were to take charge and be that leader, the leader that your wife has tried so hard to be, then your friends would flock to your aid and cause. Together you could make your whole city more peaceful and happy. It would not even take any extraordinary effort on your part. Kindness to those trod upon is like a sunray through the mists of racism. I only ask that you think about it.
I love how you were so dedicated to your family. After long hours at work you would still come home and feed your family. What was going through your head when you heard that your daughter rode the bus? I know you were kind of angry, but deep down inside, you had to have been proud that she stood up for what she believed in.	John N.
As I said before, you showed me what real courage is. Feet bleeding, legs aching, and you still get up and go to work, come home and feed your family. I now know what you had to go through, and I appreciate everything you did. Take care Odessa. I am glad I had the opportunity to ask you a few questions and tell you how I feel. Please write back soon.	
Your new friend,	
Philip	

OPTION 4: Write a poem that reveals the "essence" of a character's struggle or otherwise conveys the thematic tensions inherent in the film. Seek to attain Romantic poet William Wordsworth's definition of "good poetry" as that which is "the spontaneous overflow of powerful feelings [that] takes its origin from emotion recollected in tranquility" (Bartlett & Kaplan, 1992). The four student-written poems found in Table 2:12 serve as models of option 4. John M's poem addresses perspectives of Odessa, Miriam, Norman, and Mary Catherine balanced with the refrain "Take a long walk to get away, and walk towards a better day." Lindsey's poem also employs a refrain and allusions to other characters as they related to Miriam. Megan's poem, with an artfully balanced structure, draws comparisons and contrasts between Miriam and Odessa, while Bobbie's poem "Little Girl" illuminates the perspective of 7-year-old Mary Catherine.

Table 2:12 Examples of Option 4 (Write a Poem)

"Long Walk" by John M.	"Miriam's Song" by Lindsey
When nothing is going the way it should, and you're surrounded by confusion Take a long walk to get away, and walk towards a better day While a White woman is torn between herself and her race, Her struggle lies between her husband and maid, who are both just as afraid For the man himself, he has a choice to make, He can side with his brother or he can love one another Just take a long walk to get away, and walk towards a better day To learn from our mistakes is what each lesson will teach, Replace hate and insanity with love and humanity Times are hard and emotions are wild, Through the innocent eyes of a peaceful White child So take a long walk to get away, and walk towards a better day	I stood along the lines with you; Your Black hands intertwined with mine You sang your song of strength and triumph while I stood along the line I stood along the lines with you He watched us from the side I fought the fight that I thought was right I crossed the great divide I stood along the lines with you I'm different but feel the same Someday I hope it won't be this hard to stand up for a change I stood along the lines with you Despite the cries of ignorant hate I know my voice will be heard with yours and change the nation's fate

cont.

"Two Women" by Megan	"Little Girl" (Mary Catherine) by Bobbie
Woman	Vision, no vision
Miriam Thompson	Which is better
Mother, wife, friend	If no vision brings hate
Blonde, blue-eyed, White	Then vision is clever
Drove Odessa to her home	Divided, united
Made the cop apologize to Odessa	What would you risk
Slapped by her brother-in-law Tucker	To stay quiet and safe
Used her own car, drove Blacks to work	To gain opportunities missed
Husband left her because she drove the carpool	Could you put aside color
They held hands and sang to calm the riot, Sang loud	Religion or race
Two women, one goal, to ride in the front of a bus	Could you match respect
Her daughter trieds to ride the bus, gets harassed	To the color of a face
Had her faith and family, helped her through	Could you see what they see
Her boy got beat up real bad	Or feel what they feel
Braved the boycott with bloody shoes	Or dare to have humility
Walked to work every day	For the sake of being real
Dark-haired, brown eyes, Black	Dare you to be mature enough
Mother, wife, friend	To show compassion to these eyes
Odessa Cotter	This little girl who's so impressionable
Woman	This little girl full of why's

OPTION 5: Compose and perform a song inspired by the film. Similar to option 4, this option is added to encourage students with musical/rhythmic intelligence to express themselves through lyrics and instrumental performance. Katy, an aspiring musician and high school junior, composed "There Will Come a Day" (see Table 2:13) and performed it live in class with the accompaniment of her acoustic guitar. Through the song, Katy Grace captures Odessa's perseverance.

Table 2:13 Example of Option 5 (Compose and Perform a Song)

"There Will Come a Day"
by Katy Grace

I rise up in the morning and head out on my way
Tired, sore, and sturdy, I face another day
I walk these streets again, with my head held high
People sometimes stare at me, as they wonder why
They wonder why I walk so far, day after day
They just don't understand, it's the only way
Yes, it would be easier to pay the toll and ride
But it's not about the toll, it's about my pride

Chorus:
Why give in to those who think they're better than me?
Soon enough, my day will come, and they will start to see
They'll see I'm not so different, that I've got rights too
I am not the one who's wrong, that person is you

Until my day of glory, I will keep on walking strong
I can see the light now, I know it won't be long
It won't be long now, until I can stand right next to you
Some think I'm crazy, but I know it to be true
I'm getting closer every day, with each step I take
I feel a little stronger, even though my feet ache
If I keep on marching, I know I'll get my way
It might not be tomorrow, but there will come a day

Repeat Chorus

The day students' final artistic and written responses are due is a rich time to showcase what they gain in viewing *The Long Walk Home*. The Montgomery Bus Boycott and Civil Rights Movement are no longer regarded only as historical facts and events without emotion, but they rise, more deeply understood as benchmarks of lived experience, where people made sacrifices for the sake of equality. Having the opportunity to choose among five project options facilitates students' sense of ownership and comfort with their demonstration of learning. The day of sharing celebrates students' ability to find that which is meaningful and show it in ways that are personally relevant. Table 2:14 offers an assessment rubric for the various components of this unit; teachers may collect each assignment as it is completed or have students compile their work in a notebook for a cumulative assessment.

Table 2:14 Assessment Rubric for *The Long Walk Home* Unit

	Exemplary	Acceptable	Needs Improvement
One-Minute Vocabulary Report	Defines term in detail; Accompanies "definition" with thoughtful, neatly prepared visual that enhances understanding	Definition could include more detail or visual aid is not neatly prepared or well established in terms of relevance that will help class remember the term	"Definition" is lacking in detail or no visual aid accompanies the definition
Reflective Writing and Discussion	Thoughtful, well-developed responses to all questions; Student consistently makes use of class time to respond in writing when given opportunity to do so; Responses demonstrate personal investment as evidenced by critical thinking and relating own experience; Regularly contributes to class discussion on a volunteer basis	One or two responses are lacking in detail; Student completes all responses but does not use class time effectively (saves writing for homework even when given class time to get started); Responses tend to avoid inclusion of personal experience, thus minimizing personal relevance; Occasionally volunteers in class discussion or only contributes when asked to do so by the teacher	Three or more responses lacking in detail—approaching the prompts as short answer questions rather than paragraphs of exploration; Off-task behaviors when given time to work on written reflections in class; Rarely volunteers or not prepared to contribute when called upon
Parallel Poem	Deliberate line structure and rhythm in keeping with Chapman's song; Evident parallel in content between student's poem and the song or film	Writing employs line form consistent with lyrics and poetry but not with a rhythm that contributes to a smoothly flowing parallel poem; Evident parallel in content between student's poem and the song or film	Writing is written in sentence form or is otherwise not reflective of poetic line structure or no clear connection exists between the student's writing and Chapman's song or *The Long Walk Home*

cont.

OPTION 1: Drawing or Painting with Written Response * note that in this description collage and computer-generated art are acceptable but are not capable of earning the exemplary score	Original artwork that shows investment of time and effort; Accompanied by a detailed written response that illuminates deep thinking and symbolism conveyed by the artistic creation	Artwork is either not precisely prepared or demonstrates minimal investment of time (collage or computer-generated art) or Written response merely retells an aspect of the film's plot rather than reveals deeper symbolic thought and connections	Simple drawing, collage, or computer-generated art (elementary drawing without color, proper paper, or convincing investment of time) or Written response that is less than ½ page, failing to show serious thought or construction of meaning
OPTION 2: Collection of Artifacts with List	Each artifact is brought to class and presented in the order it is explained in the student's paper; Each item is listed, followed by an explanation that logically stems from the text; Some items are symbolic in nature, but with creative/ well-established relevance	Missing one or two artifacts in the class presentation or not including them in the paper; Explanations are not detailed beyond 2 sentences; Artifacts related to concrete happenings in the film and do not demonstrate symbolic thinking	Missing three or more artifacts in the class presentation or paper; Failure to establish a clear connection between any artifact and the film
OPTION 3: Letter to Character	Letter is personal in nature and shows either praise or criticism; Letter maintains a focus on the individual to whom it is written and demonstrates a knowledge of who that character was in the film	Letter tends to be impersonal or wanders, rather than maintaining an extended focus that demonstrates knowledge of the particular character; Letter acts as a way to retell the story rather than communicate with the character it is addressed to	Letter fails to demonstrate a clear understanding of the character to whom it is addressed; Attributing to one character actions of another character

Literature Circles to Read about the Civil Rights Movement

Having viewed and responded to *The Long Walk Home* as an introduction to the Civil Rights Movement, students will divide into groups of three to five and choose a book for their group to read, discuss, and share with the class. Harvey

Daniels' (2002) *Literature Circles: Voice and Choice in Book Clubs and Reading Groups* is a helpful teacher resource in defining characteristics and roles to facilitate Literature Circles. While broadening their exposure to various people and events integral to the Civil Rights Movement, the books (which are at the center of each Literature Circle) will also deepen students' understanding of the film and its issues. In responding to their group's book, students will write an analytical/reflective paper and a Readers' Theater, and complete a creative project of their choosing. Each group will present its work to the class—in effect, teaching their books to one another. See the bibliography of Young Adult novels at the end of this chapter for suggested books for the Literature Circle groups.

The Analytical/Reflective Paper/Presentation

After reading and discussing their assigned/chosen novel in their Literature Circle, students will work together to write an analytical/reflective paper to be presented to the class. The paper/presentation should include: 1) an overview of the book, its format and themes, 2) what the group found to be especially valuable about the book, 3) references to other literature or films the book reminded the group of, 4) a related film clip (limited to 15 minutes)—the clip should be described in the paper and shown as part of the presentation, and 5) a "new contribution"—a creative "something extra" to convey or reinforce the theme of the novel; this will also become part of the in-class presentation. See Table 2:15 for excerpts from a group's paper in response to these questions. Below are excerpts from an analytical/reflective paper (by Susan Gustafson, Caroline Knapke, Sarah Lukats, Sylvia Mallory, and Jill Robinson) for *Freedom's Children: Young Civil Rights Activists Tell Their Own Stories.*

Table 2:15 Excerpts from Analytical/Reflective Paper

Overview of the book, its format and themes:

Freedom's Children extends beyond traditional English class to cover important elements of history. The book includes such historical events as the Montgomery Bus Boycott, the Little Rock school integration crisis, Mississippi Summer, Freedom Rides, Bloody Sunday, and the Selma Movement. The book also includes extremely strong and influential figures, like Dr. Martin Luther King, Jr., Rosa Parks, Reverend Fred Shuttlesworth, and Claudette Colvin . . . *Freedom's Children* offers a different view of the Civil Rights Movement than did *The Long Walk Home* because it is broad and focuses on many aspects of the era and its struggle. It shows different opinions and views of a time in history, how evil racism and bigotry are, and what happens when hatred gets out of control . . . It is a good historical novel, showing what happened in real places at real times . . . Since the author interviewed 30 actual people who were teenagers during the Civil Rights Movement in the 1950s and 1960s, we could identify with the characters because they were close to our own age . . . *Freedom's Children* gives detailed accounts of the lives of African-American teenagers living in the South. The short stories contained in the novel describe how people felt about many aspects of racism . . . as they saw and experienced it.

What the group found to be especially valuable:

The aspect of this novel that we especially found to be valuable is the basic character strengths portrayed by the people who had participated in the Civil Rights Movement. A majority of the readers of *Freedom's*

cont.

Children will not have had the same hardships and discrimination the characters had to face. However, we could learn a lot from situations beyond our personal life experiences. Particularly influential are the character qualities of courage and confidence exemplified throughout *Freedom's Children.* When facing day-to-day trials such as standing up for religious beliefs, remembering what the civil rights activists had to endure makes it easier to face our situations with the same courage and confidence . . .

References to other literature or films the book reminded the group of:

Freedom's Children reminded us of *Oh, Freedom!* by Casey King and Linda Barrett Osborne. *Oh, Freedom!* is a nonfiction book telling the history of the Civil Rights Movement through interviews between kids and the people who were active in the movement. This book would appeal to younger readers, probably on the fourth- to sixth-grade level. The book is broken up into many short interviews, which is ideal for the shorter attention span of younger readers. In addition, there are photographs on nearly every page that help bring to life the events that are being discussed. The interviews are interspersed with pages recounting the events of the Civil Rights Movement in a more traditional, history book manner. These passages also have many photographs, and they help piece together the events at a broader level than the personal interviews provide. The books ends with a comprehensive timeline of events . . .

A related film clip:

For our related film clip, we have chosen a scene from *To Kill a Mockingbird.* Although this movie takes place during the Depression and before the Civil Rights Movement, it sets up the stage for understanding how the African-American community was treated before the 1960s. During the selected film clip, Gregory Peck's character, Atticus Finch, is making his closing statement to a court. He has courageously defended a Black man, Tom Robinson, accused of raping a White woman.

During the final argument, Atticus raises questions of social importance. Why is it that interracial relationships are taboo? Why do White men not trust the women in their lives around any Black men? These questions are important to understand the beginnings of the Civil Rights Movement, the need for fair and equal treatment. The movie clip is also important because it does not portray all Whites as being evil. Although most of the town is full with bigots, there are a select few who will stand up for what is right. This can also be related to the numerous Whites that joined the Civil Rights Movement.

New contribution:

Throughout *Freedom's Children* music was an important thread that tied many of the stories together. The songs "We Shall Overcome" and "This Little Light of Mine" were in various stories. Music helped to inspire the Black community. It gave them hope, strength, and courage. Songs were celebrated during church services, rallies, and marches.

Music could also be seen in a negative way. The song "America the Beautiful" was not seen as beautiful to one teenager because of the injustices that the African-American community had to face.

The new contribution that expands our paper and presentation is a compact disc of freedom music we compiled. Songs of freedom have been around for centuries, and the Civil Rights Movement borrowed many old songs and created many new songs. It used many gospel songs such as "Go Tell It on the Mountain." This contribution is highly effective because music is meant to be heard. The effect of hearing a song over reading about a song is dramatic. The voices and instruments bring a vivid experience to life.

In addition to the music example described as a new contribution above, other students' new contributions were visually artistic renderings (collage, pencil and crayon drawings); examples appear in Table 2:16. Jeff's drawing, in response to *I Have a Dream: The Story of Martin Luther King,* reflected the civil rights leader's dream of racial peace and unity, while Rachael's drawing illustrated pressures pulling activists in different directions. Sarah's drawing, in response to *Just Like Martin*, depicted the community's enduring sense of faith, even after the church had been bombed. Sarah built her reflections on Reverend Cable's preaching about racial harmony, depicted by the White hand touching the Black hand in prayer. Describing her drawing, Sarah wrote:

> "I think that God played a major role in the unification of the races, and I think that if the Whites' faith was as strong as the Blacks' faith back then, the Whites would have been able to see that they were treating the Blacks unfairly . . . I think that if people have a similarity in believing in God, it will help them to look past their other differences, like the color of skin."

Katie's collage, in response to *Free at Last: A History of the Civil Rights Movement and Those Who Died in the Struggle,* included pictures of Rosa Parks and Martin Luther King, Jr., two leaders of the movement who stood up for equality. Katie said she chose "words to show how I think the Blacks felt and how they needed to be heard."

Table 2:16 Example of "New Contributions"

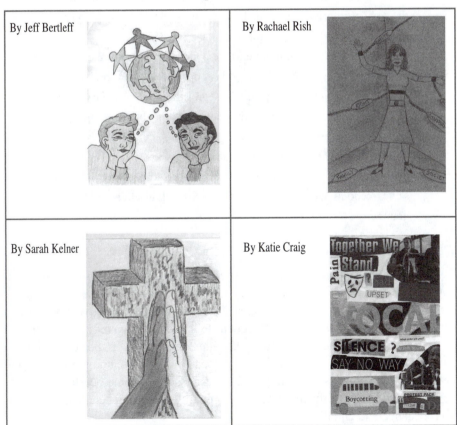

| By Jeff Bertleff | By Rachael Rish |
| By Sarah Kelner | By Katie Craig |

Readers' Theater

In addition to the analytical/reflective paper, students, working with their Literature Circle book, will compose and perform a Readers' Theater script. See the CD-ROM for a Readers' Theater from *Freedom's Children*.

Scrapbook

Asking students to imagine themselves as one of the characters in their group's book and to create a scrapbook from that character's perspective is an effective way to help them present their Literature Circle books to one another. The scrapbook should represent what the students (as the characters from the book) have seen and experienced. The scrapbook should include at least five pictures with captions, four half-page (minimum) diary entries, two letters (half-page minimum each) from others, and additional artifacts, as desired. The scrapbook can be compiled on ordinary $8\frac{1}{2}$ x 11 inch typing paper or in an actual album, if available and affordable. Sarah Schwabauer included two envelopes, each containing handwritten letters. See the CD-ROM for Sarah's scrapbook pages. In her introduction to the scrapbook, Sarah wrote:

> Although for many, the 1950s and 1960s in the South was a horrific period, a time of fear, imprisonment, and an abundance of physical and emotional abuse, these survivors can truly understand and appreciate the wonderful privilege of freedom. All of us should be so lucky as to go against the grain to fight for what we believe in and win.
>
> Let us take a look back in time to the perspective of a teenage Black girl living in the South and facing this oppression. For some, this life would be unimaginable. The ideas of segregation and prejudice against Blacks are taught in schools and social situations, but the majority of us have not personally experienced such abuse. Although we commend those who fought for freedom, most teenagers today will be stunned and shocked at what a "colored" teenager had to go through for the same freedoms and everyday rights that most White adults still take for granted.

Closing Remarks

The combination of *The Long Walk Home*—as an introduction to the Civil Rights Movement and the Montgomery Bus Boycott, in particular—and Literature Circles, in which students read and discuss Young Adult novels on various aspects of the movement, serves to deepen students' understanding of this crucial era in American history. Additionally, the range of activities immerses students in analytical, creative, and reflective experiences that facilitate comprehension and personalize the issues so that, hopefully, these issues become heartfelt and real, convincing students of the importance of speaking out, being heard, and standing up for justice and equality.

Young Adult Novels for Literature Circle Groups

Bullard, S. (1994). *Free at last: A history of the civil rights movement and those who died in the struggle.* New York: Oxford University Press Childrens.

Curtis, C. P. (1995). *The Watsons go to Birmingham—1963: A novel.* New York: Delacorte Press.

Davidson, M. (1999). *I have a dream: The story of Martin Luther King.* New York: Bt. Bound.

Davis, O. (1995). *Just like Martin.* London: Puffin.

Haskins, J. (1997). *Bayard Rustin: Behind the scenes of the civil rights movement.* New York: Hyperion.

Krisher, T. (1994). *Spite fences.* New York: Delacorte Press.

Levine, E. (2000). *Freedom's children:Young civil rights activists tell their own stories.* London: Puffin.

References

Bartlett, J., & Kaplan, J. (Eds.). (1992). *Familiar quotations: A collection of passages, phrases, and proverbs traced to their sources in ancient and modern literature* (16th ed.). Boston: Little, Brown and Company.

Bridges, R., & Lundell, M. (1999). *Through my eyes.* New York: Scholastic Press.

Chapman, T. (Performer). (1988). *Across the lines.* (Compact Disc Recording). New York: Elektra Records.

Claggett, F. (1996). *A Measure of success: From assignments to assessment in English language arts.* Portsmouth, NH: Heinemann Boynton/Cook.

Daniels, H. (2002). *Literature circles: Voice and choice in book clubs & reading groups* (2nd ed.). York, ME: Stenhouse Publishers.

Dornfield, M., Clayborn, C., & Hine, D. C. (Eds.). (1995). *The turning tide: From the desegregation of the armed forces to the Montgomery bus boycott (1948–1956).* Broomall, PA: Chelsea House.

Doyle, W. (2001). *An American insurrection: The battle of Oxford, Mississippi, 1962.* New York: Doubleday.

Glasgow, J. (2002). *Using young adult literature: Thematic activities based on Gardner's multiple intelligences.* Norwood, MA: Christopher-Gordon Publishers, Inc.

Haskins, J., & Haskins, J. (1999). *The day Martin Luther King, Jr. was shot: A photo history of the civil rights movement.* New York: Bt. Bound

Haskins, J. (2000) *Jesse Jackson: Civil rights activist (African-American biographies).* Berkeley Heights, NJ: Enslow.

King, C., Osborne, L. B., & Brookes, J. (1997). *Oh, freedom! Kids talk about the civil rights movement with the people who made it happen.* Mississauga, Ontario: Alfred A. Knopf.

King, M. L., Shepard, K. (Ed.), & Carson, C. (Ed.). (2002). *A call to conscience: The landmark speeches of Dr. Martin Luther King, Jr.* New York: Warner.

Lee, H. (1960). *To kill a mockingbird*. Philadelphia: Lippincott. *The Long Walk Home*. (1990). (Videotape). New York: Miramax.

Parks, R., & Reed, G. J. (2000). *Quiet strength*. Grand Rapids, MI: Zondervan.

Parks, R., Haskins, J., & Haskins, J. (1999). *Rosa Parks: My story*. London: Puffin.

Peck, I. (2000). *The life and words of Martin Luther King, Jr.* New York: Scholastic.

Rennert, R. S. (Ed.). (1993). *Civil rights leaders (profiles of great Black Americans)*. Broomall, PA: Chelsea House.

Ritchie, N. (2003). *The civil rights movement*. Hauppauge, NY: Barrons Educational.

Sommer, R. L. (1993). *Norman Rockwell: A classic treasury*. Greenwich, CT: Barnes & Noble.

Wilkinson, B., Young, A., Jackson, J. L., & Gallin, R. (1990). *Jesse Jackson: Still fighting for the dream (history of the civil rights movement)*. New York: Silver Burdett.

Wilson, C. (2001). *Rosa Parks: From the back of the bus to the front of a movement* (Scholastic Biography). New York: Scholastic.

Chapter Three

Celebrating Appalachian Culture and Values in Young Adult Literature

Jacqueline N. Glasgow

"No significant learning occurs without a significant relationship."
—Dr. James Comer, Education Service Center, Houston, Texas

Appalachia is both a place and a culture. As a place, Appalachia is a chain of mountain ranges that begins in Alabama and stretches all the way to North Newfoundland in Canada. The ranges include the Blue Ridge Mountains, the Great Smoky Mountains, the Allegheny Mountains, and the Cumberland Plateau. Appalachia is known for its natural beauty; it is one of the most scenic places in North America. Tradition and culture are especially important to Appalachians, and the beginnings can be traced back to the Cherokee Indians and the first European settlers. This history of these early inhabitants is an important key to understanding the people who live in the region today. Early settlers had to be self-reliant if they were to survive in a land that was still very much wilderness. In many remote areas, the pioneer way of life continued well into the 1920s. Plowing, planting, and harvesting, Appalachians have come to love the land for which they fought so hard, and they remain deeply attached to their homes. Along with this attachment comes a powerful sense of kinship. In the beginning, families needed to stick together to survive, and the feeling frequently endures today—even when the relatives aren't of the finest character. While the natural resources of Appalachia have been exploited and squandered for profit, the culture remains strong and functioning. Appalachian values need to be nurtured and strengthened in the children who remain in mountain families. Appalachian adolescents often have difficulty finding themselves in literature, yet need to see their lives represented and validated. This unit addresses those characteristics in current Young Adult novels, such as Hamilton's *M. C. Higgins The Great,* Baldacci's *Wish You Well,* Rylant's *Missing May,* and Lyon's *With a Hammer for My Heart,* that realistically portray the lives of Appalachian teens and can serve as models for young readers who are searching for their cultural values.

Table 3:1 Reading Skills Addressed in this Unit

Strategy	Set Purpose	Activate Prior Knowledge	Make Predictions	Critical Thinking	Asking Questions	Visualizing the Text	Making Connection	Monitor Reading	Cause Effect	Compare Contrast	Making Inferences	Main Idea
Parallel Poem	•	•		•		•	•				•	•
Literature Circles: Analysis of Children's Picture Books	•	•	•	•	•	•	•	•	•	•	•	•
Photographic Essay: Coal Strip Mining	•	•		•	•	•	•			•		
Open House	•	•	•	•	•	•	•	•	•	•	•	•
Mind's Eye	•	•	•	•	•	•		•			•	•
Explicit Word Study: Word in My Context	•	•		•	•	•	•	•				
Sketchbook Journal	•	•		•	•	•	•	•	•	•	•	•
Character Portrait	•	•		•	•	•	•	•	•	•	•	•
Writing Inside Photo	•	•		•	•	•	•	•	•		•	•
Whirligigs	•	•				•	•	•				
Dialect, Metaphor, and Humor	•	•		•	•	•	•	•	•	•	•	•
Understanding Poverty	•	•									•	•
Readers' Theater	•	•	•	•	•	•	•	•	•	•	•	•
Multigenre Paper	•	•	•	•	•	•	•	•	•	•	•	•

Frontloading Strategies to Understand Appalachian Culture

Parallel Poem: Where are you from?

Whether or not you or your students are from Appalachia, let's begin by inviting students to think about their childhood home. Read the poem by George Ella Lyon in *Where I'm From: Where Poems Come From* (1999), called "Where I'm From," which details her childhood memories in Kentucky. After reading the poem to the class, ask students to go through the poem line by line and notice the details Lyon remembers about her past. On a piece of paper, ask students to make a list of items they might find around their home, in their yard, and in their neighborhood. They should be encouraged to think about names of relatives who come to visit, their mother's favorite sayings, favorite foods served at family gatherings, and special places they keep their childhood treasures. After students complete their brainstorming, ask them to write a parallel poem using Lyon's structure. For instance, they should begin each stanza with, "I am from," and they should end the poem with line(s) that connects them with their family history. For more specific directions and student examples, see Christensen's lesson in *Rethinking Our Classrooms*, Volume 2, 2001, from which this lesson has been adapted. See Table 3:2 for Amy's "Where I'm From" poem.

Table 3:2 Amy's "Where I'm From" Poem

I am From
by Amy Marie Vanecko

I am from long drives to Cleveland,
from ice cream and softball fields.
I'm from home cooked meals
and late night movies.
From big wheels and bathing suits,
from talking and shopping, the color purple.
I am from mom and dad fighting,
(the angry words hurt
but are covered with twice as much love.)
I am from ant-eater teeth and the wind in the hamper,
from New Kids and broken arms.
I'm from my grandpa's hugs and my mom's example,
from the biggest stars in the sky leading my way.
I am from smiles and tears,running shoes and books.
Phone calls, letters, courage, and strength;
a door closing, a window opening.
Picnics in the living room, Christmas lights on the house.
Good, bad; all are where I'm from.
Dreams, hopes, and wishes; forever more to come.

From this poetic activity that personalizes the unit, students are ready to analyze children's picture books to begin identifying Appalachian culture and values.

Literature Circles with Appalachian Children's Picture Books

A study of Appalachian children's picture books provides students with excellent background knowledge of the values, rituals, and traditions of the culture.
Bring in as many of the books from the children's picture booklist at the end of
the chapter as are available. Divide the class into small groups to form literature
circles. Let each group select the book(s) they would like to use for this activity.
Instead of completing the task roles for Literature Circles, ask students to read
the books and then analyze them by answering the following questions:

1. How is family life represented in your picture book?
2. What chores do children perform?
3. What kinds of jobs do parents (men and women) have?
4. How is food represented?
5. How is material wealth portrayed?
6. What educational values can you find?
7. Find examples of regional dialect and humor.
8. What place do music, religion, and crafts have in your book?
9. What Appalachian imagery has been used to convey the culture?
10. What examples of stereotyping did you find?

After deliberating these questions in small groups, ask students to share their
findings with the whole group. Discuss the values and culture that students identify and compare them with their own cultural values. For homework, ask students to write an essay based on their analysis of the book. They should address
aspects of the Appalachian culture that are represented in the text and in the illustrations, giving specific examples to support their assertions. They might ask
themselves if the book accurately represents Appalachian culture and values. See
Table 3:3 for an excerpt of Mary Timm's piece for Lyon's *My Mama is a Miner.*
See the CD-ROM for a bibliography of Appalachian children's picture books.

Table 3:3 Excerpt of Mary's Analysis of *My Mama is a Miner*

Mama is a Miner, written by George Ella Lyon and illustrated by Peter Catalanotto, delves deep into the heart
of the Appalachian culture. On the front cover, we see a loving mother and daughter embrace indicating a
close relationship between them. Told from the voice of a young girl who curiously watches her mother, this
story portrays the value and strength of the family. Each illustration is carefully and strategically placed in
order to show that the home is warm, comforting, and filled with love. Along with these pictures are images
of Mama at work. "She rides the mantrip in." The darkness of the pictures in the mines makes it difficult to
distinguish mama from the rest of the workers. Each are suited up with headlight helmets and mining tools.
Though typically miners were thought to be men, women like Mama were sent deep beneath the earth in
order to provide for the family. The work was hard and dangerous. This work was essential for Mama in
order to keep food on the table and pull her family through tough times. "Hard work for hard times," Mama
says. Back home, Mama enjoys the traditional role of cooking and caring for her family.

cont.

The language of the book is rather straightforward, yet incorporates into it poetic, rhythmic lyrics which creatively express each situation. "Dig and scrape, dinner on a plate/Lift and load, coal truck on the road/ Mountain gold, black as night/Some big city's heat and light." The use of this lyrical poetry allows the reader to feel the mood of the story as though it is being told out loud at that moment. It is evident that spoken language is a very prominent part of the culture. The richness of the Appalachian culture is truly experienced through the use of simple yet descriptive images, as well as through powerful movement of the words. Though told in a very simplistic way, this book scratches the surface level and penetrates much deeper into the core of an Appalachian family experience.

—Mary Timm

To prepare students for the next activity, ask them what they know about coal strip mining. The next activity is a photographic essay that will ask them to think about environmental issues and the consequences of practices such as coal strip mining on the people who live in Appalachia.

Photographic Essay: Coal Strip Mining in Appalachia

One of the critical issues for the Appalachian community has been the destruction of their land upon which they depend for survival. First the land was destroyed by the logging industry and then by the strip mining of coal. Begin this lesson by reading aloud Lyon's (1994) *Mama is a Miner.* Discuss the lifestyle of this family. Then introduce the following quote in Baldacci's *Wish You Well.* As Cotton says in front of the jury to preserve the land to the local people:

> "Southern Valley has come in her swinging bags full of money in front
> of you, telling you that it's the savior of the whole town. But that's
> what the lumber folks told you. . . . And the coal companies told you
> the same thing. And what did they do? They came and took everything
> they wanted and left you with nothing except hollowed-out mountains,
> family with the black lung and dreams replaced with nightmares" (2000,
> p. 357).

Baldacci and Hamilton both tell stories of the consequences of the coal strip mining industry invading the sacred ground of people who have inhabited the land for generations. With their land destroyed, the people were left with a life of poverty or forced to move into a lifestyle they had resisted for years. To heighten students' sensitivity and background knowledge to these issues, ask them to view the photographic essay in the PowerPoint slide presentation, "Coal Strip Mining in Appalachia," included on the CD-ROM, which asks them to consider whether or not we should preserve the land for the Appalachian community or serve the needs of a larger community. After viewing the slide presentation, ask students to respond to the discussion questions in Table 3:4.

Table 3:4 Discussion Questions for "Coal Strip Mining in Appalachia"

1. What conflicts or contrasts are suggested or depicted in the pictures? (Energy vs. nature)
2. How do we determine what the cost is of one choice over another?
3. How should we determine the best choice?
4. Often it is difficult to understand cause and effect because they may be greatly separated by time and/or distance. Can you create a scenario in which cause and effect are immediate?
5. Write letters home from the viewpoint of these individuals: Miner, Mining foreman, EPA technicians, Appalachian land owner
6. If this goes on, imagine what the consequences would be of a world situation in which one path of choice is taken to the total exclusion of the other.
7. "Catch 22"—What is the thread (order, organization) of the pictures? What is the meaning of reversing the order? What would this mean for our lives today? What would it mean for the Appalachian community?
8. Have these changes been for the better or the worse of humankind?
9. Consider the consequences of strip mining to the culture, politics, economics, and ecology represented in the photographs.

After having considered the consequences of coal strip mining, students are ready to approach the novel. Try a prediction strategy that will help readers, especially reluctant ones, make predictions, inferences, and generalizations about the story. Use the Open House Reading Strategy before reading the first chapter of either Lyon's *With a Hammer for My Heart*, Hamilton's *M. C. Higgins, The Great*, or Baldacci's *Wish You Well*.

Open House Reading Strategy

The Open House Reading Strategy (also known as the "Tea Party") gives the students an opportunity to talk to each other about story segments of the novel and predict what will happen next. Given a paragraph of the first chapter, each student will make inferences and generalizations about the characters, setting, mood, plot, conflicts, and point of view by discussing the segments. Remind students that this is a social activity during which they are supposed to mingle, talk, and share information like a school Open House. This strategy was modeled by Kyleen Beers at NCTE, Baltimore, Maryland, November 17, 2000, in her presentation, "Strategies for Helping Struggling Secondary Readers."

Procedure:
1. Photocopy the first chapter of the novel and cut the chapter into paragraphs or natural breaks in the dialogue. Paste each segment on an index card. You will need a card for each member of the class, unless you need to pair the students in case of a large class.
2. Distribute the cards and ask the students to read their piece silently.
3. Distribute the "Open House Prediction" Sheet. (See Table 3:5 Open House Prediction Sheet.)
4. Next, ask the students to move around and interview as many students as

they can in the next 10–15 minutes. They should share the information on their card, gather the information from their classmates, and record on their sheets what they learned before moving on to the next interview.

5.   After the Open House, give students a few minutes to finish recording their predictions before opening up the discussion to the whole class.

6.   Now, ask students to read the first chapter and compare their predictions to what they read in the first chapter. Follow up with a class discussion of those discrepancies.

7.   Assessment: Students may be assessed on their participation in the Open House as well as the extent to which they completed the Prediction Sheet.

Table 3:5 Open House Prediction Sheet

Setting: Where does the story take place? What does it look like? Describe where the characters are or live.
Characters: Who is in the story? What are their names? What are they like?
Mood/Tone: Do you think that the story has a happy, sad, dark, bright, reflective, supportive feel to it?
Plot: What is going on? Are there stories within the story? What do you know?
Conflict(s):   Are there conflicts, fights, problems that are arising?
Point of View: Who is telling the story (first person, third person, third person omniscient, alternating)?
Predictions: Make an educated guess as to what is going to happen from what you learned.

Strong readers automatically make predictions, inferences, and generalizations when they read, but reluctant readers need practice with these skills. The following "Mind's Eye" strategy is designed to help students construct images and make predictions about the story they will read.

Mind's Eye Strategy

This reading strategy, described by Brownlie & Silver (1995), will engage students in constructing visual images from words that they see and hear, from which they will make predictions for Lyon's *With a Hammer for My Heart*.

Procedure:

1.   Construct a list of 20–25 words of important names, places, and objects that appear in the first two or three chapters of the novel and arrange them on an overhead transparency. (See Table 3:6 for Words from *With a Hammer for My Heart*.)

2.   As you read the words slowly and thoughtfully to the class, ask the stu-

dents to listen to the words and construct mental images of what might be happening in the story.

3.   After allowing time for visualization, ask the students to do one of the following activities:
   •   Draw a picture based on your visualizations.
   •   Formulate questions you hope the text will answer.
   •   Use the words to write a paragraph predicting the events in the story.
   •   Describe the feelings, words, and mental images called forth during the visualization. (See Table 3:7 for Visualization by Kiesha Jenkins.)
4.   Ask students to share their predictions in a class discussion before reading the novel.

Table 3:6 Words from *With a Hammer for My Heart*

Hammer	gift of healing	abuse
Heart	veteran	gas can
abandoned bus	journey	helicopter
college	Garland	Kentucky
friendship	selling magazines	"Mother Jesus"
books	ridge	pain
maps	jail	forgiveness
journal	lawyer	Lawanda

Table 3:7 Kiesha's Mind's Eye Visualization

During Reading Strategies to Enhance Appalachian Cultural Concepts

Explicit Word Study

Explicit word study is used as a way of teaching words or concepts critical to a successful experience with the text. Janet Allen (2002, May) recommends explicit word study both as a prereading strategy to help students understand "big idea words that are critical to understanding" and also as a during or after reading strategy "for helping students understand the word in the context in which they will be reading it" (p. 24). The "Word in My Context" strategy, created by Lynnette Elliott, an eighth-grade teacher at Odyssey Middle School in Orlando, Florida, uses this strategy as a way for students to activate personal background knowledge for concepts that would be difficult to understanding in the reading of the text. In the case of the Appalachian unit, there are geographical terms used throughout the novel that only those living in mountain areas would understand. Terms such as cirque, outcropping, landslide, hollow, ridge, sweetbriar, piney, thicket, gully, spoil heap, and plateau are examples of terms that appear in Hamilton's *M. C. Higgins, The Great.* For instance, without understanding the concept of "spoil heap," students would have difficulty understanding the threat to the ancestral home that M. C. Higgins is facing when he learns that the spoil heap is moving toward—and will destroy—his home. For the "Word in My Context" strategy, ask students to find dictionary definitions for these basic concepts, create a visual representation of the concept (or find one on the Internet), and then connect their feelings and personal experiences to it. See Table 3:8 for Erin Roger's Word in My Context for the word, "gully." Erin's images were taken from the Stockyard Gully Damage at http://wasg.iinet.net.au/sgully.html.

Table 3:8 Word in My Context for "Gully"

Dictionary Definition: A deep ditch or channel cut in the earth by running water after a prolonged downpour; a channel or hollow worn in the earth by a current of water.	Feelings associated with the word: Could be dangerous if hiking after a heavy rain.

My experience with the word: I've seen rushing water in the gutters of the street after a heavy rain, but I haven't seen them in the hills or mountains.

Sketchbook Journal Prompts

The sketchbook is a place where students can record their initial, global responses to literary text with pictorial maps as well as with words. According to Daniels (1998), "This is the graphic equivalent of freewriting. Students do original drawings to illustrate ideas found in their reading, discussion, and inquiry" (p. 118). The graphic element provides students with an opportunity to represent their feelings, opinions, and ideas using another dimension, enabling them to respond nonverbally and holistically, using their visual spatial intelligence as they transact with the text. See Table 3:9 for sketchbook journal prompts that are designed to help students probe passages or quotations. They may use labels or captions to accompany the drawings in response to *With a Hammer for My Heart* by George Ella Lyon.

Table 3:9 Sketchbook Journal Prompts

1. The closing line on page 1 says, "You never know who's at the door when you hear footsteps. You never know what will fall out of the sky." Create an illustration that interprets the quote.

2. After reading the first chapter of the book, ask students to visualize Garland and his buses on the ridge. What kind of person is he? What does he look like? Sketch your first impression of him or the setting where he lives.

3. Visualize Mamaw at Little Splinter Creek Church the Sunday she had her vision. Draw an image of Mamaw or her vision that got her excommunicated from the church.

4. On page 63 in the book, Garland describes Lawanda's motives for visiting him as "with a hammer for my heart." What does this mean? What is the significance of these words? Draw what you imagine she thinks about him.

5. Read the letter from Lawanda to Garland on page 73. Pretend you are Garland and write a letter with an illustration responding to Lawanda.

6. Throughout the book, the reader is given glimpses into Garland's notebook where he keeps his personal thoughts. "That's my own goddamn business! It's me, *inside*, not something out in the world" (p. 157). Illustrate one of the flashbacks of the war found in his notebooks. What was he feeling?

7. On pages 91–92, Lawanda explains her vision to Mamaw. Create an illustration of that vision giving your interpretation of what it means.

8. On the bus to Louisville, Bev Combs sits down next to Lawanda and says, "I was wondering . . . could you tell me what it feels like [to read]?" (p. 104). Create an image that captures the feeling you have when you read.

9. Create a split-open head that shows the decisions Nancy Catherine has to make about her father. Draw an oval with a line down the middle representing the left and right brain of Nancy Catherine. Draw images that show her conflict with her father. Should she get him out of jail?

10. Find Shakespearean Sonnet 29 on p. 142. Create an illustration that gives an interpretation of the sonnet. What does it mean to Garland and Lawanda?

11. "No, there was something there when he was drinking, something threatening to get out" (p. 164). Create an image that shows what Garland had bottled up inside of him.

12. Lawanda's father, Howard, says that "Lawanda's a wild plant" (p. 165). Draw an image of this metaphor interpreting Howard's comment.

Character Portrait in *Lyon's With a Hammer for My Heart*

This activity invites students to brainstorm characteristics for main characters, role play, vocabulary words, write letters, and collect evidence for their character before engaging in formal essay writing of a character portrait. This activity has been adapted from Irene Bell, English Online, New Zealand Ministry of Education.

1. Adjective Matching

Prepare a set of adjective cards and a set of character cards (one for Amos Garland, Lawanda, Nancy Catherine, and Mamaw) for each group of four students. (See Table 3:10 for adjective cards appropriate for this novel.) The set of cards is divided among the group, and each student takes a turn to place an adjective card on top of the character's name, explaining the reasons for that choice. The group agrees or disagrees. When all cards are assigned, each student writes a copy of the four lists, justifying their choices with reference to the novel.

2. Amos Garland's Personality: Brainstorming and Vocabulary Extension

Taking the adjectives students chose for Garland, write them on the board. Add other adjectives as students mention them. Encourage students to use a thesaurus to find more adjectives for Garland. Discuss the meanings of unfamiliar words. Then ask students in each group to do one of the following activities:

1. Role play: Students mime a difficult word, such as "eccentric."
2. Tableau: A group of students interprets a word by freezing in positions that show the words by using body language and facial expressions.
3. Talk Show Interview: The host interviews Garland to discuss his eccentricity.
4. Ask class members to guess the vocabulary word represented in the role play and tableaux.

Table 3:10 Adjective Cards

lonely	selfish	sensitive	careless	irresponsible
insecure	extroverted	misunderstood	sad	intelligent
creative	perceptive	hermit	innocent	generous
eccentric	intellectual	religious	troubled	imaginative
ambitious	suffering	resourceful	possessive	determined
musical	infuriating	intellectual	abusive	hurt

3. Static Image: Ranking Ideas

Static images are images that don't move. They include greeting cards, posters, slides, paintings, photographs, comics, collages, and tableaux. In this case, ask each group of students to draw an image or cartoon of Garland and arrange the adjectives on or around him in order of importance. Students need to decide how to display their words. For instance, some words could be larger than others, more important words could be nearer his heart, or more important words could be closer to his body, while less important words are nearer the edge of the page. See Table 3:11 for a student example of static images for Amos Garland by Adam Basch.

Table 3:11 Static Image of Amos Garland

4. Letter Writing

Using the adjectives students have generated for Garland, ask them to write two letters:

- Write one letter as Lawanda to her Mamaw, describing Garland.
- Write one letter as Howard Ingle to Galt, describing Garland. (See Table 3:12 for Adam Basch's letter.)
- Write a letter from Garland to Howard to persuade him to permit Lawanda to visit him.
- Write a letter from Lawanda to Nancy Catherine convincing her to return and visit her father, Garland.
- You see Howard on his way to set fire to Garland's buses. Persuade him not to do it based on Garland's character.

Table 3:12 Letter to Galt from Howard Ingle

To Galt,

That Garland is no-account. What business can that man want with my girl that ain't even through the schooling yet? He's a troubled man. A selfish, lonely man. Just because the man couldn't love his own family don't give him no right to a tryin' again with my girl. I don't like to talk bad about no one with no reason, but he's a rotten pervert, thinkin' about what ain't right. You make sure and do your job and keep that sneaky Garland under lock and key. We need to have that book he wrote in about my girl and then go throw the book at him—no dishonest hermit got a right to mess with my daughter. Lawanda? She's too young to know what she wants and that crazy coot's not about to fill her head with foolishness. You come by and let me know before he leaves that jail. Garland is a dangerous eccentric, liable to hurt himself or anyone what gets mixed up with him.

—Howard Ingle

5. Evidence Collecting

Ask students to highlight the main points about Amos Garland in these two letters. Ask students to put their ideas up on the board and copy any new points they did not include. Then, assign chapters to small groups. Each group should find examples and quotations from their chapters to illustrate Amos Garland's personality. These should be recorded with page references on newsprint paper or large post-it paper headed with the chapter number. Place these charts in order around the room for easy reference by everyone. Each group justifies its chart and entertains comments from the class. This might lead to crossing out items that are not relevant or important.

6. Writing the Character Portrait

The individual assignment is to choose one of the other characters—Lawanda, Mamaw, or Nancy Catherine—to compose the character portrait. Students may refer back to activity 1 and add more adjectives, draw a picture of the character, or arrange words in order, as in activity 3. They should then collect quotes and examples from each chapter. Afterwards, they should choose the four most important adjectives, with supporting quotes and evidence for each. With this information, ask students to write a character portrait for their chosen character. See Table 3:13 for Adam Basch's Static Image and Character Portrait of Lawanda.

Table 3:13 Static Image and Character Portrait of Lawanda

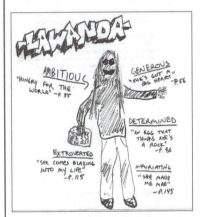

Lawanda Ingle is one of the more ambitious characters in George Ella Lyons' *With a Hammer For My Heart.* Lawanda's Grandma, Mamaw, recalls the birth of her granddaughter fondly on page 55 when she says, "That baby was a sight — long-legged, smiling, and hungry for the world. Hasn't changed a bit." Mamaw knows her granddaughter so intimately that this insight carries a lot of weight. This reading of Lawanda's character is corroborated by her father who, ruminating on the family, uses a colorful metaphor to clarify just how determined Lawanda is. "Lawanda's an egg that thinks she's a rock," he says while trying to keep her safe on page 86. This determination and ambition can also be infuriating, as Nancy Catherine finds out when she and Lawanda go pay a visit to Garland's buses. When Lawanda tried to tell Nancy Catherine why she must act a certain way, Nancy Catherine almost explodes. "She made me mad," she realizes, and then tells Lawanda, on page 145, that, "You can't control the world." Since all three of these characters have intimate relationships with Lawanda, their thoughts, feelings, and actions toward and about her offer a clear window through which to see her character traits.

—Adam Basch

Writing from Inside the Photograph

One of our goals as teachers is to enable students to explore, through the dimensions of the senses, the power of the mind. It involves all the natural dimensions of our experience, including aspects of our sense experiences: color, shape, texture, and sound. Books in the form of photo essays provide students with the opportunity to look deeper into the experiences of photographic images. In this assignment, students are asked to choose a photograph and write the story of the person(s) they are viewing. Two excellent books that depict the lives of Appalachian people are Adams' *Appalachian Legacy* (1998) and Bartoletti's *Growing Up in Coal Country.* Either pass the books around and have students choose the photo that they connect with or tear the pages out of the book or scan them to make a bulletin board, as I did. Students need time to dwell in the photo and imagine the circumstances of the person they are viewing. Ask them to write the story that they "see" in the photograph. See Table 3:14 for Theresa McClain's writing from "inside" the photograph of Adams' "Sixty-Four Years of Marriage."

Table 3:14 Writing "Inside" the Photograph in Adam's "Sixty-Four Years of Marriage"

"Reece, I'm so glad that bullet missed its target. Funny, I almost hoped and prayed that rifle shot would be the end of you and the end of my stupidity . . . taking your sorry butt back every time you dragged yourself down the mountain just in time to fill me up with another child. How fitting that bullet tore out your manhood—tweren't no more polecatting around for you, and I learnt much about forgiveness."

"Forgiveness, I say you've had enough of that for a lifetime; but here you stand on the back porch takin' care of me."

"Forgiveness, well that sho' is a sweet thing. I'm so glad when after sellin' all those paintings, we stayed on this mountain, on this back porch—growin' old together. Yep, no price on forgiveness."

—Theresa McClain

After Reading Strategies to Understand Appalachian Dialect and Poverty

Building Whirligigs in Rylant's *Missing May*

Missing May is a Newbery Metal Award–winning novel that demonstrates how love overcomes grief. Once an orphan, Summer has lived the last six years with Aunt May and Uncle Ob. When Aunt May passes, Summer must not only deal with her own loss, but also comfort Uncle Ob, who doesn't have much will to live after Aunt May passes. Yet, Uncle Ob was unique in that he used his artist talent to create *whirligigs*. These were not farm animals or cartoon characters as most think of whirligigs, but rather they were artistic pieces that he called "The Mysteries" (p. 6). As Summer says, "One whirligig was meant to be a thunderstorm and it was so like one, black and gray, beautiful and frightening" (p. 6). Whirligigs have moving parts that blow in the wind and can be made of paper and popsicle sticks, pop cans, plastic milk jugs, or just about any other media. Ask students to create a whirligig to represent one of their mysteries in life.

Appalachian Dialect and Metaphor

Regardless of the book(s) your students have been reading, the beauty of the Appalachian dialect and metaphor has been part of the reading experience. In order to help students appreciate the language, ask them to find colorful phrases spoken by the narrator. For instance, in Rylant's *Missing May*, they might find the following:

- "Back in Ohio, where I'd been treated like a homework assignment somebody was always having to do, eating was never a joy of any kind" (p. 7).
- "But I felt like one of those little mice who has to figure out the right button to push before its food will drop down into the cup. Caged and begging. That's how I felt sometimes" (p. 7).
- "While Ob and me were off in our dreamy heads, May was here in this trailer seeing to it there was a good home for us . . . " (p. 15).
- "If Cletus gets wind that May's back, I know he'll take it and run with it" (p. 17).
- "Ob needed somebody to fill the empty hole she left, and I reckon I thought if I aged about fifty years, I might could fill it for him" (p. 24).

In another place, a classmate described Summer as being "like some sad welfare case, in the sorry way her clothes and hair were described" (p. 46). However, this was not the way Summer thought of herself. After collecting these phrases, ask students to describe the Appalachian values conveyed in the language.

In desperation to make contact with May, Uncle Ob takes Summer and Cletus on a trip across Virginia to find "Miriam B. Conklin: Small Medium at Large." The journey seems to fail, since Rev. Conklin has died, but Ob finally agrees to put aside his grief and take the children to the Capitol as he had promised. The trip is upbeat, and their language is humorous. Ask students to find examples of humorous language. The following are some examples to get you started:

- "Deep Water needs itself some Renaissance Men," says Cletus. "Ha! After our little trip, you might be calling yourself a Rent-a-Seance Man!" said Ob (p. 55).
- "You two stop that jawing and get on in the car" (p. 67).
- "Best reading I ever done was in my daddy's old johnnyhouse. And I don't mean dirty stuff, neither. He kept him some books on auto mechanics, fishing, Civil War—you name it. I used to love to get the diarrhea" (p. 68).
- "Right out of the blue, he wanted to live again" (p. 80).

Talk about humor. How does the language contribute to the humor? Some students may want to design cartoons based on the imagery of the selected passages. Ask students if they can identify the positive qualities of Appalachian humor. Show how Appalachian humor includes the use of metaphors, similes, and idioms specific to the mountain people. This might lead to a study of hillbilly jokes. Ask students to tell jokes that they already know and figure out what makes them funny. Ask them to distinguish between jokes told by an outsider vs. one told by an insider. What is the difference in their motives? This discussion could lead to having students collect cartoons and jokes representing Appalachian humor. There are many Internet sites that can be located through the "google" search engine. Ask students to sort the jokes and cartoons by speaker—insider or outsider. Discuss the differences between them. Which jokes and cartoons appear to promote the hillbilly stereotypes, and which ones turn the joke on the speaker?

Understanding Appalachian Poverty

Typically, Appalachians have resisted the modern way of life. They have lived like pioneers in remote areas of the mountains, surviving on their land, living independently, and making do with what they have or going without. These folks have lived a successful, satisfying life as they raise their families and enjoy the fruits of the land. It wasn't until the timber, coal, and gas companies came along that their lifestyle was threatened. Louisa Mae Cardinal in Baldacci's *Wish You Well* is a prime example of a woman who has lived a full life in the mountains, although most modern people would be appalled by her poverty. We see similar stories of resilience in generational poverty in Lyon's *With a Hammer for My Heart*, Hamilton's *M. C. Higgins, The Great*, Rylant's *Missing May*, and Creech's *Chasing Redbird*.

Ruby Payne, in her book, *A Framework for Understanding Poverty*, gives us a model to begin examining poverty in Appalachian Young Adult literature. Payne (1998) defines poverty as "the extent to which an individual does without resources" (p. 16). While most of us think in terms of financial resources, Payne tells us that the ability to leave poverty is more dependent upon other resources. Payne outlines the various types of resources that one needs to survive poverty: financial, emotional, mental, spiritual, physical, support systems, relationships/role models, and knowledge of the rules of society.

Ask students to write a persuasive essay using textual evidence to show how the protagonist sustains a satisfying lifestyle living in the poverty of their lives. Use Payne's definitions of resources as the basis for collecting textual evidence. See Table 3:15 for a Student Example of Collecting Textual Evidence for Louisa Mae Cardinal in Baldacci's *Wish You Well*. Louisa Mae Cardinal lived on a remote farm in the mountains of Virginia, where there were no phones, no electricity, and no indoor plumbing or running water. At age 80, she raised chickens, cows, hogs, mules, and sheep as well as maintaining a vegetable garden to sustain her life there. She took in a Black man, Eugene, when he lost his home. She took in Diamond after his father was killed in a mine. Then she took in her two great-grandchildren, Lou and Oz, and their comatose mother, Amanda, whom she had never before met. Louisa Mae Cardinal gets along no matter the weather, no matter the fertility of the land. " I find water where there ain't supposed to be none, I get on" (p. 275), and she's not afraid to take in others.

Table 3:15 Textual Evidence of Sustaining Life in Poverty for Louisa Mae Cardinal

Resource	Textual Evidence
Financial	"What about the car?" "T'ain't practical. Take money we surely ain't got . . . wouldn't have the durn thing, cept William . . . give it to us . . . can't drive it, no plans to ever learn" (p. 63). "I got me a problem, Cotton. Last three years of drought and ain't no crops come in. Down to five hogs and gotta butcher me one purty soon . . . and McKenzie on down at the store, he ain't giving me no more credit to us folk up here" (p. 95). "That little boy [Jack] always run circles round me. But giving me money when he ain't got it. And curse me for taking it" (p. 95).
Emotional	"Fact is," Louisa continued, "you and Oz coming here is a blessing. Some folk might say I helping you out, but that ain't the truth. You helping me a lot more'n I can you. For that I thank you" (p. 71).
Mental	"It be a hard life up here, 'specially for a child. And it hard on husband and wife, though I ain't never suffered that. If my momma and daddy ever said a cross word to the other, I ain't never heard it. And me and my man Joshua get along to the minute he took his last breath" (pp. 274–275).
Spiritual	"Miz Louisa, she believe in God with all her soul. But she don't subscribe to church much. She say the way some folk run they's churches, it take God right out cha heart" (p. 231).
Physical	"She was tall, lean, and looked strong enough to strangle a bear, and determined enough to do so" (p. 57).
Support Systems	"And Eugene. He my family. He work hard. He getting some of this land so's he can have his own place, raise his own family. Only fair" (p. 96). Cotton said, "You need me for anything, come up and help with the planting, the children, you must let me know. I'd be beyond proud to help you" (p. 96). Cotton looked at Amanda, "It'll be my real privilege to read to you" (p. 98). "Your daddy did come back. I got me the three people he loved most in the whole world" (p. 206). They spent a solid hour loading bags of cornmeal, canning jars full of beans and tomatoes, and buckets of rutabagas . . . and even some cuts of salted hog meat on that wagon [for Billy to drive home]. "They can't hide all that food from George Davis," Lou said. "I been doing this many a year now. Man never once fretted about where the bounty come from" (p. 244).
Relationships	Cotton unveiled the gramophone . . . music . . . and dancing . . . and laughter (p. 188). "He [Diamond] a wild bird. Put him in a cage, he just shrivel up and die. He need anythin', he know to come to me" (p. 193). "What's wrong, Billy?" "Ma's baby coming . . . say baby ain't feel right. Rode the mule come get you" (p. 213).
Knowledge of Hidden Rules	Louisa pulled the rifle from behind her back and leveled it at George Davis. The man stopped halfway off his wagon when he saw the Winchester's long barrel pointed at him (p. 185).

cont.

Destruction of the Land	"Lou could see loaded coal trucks far below them inching down one side of the road, while on the other side empty trucks flew hell-bent back up, like honeybees, to gorge some more" (p. 51).
	"All around here the face of the mountains had been gashed open in places, exposing rock underneath, the topsoil and tree all gone" (p. 51).
	"Lou watched as coal trolleys emerged from these wounds in the mountains, like drips of blackened blood, and the coal was tippled into the truck beds" (p. 51).
	"Cotton, Diamond said some men coming round folks' coal mines." "Surveyors, mineral experts, so I've heard" (p. 97).
	"Coal mining pays pretty good, but the work is terribly hard, and with the way the company stores are set up the miners end up owing more to the company than they earn in wages . . . and the men also get sick and die of the black lung, or from cave-ins, accidents, and such" (p. 151).
	"Coal is king," the mayor announced . . . "And what with the war heating up across the Atlantic and the mighty United States of America building ships and guns and tanks for our friends fighting Hitler, the steel mill's demands for coke, our good, patriotic Virginia coke, will skyrocket" (p. 200).
	"'Cept I ain't selling it to you. You ain't scalping this land like you done everywhere else" (p. 260).
Dependence on the Land	"Land don't help none who don't never bother to learn it" (p. 70).
	"I can't complain none, this old mountain give me all it can over the years" (p. 96).
	"Well the one thing you do have, Louisa, is land. Now, there's an asset" (p. 96).
	"God made these mountains so's they last forever. Yet he put us people here for just a little-bitty time. Now, what does that tell you?" (p. 260).
	"You ask me why I don't never leave this place? I love this land, Lou, 'cause it won't never let me down . . . Me and the land. Me and this mountain . . . it means everything to me . . . And the mountain is my home" (p. 275).

However resourcefully Louisa Mae Cardinal has managed to live, she will have no chance of survival if the Southern Valley Coal and Gas Company wins the legal battle for mineral rights to her land and neither will her great-grandchildren, to whom she left her land.

Readers' Theater for Baldacci's *Wish You Well*

Readers' Theater is a way to involve students in an oral performance of the novel they are reading. While there are various ways of creating a Readers' Theater, this one was designed to focus on the struggle of Louisa Mae Cardinal to keep her land against the Southern Valley Coal and Gas Company in Baldacci's *Wish You Well*. The script covers highlights of the last 100 pages of the novel, taking many of the lines verbatim from the text. The narrator functions to fill in the gaps, provide transitions between events, and move the action forward. The script begins with a visit of the Southern Valley Coal and Gas Company executives on Louisa Mae Cardinal's property. It takes the audience from her stubborn position of refusing to sell the property to the final courtroom scene, in which Cotton Longfellow is pleading with the judge and jury to vote in Cardinal's favor. Read the script for the Readers' Theater based on *Wish You Well* on the CD-ROM.

Readers' Theater for Hamilton's *M. C. Higgins, The Great*

After completing the reading for *M. C. Higgins, The Great*, ask students to create a script for a Readers' Theater. Divide the class into small groups and assign each group a chapter or chapters (depending on class size), which they will write in Readers' Theater format. If students have not had prior practice in such an activity, remind them of the following principles:

- Write as a play script with the characters name on the left side.
- Create short dialogues by turning indirect speech into direct speech (i.e., "M. C. was feeling tired and hungry" indirect speech to "I am feeling tired and hungry" direct speech).
- Think of ways to use a chorus of several voices to add drama to your Readers' Theater.
- Use a narrator to explain reasons for events and transitions from one event to another. Do not overuse this character.
- Use poetic devices, such as rhyme and repetitive structure, to appeal to the ears of the audience.
- Your Readers' Theater should make a clear point, and should maybe even have rising action, climax, and falling action.
- You may add sound effects, props, or music to enhance your performance.

When students have finished preparing their scripts, set aside time for them to perform them for the rest of the class. If this is the first time your students have ever performed Reader's Theater or if you would like to see a model, find the Readers' Theater for *M. C. Higgins, The Great*, Chapter 6, written by Erin Rogers, on the CD-ROM.

Exploring Social Issues Through Appalachian Young Adult Literature

The following books can be used to extend students' understanding of Appalachian literature by exploring concepts related to race, ethnicity, and social inequality. These books could be used for comparison to other books they have read or chosen as a focus for their multigenre research papers.

1. Racial Prejudice in *M. C. Higgins, The Great* by Virginia Hamilton

While prejudice is not the main focus of the book, the protagonist in the novel follows M. C.'s unresolved struggle to decide whether or not to buy into his father's stereotypes about the family that lives at the foot of the mountain. "Those people aren't right, wash your hands, you let one of them touch you," says M. C.'s father (p. 195). The Kilburns have red hair, six fingers on each hand, and six toes on each foot. Although Hamilton does not refer to them as such, the Melungeon people fit this description. Melungeons are a mixed race of people who don't fit in with White society, but neither are they part of Indian or Black society. There are many groups that live in Appalachia, although others have migrated out of the region. Therefore, their features identify them as the closeness and oneness of a clan, rather than the product of inbreeding. Are they the "witchy" people that M. C. has been led to believe they are?

2. Superstitious Stereotypes in *Clara and the Hoo Doo Man* by Elizabeth Partridge

Partridge's novel tells of everyday experiences of a young African-American girl growing up in mountain traditions of ginseng gathering, home births with midwives, and healing illnesses with herbs. Clara must also struggle to decide whether or not to buy into her mother's stereotypes concerning the Hoo Doo Man. Her mother warns her against an encounter with him saying, "a hoodoo man could put a hex on you real bad" (p. 27). However, her experience with Old Sugar Johnson up on Red Owl Mountain is quite different. He befriends her and her sister and helps them dig the ginseng plants that she needs to trade for a new crock to replace the one she broke. Then, when Clara's sister becomes seriously ill with an unrelenting fever, Clara has to decide if it is Hoo Doo's fault or her own. When mother goes for the White doctor and his expertise fails to bring her sister relief, Clara confronts the prejudice, risks her mother's wrath, and seeks the Hoo Doo Man's healing. When her sister is healed, the negative stereotype Clara's mother has of this outcast man is dispelled—it is this stereotype of the Hoodoo Man, and not racial conflict, that serves as the educational point about prejudice in this book.

3. Prejudice toward the Cherokee in *Soft Rain: A Story of the Cherokee Trail of Tears* by Cornelia Cornelissen and *Cherokee Sister* by Debbie Dadey

The Cherokee Nation is another racial-ethnic group which offers richness to the Appalachian experience. Both novels introduce the life of the Tsalagi in their homeland in North Carolina just prior to the moment families are torn apart with the onset of the Trail of Tears. The families of both protagonists are displaced from their mountain homes and required to take the long, perilous journey beyond the Mississippi River. Readers learn about historical figures—such as Sequoyah—the complexities of the westward movement, and the impact that schooling had on assimilation. While these authors do not diminish the horrors of the removal of the race relations, neither do they vilify the United States soldiers and Euro-American civilians they meet along the way. Readers not only experience the tragedy of these historical events, but also share the strength, courage, and bonding of the characters.

4. Prejudice Against Integration of Cherokee Children in *Music from a Place Called Half Moon* by Jerrie Oughton

Prejudice and reactions to prejudice take place in a small North Carolina town near Asheville, when Edie Jo Houp's father opens his Vacation Bible School to all the children in Half Moon—including the Cherokee children. As nearly everyone in the town turns on the Houps and Edie Jo has a frightening run-in with some Indian boys, she decides that integration is not for her. It isn't until she gets to know an Indian boy named Cherokee Fish that Edie Jo comes to a deeper understanding of friendship that crosses racial boundaries and understands for herself that "friendships don't shape on color" (p. 130). Readers learn tolerance from the ethnocentric mistakes of the characters in this novel.

5. Prejudice toward the Chinese-Americans in *The Star Fisher* by Laurence Yep.

Yep based his novel on the experience of his Chinese-American grandmother, who moved to West Virginia from Ohio, when her father decided to open a laundry in Clarksburg. In the novel, the Lees are the first Chinese-Americans to arrive in Clarksburg. Since the family speaks Chinese to one another, Yep italicizes the text when his characters speak English and uses the plain type when they speak their native tongue. Due to this technique, it is the English speakers who seem out of the norm. Yep normalizes the presence of his people in this Appalachian town, even though residents are reluctant to frequent their business. Even though Joan Lee was born in America and speaks fluent English, her teacher and classmates never look beyond her surface features. Joan struggles with her identity, finally coming to the proud realization that "We may talk and dress and act like Americans, but in our hearts we'll always be Chinese" (p. 146). This book celebrates diversity and focuses on the assimilation process.

Multigenre Research Paper

As found in chapter 1, the multigenre research paper is the culminating project for this chapter as well. The assignment for this unit was different in that it comprised a service-learning component. Students were asked to volunteer at a local soup kitchen, homeless shelter, school, or church group, serving the needs of this Appalachian community. Students were asked to write on their experiences in journal entries or as a short story and include their pieces in the multigenre paper. The instructions for students are found in Table 3:16. See Table 1:11 for Assessment Rubric for the Multigenre Research Paper.

After students have completed the writing of their Multigenre Research Papers, set aside a date and time for presenting them to the class. You may want to invite other school personnel, parents, and community members to join in the celebration of these presentations. See the CD-ROM for this chapter for a student Multigenre Research Paper written by Katie Ellis entitled, "Appalachian Poverty." Also, listen to Megan Steven's performance of "Miner's Prayer" by Dwight Yoakam. There is a bibliography of Appalachian children's literature also on the CD-ROM.

Table 3:16 Multigenre Research Paper Requirements

1. Select a topic related to the Appalachian literature unit for your research. Prepare a Prospectus that states your topic, interest, purpose, audience, and materials you will use for information.

2. Choose the service organization for which you prefer to volunteer at least 5–10 hours. Confirm your arrangements with me. Include a time sheet with your project that documents your hours. Keep a journal of your experiences in the field. An interview or journal entry could be one of the creative pieces for your multigenre paper.

3. In addition to the novel you've been reading for class, read another book of poetry, autobiography, biography, or children's book in order to compare ideas and different perspectives of your topic. At least one of your creative pieces should reflect this comparison.

4. As you begin drafting your creative pieces, think about what you will use as repetends to connect your ideas and create a main point to your paper. These might be statistics, quotes, photographs, drawings, or other ideas that will make your paper cohesive.

5. Your final paper should include a minimum of five creative pieces written in at least three different genres (letters, journal entries, poems, news articles, etc.).

6. As you prepare to present your project to the class, think of musical selections from Appalachian folk music that might be performed or played as background music.

Appalachian Young Adult Literature

Baldacci, D. (2000). *Wish you well*. New York: Warner Books.

Bartoletti, S. C. (1996). *Growing up in coal country*. Boston: Houghton Mifflin Company.

Caudill, R. (1966). *Did you carry the flag today, Charley?* Illustrated by Nancy Grossman. Austin, TX: Holt, Rinehart and Winston.

Cornelissen, C. (1998). *Soft rain: A story of the Cherokee trail of tears*. New York: Delacorte Press.

Creech, S. (1997). *Chasing Redbird*. New York: HarperCollins.

Dadey, D. (2002). *Whistler's hollow*. New York: Bloomsbury Children's Books.

Hamilton, V. (1974). *M. C. Higgins, the great*. New York: Aladdin Paperbacks.

Hamilton, V. (1990). *Cousins*. New York: Scholastic.

Hamilton, V. (1998). *Second cousins*. New York: Scholastic.

Hesse, K. (1998). *Just juice*. New York: Scholastic.

Houston, G. (1994). *Mountain valor*. New York: Putnam & Grosset Group.

Lowry, L. (1987). *Rabble Starkey*. New York: Bantam Doubleday Dell.

Lyon, G. E. (1997). *With a hammer for my heart*. New York: Avon Books, Inc.

Lyon, G. E. (1999). *Borrowed children*. Lexington, KY: The University Press of Kentucky.

Naylor, P. R. (1991). *Shiloh*. New York: Atheneum Books for Young Readers.

Naylor, P. R. (1996). *Shiloh season*. New York: Atheneum Books for Young Readers.

Naylor, P. R. (1997). *Saving Shiloh*. New York: Atheneum Books for Young Readers.

Oughton, J. (1995). *Music from a place called Half Moon*. Boston: Houghton Mifflin.

Partridge, E. (1996). *Clara and the Hoo Doo Man*. New York: Dutton Children's Books.

Paterson, K. (1985). *Come sing, Jimmy Jo*. London: Puffin Books.

Rylant, C. (1992). *Missing May*. London: Orchard Books.

Stuart, J. (2000). *The best-loved short stories of Jesse Stuart*. Ashland, KY: Jesse Stuart Foundation.

Stuart, J. (1949). *The thread that runs so true*. Carmichael, CA: Touchstone Books.

White, R. (1996). *Belle Prater's Boy*. New York: Bantam Doubleday Dell Books.

White, R. (2000). *Memories of summer*. Vancouver, BC, Canada: Douglas and McIntyre, LTD.

Yep, L. (1991). *The star fisher*. New York: Morrow Junior Books.

References

Adams, S. (1998). *Appalachian legacy*. Jackson, MS: University Press of Mississippi.

Allen, J. (2002, May). "I Am Thorgood, King of the Orgies": The reading challenge of content vocabulary. *Voices from the Middle, 9*(4), 22–27. Urbana, IL: NCTE.

Bartoletti, S. C. (1996). *Growing up in coal country*. Boston: Houghton Mifflin Company.

Beers, K. (2001, November 17). *Help struggling secondary readers*. Baltimore: NCTE.

Bell, I. (1998). *Character building in Zindel's Pigman*. English Online. New Zealand Ministry of Education. Brownlie, F., & Silver, H. G. (1995, January). *Mind's eye*. Paper presented at the seminar "Responding Thoughtfully to the Challenge of Diversity," Delta School District Conference Center, Delta, British Columbia, Canada.

Christensen, L. (2001). Where I'm from: Inviting students' lives into the classroom. In B. Bigelow, B. Harvey, S. Karp, & L. Miller (Eds.), *Rethinking our classrooms: Teaching for equity and justice*, Vol. 2. Milwaukee, WI: Rethinking Schools, Ltd.

Daniels, H. (1998). Jotting and sketching: Twenty-three ways to use a notebook. In H. Daniels & M. Bizar's *Methods that matter: Six structures for best practice classrooms*. Portland, ME: Stenhouse Publishers.

Hamilton, V. (1974). *M. C. Higgins, the great*. New York: Aladdin Paperbacks.

Lyon, G. E. (1994). *Mama is a miner*. Paintings by Peter Catalanotto. New York: Orchard Books.

Lyon, G. E. (1997). *With a hammer for my heart*. New York: Avon Books, Inc.

Lyon, G. E. (1999). Where I'm from. In Lyon's *Where I'm from: Where poems come from*. Photographs by Robert Hoskins. Spring, TX: Absey & Company.

Payne, R. K. (1998). *A framework for understanding poverty*. Highlands, TX: RFT.

Chapter Four

Homeless Children: America's Newest Outcasts

Jacqueline N. Glasgow

W hat does a homeless person look like? How many of the following statements have you heard? (Rozakis, 1995, p. 8).

- Some people like the homeless lifestyle.
- Middle-class people can't become homeless.
- Children can't be homeless.
- The homeless are mainly men.
- Homeless people only live in cities.
- The homeless are all either mentally ill, alcoholics, or drug abusers.
- The homeless are dangerous.

The reality of homelessness is that homeless people are all ages, live in all parts of the United States, and are of all races and backgrounds. What they have in common is that they are all people who have nowhere to live. As Rozakis says, they don't choose their lifestyle—they are victims of circumstances beyond their control. Many homeless people have jobs, but they cannot earn enough to support themselves or their families. Approximately 25% are mentally ill, and some abuse substances. However, they are not threatening, as they tend to be victims of crime, not criminals themselves.

Through Young Adult novels in which the protagonist is homeless, this unit is designed to examine the coping strategies, support systems, learning structures, relationships, and resources that enable survival in these harsh circumstances. This unit provides us with an opportunity to understand homelessness in a way allowing hope for helping children and youth to leave it behind, sensitizing other readers to these dire circumstances, and suggesting community service projects. Reading strategies include using the report sack for predicting character traits, creating a sun/shadow mandala to provoke rich imagery, and a photo essay to make connections and meaning among many others. See Table 4:1 for a comprehensive list of reading strategies for this unit.

Major goals for this unit include opportunities for students to:
1. explore the importance and nature of family ties,
2. understand the importance of preserving individual dignity,
3. examine survival coping skills through cohesion and forming close relationships, and
4. discover the aspects of hope that enable survival and reconciliation.

This unit may be implemented as a whole-group reading of the same novel or in Literature Circles, in which each group of students selects the book they'd like to read from the reading list. The reading strategies for this unit will be described for one of the following novels: *Monkey Island* (1991) by Paula Fox, *The Family Under the Bridge* (1958) by Natalie Savage Carlson, *Maniac Magee* (1990) by Jerry Spinelli, *The Crossing* (1987) by Gary Paulsen, and *December Stillness* (1988) by Mary Downing Hahn. Even though the reading strategies are described for these different books, they can also be adapted for any particular novel. The primary novel for this unit is Fox's *Monkey Island*.

The story takes place at Monkey Island, a homeless settlement in New York City, which is the locale for much of the action in this book. It is where 11-year-old Clay Garrity ended up after first his father lost his job as art director for a prominent magazine and then his mother lost her job in a Wall Street firm after discovering her pregnancy. Abandoned by both his desperate father and distraught mother, he was left to fend for himself in an unsavory welfare hotel. Clay left the place when a neighbor threatened to call the police. He didn't want to risk not finding his mother again. He hit the streets in Monkey Island and ended up befriending a one-time math teacher named Calvin, who lost everything in a fire, and a young Black adult, Buddy, who couldn't earn enough money for a rent deposit in order to survive on Monkey Island while he searched for his missing mother. Sometime later, their tentative existence was destroyed by a group of angry mobsters (the stump people) determined to drive out the homeless from the area. In the end, Calvin dies after a drinking spree and Clay is hospitalized with pneumonia. After the birth of a baby, his mother found him in a foster home and Clay came to live with her and began to forgive her for leaving him. Paula Fox sends a clear message: this situation could happen to anyone. To introduce students to the concept of homelessness, begin with the frontloading activities.

Table 4:1 Reading Skills Addressed in the Homeless Unit

Strategy	Set Purpose	Activate Prior Knowledge	Make Predictions	Critical Thinking	Asking Questions	Visualizing the Text	Making Connections	Monitor Reading	Cause Effect	Compare Contrast	Making Inferences	Main Idea
Anticipation Guide	•	•		•		•	•				•	•
Report Sack to Predict Characters	•	•	•	•	•		•		•	•	•	•
Prediction Cards	•	•	•	•	•	•	•		•	•	•	•
Word in My Context	•	•		•	•	•	•			•	•	•
Chapter/Story Portrait	•	•	•	•	•	•	•	•	•	•	•	•
Two-Voice Poem	•	•		•	•	•	•		•	•	•	•
Making Inferences	•	•		•	•	•	•	•			•	•
Story Web	•	•		•	•	•	•	•	•	•	•	•
Journal Beyond Stereotypes	•	•	•	•	•	•	•	•	•	•	•	•
Sun/Shadow Mandalas	•	•		•	•	•	•	•	•	•	•	•
Photo Essay	•	•		•	•	•	•			•	•	•
How Much Does It Cost to Live?	•	•			•		•	•			•	
Readers' Theater	•	•		•	•		•		•	•	•	•
Multigenre Paper	•	•	•	•	•	•	•		•	•	•	•

Frontloading Strategies to Draw on Students' Prior Knowledge of Homelessness

Anticipation Guide

An *anticipation guide* is a series of statements to which students must respond individually before reading the text. These statements focus on the major themes of a work. Their value lies in the discussion that takes place after the exercise, in which students explore what they believe about the statements. The teacher's role during discussion is to activate and agitate thought. As students connect their knowledge of the world to the prediction task, you must encourage a wide range of responses. This activity will encourage poor comprehenders to acquire the skill of anticipating and predicting meaning, just as good comprehenders have already learned to do. Students must think about a set of generalizations related to the main theme of the novel. Students decide whether they agree or disagree with each statement presented in the guide. These guides activate students' prior knowledge, help them make personal connections with the text, and help them become an active participant from the beginning of the reading experience.

Guidelines for Constructing Anticipation Guides

Anticipation guides vary in format but not in purpose. In each case, the readers' expectations about meaning are raised before they read the text. Keep these guidelines in mind when constructing and using an anticipation guide (adapted from Vacca & Vacca [1999, p. 373]).

1. Analyze the material to be read. Determine the major ideas—implicit and explicit—with which students will interact and can decide whether they agree or disagree.

2. Write those ideas in short, clear declarative statements. These statements should in some way reflect the world that the students live in or know about. Make sure there is not a right or wrong answer or the guide will be ineffective.

3. Put these statements in a format that will elicit anticipation and prediction.

4. Discuss the students' predictions and anticipations before they read the text selection.

5. After reading the assigned text, have the students evaluate the statements in light of the author's intent and purpose, and contrast their predictions with the author's intended meaning. See Table 4:2 for Anticipation Guide for Fox's *Monkey Island*.

Table 4:2 Anticipation Guide for Fox's *Monkey Island*

Before Reading		After Reading
Directions: Read each statement and write "Yes" in the blank if you believe the statement and could support it or put "No" in the blank if you do not believe the statement and could not support it. After you finish reading the selection, revisit the statements. This time, decide how a character in the story would react to each statement.		
	1. If you work hard, you will keep your job.	
	2. Some folks are forced to rely on welfare.	
	3. The government should provide shelters for the homeless.	
	4. Adults should take care of children even if they are not their own.	
	5. Fathers are responsible for providing for their families.	
	6. If you lose your job, you will be able to find another.	
	7. Parents do not have the right to desert their children.	
	8. Children should be removed from dysfunctional parents.	
	9. It is shameful to rely on welfare.	
	10. The homeless are beggars.	

Report Sack

While there are many ways to implement the Report Sack activity (Glasgow, 2002), the purpose here is to encourage students to think about character attributes, share impressions with classmates, and predict character development in the novel, *Monkey Island*, by Paula Fox. This activity helps students draw conclusions and form generalizations about the book.

Report Card Activity
1. Before students read the book, make a list of the main characters for the book.
2. Brainstorm a list of personality traits exhibited by each character.
3. Find or construct at least five objects that represent your character's personality.
4. Put those items in the standard brown paper lunch sack. (See Table 4:3 for sample objects.)
5. In class, ask students to examine the report sacks and brainstorm attributes of the character represented by the objects in their particular sack. They

could complete a worksheet with the following columns: "What it is," "What it Represents/Means," "Why You Think That."

6. Ask students to write a paragraph predicting the character's personality, function, and possible events that character might participate in.

7. As students read the novel, ask them to refer back to their predictions and compare them to actual events and characters in the story.

Prediction Cards

Prediction cards allow students to tap into their background knowledge about the topic of a book, share that information with classmates, and make predictions about the content of a piece of literature. At the same time, students can manipulate their vocabulary and share ideas related to word study and comprehension of text. Here is the procedure:

1. Before students read a book, select 20–25 words from the book. It is preferable to have words from the beginning, middle, and end of the book. Include words you know students are familiar with, words essential to comprehension of text, and a few unknown words.

2. Print each set of words on index cards and distribute each set of cards to a small group of students. See Table 4:4 for Labels for Prediction Cards for Fox's *Monkey's Island*.

3. Invite students to assemble the cards into categories of their choosing. (Note: Do not tell them a specific number of categories or number of "word cards" that should be in each grouping.) Encourage students to place words in categories according to their own knowledge of those words or their predictions of how those words might be used in forthcoming text.

4. Invite student groups to share their various categories and groupings and provide their rationale for the placement of word cards within specific groups.

5. Invite students to read the text, looking for the words on the index cards. After reading, encourage students to rearrange cards or manipulate words into new categories or groupings based on the information gleaned from the text. Afterward, invite students to discuss reasons for any rearrangements and compare their placements with those of other groups.

Table 4:3 Report Sack Objects for *Monkey Island*

Angela (Mother)	Clay Garrity	Buddy Meadowsweet	Calvin Bosker	Gerald
potholder to represent domestic duties legal pad to show her job baby bottle to show infant care advertisement for mental health and recovery services advertisement for help with pregnancy	*Robinson Crusoe* model of red double-decker bus book bag library card *David Copperfield* $28.75 (play money) his mother left with him	newspaper to represent the hut he made for shelter soda cans that he collected and sold to make money 5-cent pieces to represent what they lived on Rags used to keep warm Photo of father and son to show caregiving	calculator to represent he is a retired math teacher matches to represent his house burned up in fire ambulance that he was taken to hospital in notebooks—the journals of his life slippers cut out of an old pink carpet Rye whiskey to represent alcoholism	Van with Salvation Army emblem on the roof to show he helps the homeless coffee and doughnuts that he serves model sports car to show his affluence photos of wealthy homes that he owns

Table 4:4 Labels for Prediction Cards

stationery store	coffee & doughnuts	stump people	double-decker bus
Father	red crayon	Art director	pneumonia
Wall Street Office	Miss You-Can't-Fool-Me		hospital
police	wooden crate	lice	food van
battery-run radio	Writing in notebooks	Clay	Monkey Island
hotel	social services	Buddy	taxi
Mother	gathering soda cans		foster home
"Nigger"	lice	Calvin	baby sister
welfare hotel	police	ambulance	Forgiveness

Word in My Context

The prereading word study is a way for students to activate personal background knowledge in preparation for their reading. "Word in My Context" is a graphic organizer suggested in Janet Allen's forthcoming book, tentatively titled *Common Ground* (2003), which provides opportunity for whole-class predictions of content based on their own background knowledge. Megan Stypinski used this strategy with seventh graders who would read Cynthia DeFelice's novel, *Nowhere to Call Home* (1999). First, Megan asked the students to predict what the story would be about, based on viewing the cover of the book. They could see one boy pulling the other into a boxcar of a train. Along with the quote on the bottom of the cover, "Wealthy Frances Elizabeth Barrow is about to become a hobo . . . ," they could predict that this person was running away from home and would be living like a hobo. Then, Megan developed vocabulary words based on key concepts that she would teach explicitly. She asked students to select an index card with a key concept written on it: boxcar, cooperation, freedom, freight train, friendship, hobo, homeless, hungry, poverty, or runaway. In Megan's example (Table 4:5, Word in My Context), students looked up dictionary definitions of the word and then connected those definitions to feelings that could be associated with the word, given their predictions of homelessness from the book cover. After students completed the graphic organizer, Megan facilitated a discussion, and students then wrote about their personal experiences.

Table 4:5 Word in My Context for "Boxcar"

Dictionary Definition:	Feelings Associated with the Word:
Webster's defines boxcar as an enclosed railway car for freight.	It is so sad that some people do not have any place to live but a cold, dirty boxcar.

 **Word Visual**

My Experiences with the Word

While I've only seen pictures of boxcars, I remember reading stories about the Boxcar Children when I was in elementary school. After reading the book, each student made a mobile which represented the most important parts of the story. I made mine how happy the children were in their boxcar home.

During Reading Strategies:
Tasks for Literature Circles on Homelessness

Chapter/Story Portrait (Elaine Henderly, Amanda-Clearcreek Middle School)

This visual/spatial activity provides an opportunity for students to use higher-level thinking skills to summarize a chapter by using pictures (magazine cutouts, computer graphics, or clip art) to illustrate critical parts of the chapter of a novel, as well as descriptive sentences to match the pictures.

1. Decide on the media for the activity—newspaper, magazines, computer clipart, Internet graphics.
2. Have the students take out two sheets of paper (one on which to glue pictures and words, the other on which to write sentences).
3. Assign chapters/sections over which the portrait is to be done to groups or to individuals, whichever meets your goals.
4. Assign the number of pictures/words and matching sentences (10–15 is a reasonable goal for middle schoolers).
5. Students cut out words/pictures which describe something that happened in the chapter/section. The teacher must be "open" to some of the unusual pictures/words that are submitted by students, since they are limited by the available graphics.
6. On one sheet of paper, students glue the word/picture. Be sure to have them number the item.
7. On another sheet of paper, students write a sentence that corresponds with the word/picture and underline what was used from sheet #1. In their sentences, students must demonstrate knowledge of the assigned chapters/section. They need to write descriptive sentences, not simplistic ones.
8. Encourage students to summarize the assigned chapter/section.
9. If students are reading different books, encourage trading of magazines, newspapers, etc. and an open discussion of things they might need in order to help others.
10. Students hand in both pages stapled together.
11. A final activity, once it's complete, is to trade the picture/word sheet with another student. Have that student write their own sentences and then compare/contrast to see how the two sets of sentences match up.

Two-Voice Poem for Spinelli's *Maniac Magee*

Using the delightful structure of poetry first developed by Paul Fleischman in *Joyful Noise: Poems for Two Voices* (1988), students will write poetry for oppositional characters in Spinelli's *Maniac Magee* (1990). In the poem for two voices, students will explore the themes of homelessness, racial issues, and/or prejudices through the voices of the characters they choose to represent them. If students are unfamiliar with this form of poetry, read aloud some of Fleischman's poems, discussing the effects of the sounds, rhythm, and format.

Poem in Two-Voice Activity for Spinelli's *Maniac Magee*

1. Ask students to choose the characters for their two-voice poem from the following list:

    John McNabb and Mars Bars

    Maniac Magee and Grayson

    Maniac Magee and any of the McNabb family

    Maniac Magee and the old man (the one who told him to go back to his own "side")

    Maniac Magee and any member of the Beale Family

2. Pair students so that they can each write from a different character's point of view. Ask them to decide what theme they want to portray in their poem: racial issues, prejudice, homelessness, belonging.

3. Ask students to use the prewriting handout to scaffold their thinking and organize their words and phrases about the two characters. As an alternative, you may even ask the students to document the words and phrases they use straight from the text in a found poem type of word/phrase collection. (See Table 4:6 for Student Prewriting Handout for Two-Voice Poem developed by Kelly Gambor.)

4. Next, ask students to decide what lines the characters will say together as a refrain or choral effect, and which lines do each need to say separately. Ask them to use lined paper to set up their final draft, so that it is clear which lines are said together and which are not.

5. Perform and critique the poem in two voices. See Table 4:7 for Kelly Yambor's teacher model for Maniac Magee and Grayson.

Table 4:6 Student Prewriting Handout for Two-Voice Poem

Character 1 is: _____	Character 2 is: _____
Lives: _____	Lives: _____
Favorite thing to do: _____	Favorite thing to do: _____
Fears that _____	Fears that _____
Hopes that _____	Hopes that _____
Personality traits: _____	Personality traits: _____
Dislikes: _____	Dislikes: _____
Preconceived ideas: _____	Preconceived ideas: _____
Other thoughts: _____	Other thoughts: _____
Quote: _____	Quote: _____
Major Theme: _____	Major Theme: _____

Table 4:7 Two-Voice Poem for Maniac Magee and Grayson

Maniac Magee	Grayson
Where am I?	Where am I?
Hiding.	Hiding.
	Who from?
	Memories.
Somewhere out there	
I did live on Sycamore Street.	
	I live at Two Mills YMCA.
Don't you want to know what I was	Don't you want to know what I was
doing at the zoo?	doing at the zoo?
I live there.	I work there.
	Where are you going to live?
In the baseball room.	
It's perfect.	It's perfect.
	Why don't you go to school?
You must have a home address to go to school.	
Your past?	
	Something deep.
	I've never held
	a kid's hand before.
I've never had	
a real home before.	
	The ballroom came to be homier than
	my room at the Y.
Will you move in with me?	Outside the ball room door
I'll paint with brown paint.	101
	One 'o one Band Shed Boulevard
	God I want to thank you
101	
One 'o one Band Shed Boulevard	
God I want to thank you	
for this warm house	for our own little family.
Amen!	Amen!

Making Inferences about the Homeless in Carlson's
The Family Under the Bridge

Learning to make inferences is one of the reading strategies that independent readers do well and dependent readers do poorly. Teaching readers to make inferences is a challenge in that good readers tend to anticipate content and make predictions about upcoming material as they "fill in the gaps" in the material during reading, while poor readers struggle with basic comprehension. In Beers' (2003) words, "an inference is the ability to connect what is in the text with what is in the mind to create an educated guess" (pp. 61–62). This activity is designed to help students make inferences about the homeless from passages in Carlson's *The Family Under the Bridge.*

1. Ask students, "What are some common perceptions of the homeless? What are your perceptions of the homeless? Where do these perceptions derive from? Are these perceptions based on facts, or are they inferences?

2. Pair up students and give each pair a textual example. Instruct the students to identify the inferences about homeless stereotypes from each example. See Table 4:8 for Identifying Inferences about the Homeless in Carlson's *The Family Under the Bridge*.

3. After students have had an opportunity to think about their passages, have them reconvene as a whole group. Ask each group to discuss the inferences they made about the homeless from the passages.

Table 4:8 Identifying Inferences about the Homeless in Carlson's *The Family Under the Bridge*

---

1. Context of the scene: Armand (the hobo) and the children are walking out of a department store in downtown Paris:

   The main floor was less crowded as they walked between the counters. An elegant floorwalker caught sight of the vagabonds. He hurried to them. He made a little noise as he tapped the immaculately white handkerchief peeping from his breast pocket.
   "Aren't you in the wrong store?" he asked haughtily.
   "I should say we're in the wrong store," replied Armand, just as haughtily (p. 28).

2. Context of the scene: Armand takes the children downtown and has them sing for people on the streets. People give them money for their performance. They return to the bridge and their mother finds out:

   Madame Calcet flung the children's gifts to the ground. She angrily advanced toward the hobo, who was stretched out on his canvas. "You've turned my children into beggars," she accused. "You've been using them for begging on the streets."
   "Now, now, madame." Armand tried to quiet her. "When the grand singers at the Opera get paid for their songs, is that begging? I'll give you your share."
   But Madame Calcet was busy tearing down canvases and gathering up blankets. "I don't want any of your ill-gotten money," she retorted. "We are going to leave here," she cried to the children. "I forbid you to have anything more to do with him" (p. 37).

3. Context of the scene: Armand is walking along the river toward the bridge:

   So back he trundled his buggy, and the wheels left wet black lines in the snow. There was no sign of life around the fireboats. But as he neared the old bridge tunnel, two women in fur coats came walking down the quay. In alarm Armand noticed that the trail they were leaving behind them ended at the canvas propped against the wall. He quickened his shuffling steps. As the two women passed, they turned their heads toward him.
   "Poor, wretched creature!" exclaimed the woman in the black fur coat.
   "Perhaps we could save him," said the woman in the brown fur coat.
   "Oh, go feed the pigeons," jeered Armand (p. 42).

---

cont.

4. Context of the scene: Suzy is teaching Tinka, a gypsy girl, how to read and write by showing her the alphabet. Tinka shows Suzy some gypsy symbols:

Tinka gave Suzy a foxlike grin. Below Suzy's letters she quickly drew two circles, one inside the other.
Suzy frowned. "That isn't a letter. It doesn't mean anything."
"Oh, yes it does," said Tinka, grinning. "If you see that sign near a gate, it means that the people who live inside are good and generous." She quickly scratched an upright line, then crossed it with two short bars. "But that sign means that beggars will be badly received. Perhaps the people will even set the dog on them" (p. 59).

5. Context of the scene: After Armand cleaned himself up, he went to check a job opportunity:

Armand helped Jojo [the dog] through the glass doors of which the store was so proud. He walked to a saleslady. "Is there a Monsieur Latour here?" he asked. "He's on the mezzanine now," she answered. "Oh no. Here he comes. Monsieur Latour! Monsieur Latour!"
Armand turned to face the haughty floorwalker. His first idea was to grab Jojo in his arms and run through the glass doors again. But the haughty monsieur did not recognize them (pp. 114–115).

After Reading Strategies to Engage Students in Higher Order Thinking

Story Web: Themes, Motifs, and Symbols

A *story web* is, by definition, a visual map that serves to structure information into major ideas and supporting details of a text. As an after reading strategy, this activity may be completed collaboratively in Literature-Circle formations or as an individual activity. While there are different ways to form a story web, this one begins by placing the fundamental idea explored by the text in a center circle of the web. In the case of Carlson's *The Family Under the Bridge* (1958), a group of teachers, Adam Remnant, Sarah Lukats, and Amanda James, chose the central concept, "Home." Branching out from this circle should be three rectangular boxes, each containing related information, or *motifs,* of the story. Motifs are recurring structures, contrasts, or literary devices that can help develop and inform the text's major themes. This group chose "friends," "territory," "work," and "family" as motifs for their story web. Branching out from these three rectangles should be at least two circles, each containing supporting details in the form of symbols, such as objects, characters, figures, or colors used to represent abstract ideas or concepts. See Figure 4:1 for Story Web for *The Family Under the Bridge*.

Figure 4:1 Story Web for *The Family Under the Bridge*

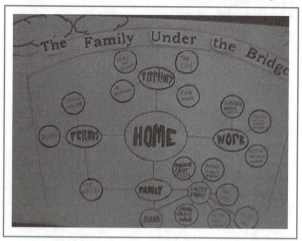

Journaling Beyond Stereotypes

This activity is designed to help students compare the stereotypes of homeless people with characters in the book. Sarah Lukats designed this activity to use with seventh graders who had just finished reading Carlson's Newbery Honor Book, *The Family Under the Bridge*. This book is about a struggling mother and her three children who became homeless and took shelter under a bridge in the streets of Paris. The Calcet family had invaded the space of a hobo, Armand. Though he tried to dismiss their troubles, Armand soon became attached to the family and shared his unusual home. As Christmas approached, he tried to find a warmer, more permanent shelter for them all.

In order to prepare students for the journal assignment, brainstorm stereotypes of homeless people. Ask students if Armand fits into any of the stereotypes mentioned. (They might note that he carries all his possessions around in an old baby buggy.) Then brainstorm characteristics of Armand on the blackboard. Next, ask students to find any clues in the text that hint to Armand's life prior to the Calcets. (For instance, they might pick up on the fact that "he wanted nothing to do with children. They meant homes and responsibility and regular work—all the things he had turned his back on so long ago" p. 8.) Ask students to give possible predictions of what Armand's life was like before he became a hobo. Then give students the following journal prompt:

"Pretending to be Armand (therefore, writing in first person), write a two- to three-page journal entry using characteristics, predictions, and knowledge of the text to explain what life was like for Armand before meeting the Calcets."

Explain to the students that the journal should include specific references from the text. Students can write as far back in his life as they can imagine in order to reveal as much as possible about Armand. They are especially encouraged to write against the stereotypes. They should imagine Armand's life based on real causes of homelessness. See Table 4:9 for Sarah's Journal Entry.

Table 4:9 Sarah's Journal Entry

September 23, 1930

My life is gone, vanished in a matter of minutes. I shouldn't have let my wife step onto that boat. I had a strange feeling that something was going to happen . . . and it did. She's gone forever, and I don't know how I can go on living this meaningless life. What use do I have now for all of the money I have acquired? I can no longer spend it on the one I loved so dearly.

After Annabelle's death, I no longer see the point of going to work at that stupid bank. Everyday I am forced to look at happy couples who come in as if there isn't a care in the world. Not only do I see these carefree couples at work, but at the Place Maubert, the old Court of Miracles, and strolling under the Paris bridge. Annabelle and I used to be just like those couples. We used to walk hand-in-hand under countless bridges in Paris. I relive some of my fondest memories of Annabelle when I stroll past those bridges. I would give anything to just be able to hold her again. I would give away all of my riches, my clothes, and my house. Who needs these trivial things anyway? These things are merely possessions that distract people from the things . . . the people who are really important.

Annabelle and I even talked about starting a family in the year to come. We both love children so much that we could hardly wait to have some little ones running around the house. I even surprised her one day when I bought the most expensive, beautiful baby buggy at The Rue de Rivoli. She was so thrilled to see that baby buggy, because it meant that soon we would have a precious little baby to put in it. I can't even look at children the same anymore. I can't abide them now . . . to me they are just little starlings . . . little pests. Every child I see, I am reminded of Annabelle's desire to have children and start a family. I know that if I would as much as look at a child, my heart would be stolen. Therefore, I must keep my heart well hidden.

So now I am alone. I've been thinking about this for a while, and I've decided to get rid of everything. I plan to go to the one place that makes me happy, and that makes me remember Annabelle. I've decided to live under the bridge that we'd walked under so many times. Everything that I need can be carried in that stupid baby buggy that will never fulfill its true purpose. I won't have to worry about wearing those silly work suits that I have come to despise. I won't have to worry about seeing those happy couples ever again . . . because I used to be half of a happy couple, and now I never will be again.

Literary Character Sun/Shadow Mandalas

The concept of the *mandala* is drawn from the ancient idea of the circular shape as an archetype, denoting the integration of a number of elements to make a whole. Rose windows in cathedrals and sand paintings of the Navaho are examples of mandalas. For this activity, created by Fran Claggett in *Drawing You Own Conclusions* (1992), students plan and draw the mandala for a literary character, weaving both sun (external) and shadow (internal) metaphors into sentences which frame the drawing. Students select their sun images by thinking analytically and considering alternatives. They select shadow images by moving through a process of word choices, arriving at their images by opposition. Then, within the framework of a circle, using color and shape—but no words—they draw or symbolize all the sun and shadow images. After completing the mandala, students can write poems, interpretive character studies, or reflective or analytic papers on concepts derived from the literary work.

Sun-Shadow Mandala Activity
1. Select a literary character for the project.
2. Select sun/shadow image qualities (See Table 4:10 for Armand in *The Family Under the Bridge* by Amanda James).
3. Write the sun sentences for each of your specific symbols: "_____ (character's name) is like the _____ (sun image) because, like the _____ (item), she/he _____."
4. Write the shadow sentences moving from the outward, or sun images, to the inward aspects of your character's life, and generate a shadow image for each of the seven categories that will make up the mandala: "Inwardly _____ (character's name) is like a _____ because _____."
5. Draw the sun/shadow mandala. Within the framework of a circle, using color and shape—but no words—draw or symbolize all of your sun and shadow images. Arrange them in any way that you like. You may want to consider how you place things in relation to each other, or only the way the colors and shapes look together. Consider the size of the objects to connate importance in the character's personality.
6. To frame the mandala, write sun/shadow sentences. Write a single sentence using all of your sun signs. See how you can weave all of these images together in one sentence. Then weave your seven shadow signs into a sentence. Write both of these sentences around the outside of your mandala. (See Figure 4:2 for Amanda's Sun/Shadow Manadala.)
7. From mandala to extended writing activities—ask students to write poems or interpretive character studies based on their mandala experiences.

Table 4:10 Selecting Sun/Shadow Image Qualities For Armand in
***The Family Under the Bridge* by Amanda James**

	Sun-Symbol		Shadow-Symbol	
	Column 1 Most Like	Column 2 Adjective Describing Column 1	Opposite of Word in Column 2	Most like Column 3
Animal	vulture	selfish	helpful/giving	dolphin
Plant	old oak tree	solid/static	free/growing	sun flower
Color	red	judgmental	spiritual	purple
Number	one	lonely	complete	five
Shape	circle	internal unity	fragmented	scattered
Gem & Mineral	diamond	rigid, rough edges	soft	circular
Element (Air, Earth, Fire, Water)	wind	relentless	replenishing	Water

Figure 4:2 Amanda's Sun/Shadow Mandala

Photo Essay

(adapted from http://kenston.k12.oh.us/khs/english/english2.htm)

Create a photo presentation using 10 photos that you take solely for this project to demonstrate your understanding of 10 life lessons found in your novel for the homeless unit.

- Choose 10 life lessons (survival, coping strategies) that made an impression on you while reading your book on homelessness. Record page numbers and quotes from each lesson that you choose from the book.
- Decide on possible subjects to take photographs of that will illustrate the

lessons you have chosen. You may choose to take two photographs for each lesson, so that later you will have the option of picking the most appropriate photograph for each lesson.

- Take the photos and have the film developed.

- Create a written explanation for each photo, beginning with the quote and page number of the lesson. Explain clearly how the photo illustrates the lesson. You may wish to print written explanations on colored or graphic paper.

- Create a neat, organized method for displaying your photographs and explanations. You might wish to paper frame your work.

- On the due date, hang your display on the wall of the room alongside your classmates for everyone to enjoy. (See Figure 4:3 for Photo Essay on Homelessness by Melisa Bushong.)

Figure 4:3 Melissa's Photo Essay on Homelessness

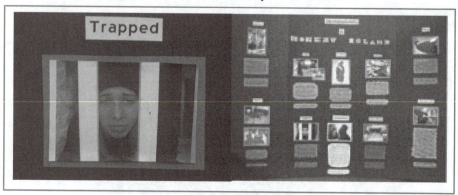

Readers' Theater

The Readers' Theater for this chapter, *Survivor*, is based on Fox's *Monkey's Island*, written by Janie Reinart, Language Arts Consultant in Cleveland, Ohio. It is a combination of Clay's survival story, along with statistics taken from the *New York Times* about the increase in homelessness in New York City. The central message is that homelessness can happen to anyone. See the CD-ROM for this chapter.

Multigenre Research Paper

One of the culminating project choices for this unit was a multigenre research paper. Students were asked to research any aspect of homelessness that interested them. Some chose to focus on the children's experiences, while others chose to study voluntary homelessness. See the CD-ROM for Megan Stypinski's Multigenre Paper about Homelessness during the Depression that was inspired by DeFelice's *Nowhere to Call Home*. See Table 1:10 for the requirement sheet and Table 1:11 for the Assessment Rubric for the Multigenre Research Paper.

Zines—The Ultimate Mode of Self-Expression

Another option for the culminating project for this unit was a zine assignment. Everyone at one time or another has a burning idea or obsession (in the case of this assignment, homelessness would be the topic) they would like to share with a sympathetic and like-minded audience. Thanks to the evolving computer and Internet technologies, anyone now has an opportunity to create their own zine (independently created and published personal magazines). Zines produce erratic, erotic, and controversial literature. They also provide strikingly uninhibited analyses of popular culture and society. Free from the restraints that burden traditional media, they can stimulate the minds of those in emerging and peculiar cultures. They range in design from publishing by photocopying to e-zines published solely on the Internet. In terms of form and content, there are no rules to follow. Editors make up the rules as they go along, which gives small publishers even more possibilities for self-expression. The possibilities are endless! The Zine Assignment has been adapted from Christie Bott's assignment (*English Journal*, November 2002). See Table 4:11 for Zine Assignment and Table 4:12 for Zine Assessment Rubric.

Table 4:11 Zine Assignment

• Cover/Title page (You need a GREAT title!)
• Introduction to the readers
• Table of contents
• Minimum of 4 sheets of paper folded in half, if making by hand.
• Zine may be composed using software for making a brochure.
• Zine contents must use a variety of magazine formats (such as reviews, editorials, graphics, drawings, cartoons, music, sports, etc.).
• Zine must present evidence of research into the topic.
• Zine must provide documentation of research source.
• Prepare to present your zine to the class.

See the CD-ROM for Matthew McManus' Zine, *Streetwise in Jurez*, based on Paulsen's (1987) *The Crossing*.

Table 4:12 Zine Assessment Rubric

	5 points	4 points	3 points	1 point	Total
Front Matter: Cover/ Title Page, Table of Contents	Organizes material in a creative, clear, appropriate, and precise manner	Organizes the material in an effective manner that is appropriate and precise	Organizes the material in an appropriate manner, but may lack some clarity or consistency	Little evidence of a cohesive plan. Little or no description or detail.	___ x 2 =
Introduction	Creatively catches the reader's interest and gives important information for understanding the zine	Catches the reader's attention and provides important information for understanding the zine	Does not catch the reader's attention and fails to give the reader enough information to understand the zine	Does not acknowledge that the reader needs certain information to make the most of the zine	___ x 1 =
Zine Design	Creative presentation of zine format and design. Captures readers' attention.	Excellent presentation of zine format and design. Appealing to the reader.	Good presenta-tion of zine format and design. Interesting to read	Does not resemble zine format and design. Does not hold readers' attention.	___ x 2 =
Nine Creative Writing Pieces	Unified, focused compositions; topic or ideas consistently clear; details varied and vivid; pieces are personal and meaningful	Generally well-organized; topics or ideas generally clear; details generally varied and vivid; pieces are personal and relevant	Topics, ideas, or plans may not be clear; minimal use of supportive detail; pieces are impersonal	Topic may be clear but no overall organizational plans; little development of ideas; pieces are impersonal	___ x 5 =
Research	Research evident from a variety of media, reference, and technological sources	Research evident from Internet and print material	Research from only one source	No research evident	___ x 4 =
Conventions	Correct grammer, punctuation, and spelling	Mostly correct grammar, punctuation, and spelling	Frequent errors in grammar, punctuation, and spelling	Numerous problems with grammar, punctuation, and spelling	___ x 1 =
Bibliography/ Documentation	Accurately documents sources using MLA format	Documents sources with minor errors using MLA format	Documents sources with many errors using MLA format	Does not documnet sources correctly; missing sources	___ x 1 =
Presentation	Student presents the topic creatively and provides vivid examples to illustrate the highlights of the project	Student presents the topic clearly and provides interesting examples to illustrate the highlights of the project	Student does not present the topic clearly and provides few examples to illustrate the highlights of the project	Student does not present the topic clearly and provides weak examples to illustrate the highlights of the project	___ x 2 =
			TOTAL (90/3 = 30 average points)		

Homelessness in Young Adult Literature

Carlson, N. S. (1958). *The family under the bridge*. New York: HarperTrophy.

Collier, J. L. (2001). *Chipper*. New York: Marshall Cavendish.

DeFelice, C. (1999). *Nowhere to call home*. New York: HarperTrophy.

Ellis, D. (1999). *Looking for x*. Toronto, Canada: Groundwood Books.

Fenner, C. (1998). *The king of dragons*. New York: Margaret K. McElderry Books.

Fox, P. (1991). *Monkey island*. London: Orchard Books.

Grove, V. (1990). *The fastest friend in the west*. New York: G. P. Putnam's Sons.

Hahn, M. D. (1988). *December stillness*. New York: Avon Books.

Hughes, D. (1989). *Family pose*. New York: Atheneum.

Johnson, L. L. (2002). *Soul moon soup*. Asheville, NC: Front Street Press.

Letts, B. (1998). *Where the heart is*. Victoria, Australia: Warner Books.

McDonald, M. (1993). *The bridge to nowhere*. London: Orchard Books.

Nelson, T. (1992). *The beggars' ride*. London: Orchard Books.

Oldham, J. (1996). *Found*. London: Orchard Books.

Paulsen, G. (1987). *The crossing*. London: Orchard Books.

Snyder, Z. K. (1997). *The gypsy game*. New York: Delacorte Press.

Spinelli, J. (1990). *Maniac Magee*. New York: HarperTrophy.

Tolan, S. (1992). *Sophie and the sidewalk man*. New York: Four Winds Press.

References

Allen, J. (2003). *Common ground*. Portland, ME: Stenhouse Publishers.

Beers, K. (2003). *When kids can't read, what teachers can do: A guide for teachers, 6–12*. Portsmouth, NH: Heinemann.

Bott, C. (2002, November). Zines—the ultimate creative writing project. *English Journal, 92*(2), 27–33.

Claggett, F. (1992). *Drawing your own conclusions*. Portsmouth, NH: Heinemann.

Fleischman, P. (1988). *Joyful noise: Poems for two voices*. New York: HarperCollins.

Glasgow, J. (2002). *Using young adult literature: Thematic activities based on Gardner's multiple intelligences*. Norwood, MA: Christopher-Gordon Publishers, Inc.

Guthrie, W. (1940). "I ain't got no home in this world anymore.Æ On *Dustbowl Ballad* (CD). Camden NJ: RCA Victor.

Rozakis, L. (1995). *Homelessness: Can we solve the problem?* New York: Henry Holt and Company, Inc.

Vacca, R., & Vacca, J. (1999). *Content area reading: Literacy and learning across the curriculum* (6th ed.). New York: Longman.

Chapter Five

The Gang of Five:
There is Always Room for One More

Allison L. Baer

> *"Sticks and stones*
> *may break our bones,*
> *but names*
> *will break our spirit."*
> —*The Gang of Five*

Middle schools can be electric. Hallways are filled with hormone-riddled bodies jostling for position and attention. Young girls try out make-up in the hopes that the boy in the third row over will notice them. Young boys swagger down hallways slightly tipping their heads as a sign of recognition. Shouts fill the air as they all try to be heard over the din of the between-class bustle.

Middle schools can also be cruel. In the midst of the bustle, there are young people hugging the walls hoping not to be seen by those bigger and more powerful students. The less popular are often chosen by the more popular to bear the brunt of jokes and ridicule. Those who are different—the very tall girl or very short boy, the fat girl or the skinny boy, the mixed race or the dark-skinned child—frequently find middle school to be intolerable. They wake up in the morning sick to their stomachs at the prospect of facing yet another day of school.

Paintbrush Falls Middle School is a school of both vibrant electricity and routine cruelty. James Howe (2001) in his book, *The Misfits*, uses the setting of Paintbrush Falls Middle School to tell the story of four young people—Bobby, Addie, Skeezie, and Joe—known as the Gang of Five, so called because:

> "Kids who get called the worst names oftentimes find each other. That's
> how it was with us. Skeezie Tookis and Addie Carle and Joe Bunch and
> me. We call ourselves the Gang of Five, but there are only four of us.
> We do it to keep people on their toes. Make 'em wonder. Or maybe we
> do it because we figure that there's one more kid out there who's going
> to need a gang to be a part of. A misfit, like us" (p. 13).

Told from the perspective of Bobby Goodspeed, a shy, 12-year-old overweight boy who sells ties at Awkworth & Ames Department Store and lives in a trailer with his ever-working father, *The Misfits* (2001) follows these four adolescents through the first few months of seventh grade and the ever-important Student Council elections. Addie is a liberal, social activist who takes word-for-word notes at their weekly Floating Forums, at which they discuss important issues "in the back booth with the torn red leatherette upholstery at the Candy Kitchen" (p. 39). Joe Bunch, once a 4-year-old cross dresser, is now a flamboyant, gay seventh grader that paints one pinky fingernail, frequently changes his name, and insists that those who write "fagot" on his locker spell it correctly. The last of the Gang of Five, Skeezie Tookis, is fond of black leather jackets and slicked-back hair, does not care for personal hygiene, eats like a pig, and has "as big a heart as was ever produced by the little town of Paintbrush Falls, New York" (p. 2).

When Ms. Wyman, the Student Council advisor, tells Addie that there will be only two parties up for Student Council elections, Addie makes it her (and her friends') mission to form a third party that stands for those who have no voice. One day, after being turned down as an independent party and being told that they needed a real platform to form a third party, the Gang of Five sat discouraged at the lunch table. Bobby heard Kevin Hennessey once again mimic Daryl Williams' stutter and realized that they did have a platform. He grabbed pen and napkin and hurriedly wrote a list of all of the names he had been called over the years. Bobby told his friends to do the same, and they came up with a list of over 60 different names, from loser to homo to fatso to Godzilla. The No-Name Party was born. Their motto: "Sticks and stones may break our bones, but names will break our spirit" (p. 142).

The subject of tolerance and peer pressure is a vital, yet often awkward, one for middle school students to confront. While they may experience bullying and name-calling on a frequent basis, they may not be comfortable talking about it in the classroom. By using the book, *The Misfits*, opportunities arise for open and honest discussion, and the possibility for affecting real change in the lives of adolescents is very real. In light of the personal nature of the contents of this book, it may be best to read it later in the school year after a safe, risk-taking environment has been established in the classroom. With this in mind, it is important to include solid frontloading activities to prepare the students for this humorous, yet demanding, book. See Table 5:1 for Reading Skills addressed in this unit.

Frontloading Strategies to Motivate Students to Read Howe's *Misfits*

Brainstorm and Categorize

Brainstorm and Categorize (Robb, 2000) is an activity that involves brainstorming about a topic, concept, or a key word. Students are given one of the above and asked to brainstorm as many words and ideas as they can that relate to the given word. After creating a rather large list, the students then put these words

Table 5:1 Reading Skills in this Unit

Strategy	Set Purpose	Activate Prior Knowledge	Make Predictions	Critical Thinking	Asking Questions	Visualizing the Text	Making Connections	Monitor Reading	Cause Effect	Compare Contrast	Making Inferences	Main Idea
Brainstorm and Categorize		•	•	•			•					•
Probable Passage	•	•	•	•	•		•		•	•	•	•
Dialogue Journal	•	•	•	•	•	•	•	•	•	•	•	•
Signal Words		•	•	•	•		•	•	•	•	•	•
Poetry Notebooks		•	•	•	•		•				•	•
Literature Circles	•	•	•	•	•	•	•	•	•	•	•	•
Sticky Notes	•	•	•	•	•	•	•	•	•	•	•	•
Character Bulletin Boards	•	•	•	•	•	•	•		•	•	•	•
Report Sacks	•	•	•	•	•	•	•		•	•	•	•
Copy Change Poetry	•	•	•	•	•		•			•	•	•
Book Report Puzzles	•	•	•	•	•	•	•	•	•	•	•	•
No-Name Signs	•	•	•	•	•		•		•	•	•	•

into categories that, again, they have chosen. This activity allows the students to see what they already know about the subject so they have confidence in their own prior knowledge and gives them a base on which to build new knowledge.

Brainstorm and Categorize Activity
1. Choose a topic, concept, or key word relating to the book.
2. Break up into groups of four or five and allow time for them to discuss the topic.
3. As a group, students should brainstorm a list of related words and ideas.
4. Bring the class back together and create a large list from all of the smaller lists.
5. Model how to create categories. Use the created list to give a suggested category.
6. Brainstorm categories from the words on the list, and place words in the appropriate categories.
7. Point out that some words may go in multiple categories. This is acceptable as long as students can defend their decisions.

In the case of *The Misfits*, the key concept was *tolerance*, and the students brainstormed the categories and words/ideas found in Table 5:2.

Table 5:2 Brainstorm and Categorize—Key Concept: Tolerance

Category	Brainstormed Words/Ideas
Name-calling	weak, cool, freak, nice, fishbelly, loser, jerk, dumb, moron, geek, weird, stinky, dumbo ears, ugly, stupid, cool, nerd, retard, four-eyes, cross-eyed, idiot, jerk
Opinions	All redheads are cute, All brunettes are smart, All people that live down South are dumb, We should separate people by color
Synonyms	segregation, racism, judgment, bigotry, separating, name-calling, opinions
Feelings	unfriendly, hurtful, painful, harmful, hateful, ignorant, stubborn, no trust, uncool, mean

Probable Passage

The objective of Probable Passage (Wood, 1984; as cited in Beers, 2003) is to engage the students in making predictions and writing a predicted summary when given words taken from the text. The students are given words and basic categories, such as "characters" or "problem." "As students work through this process, they use what they know about story structure, think about vocabulary, look for causal relationships, and predict what they think will happen" (Robb, 2003, p. 87). When done in small groups, the students also practice collaboration and group problem-solving skills.

Probable Passage Activity

1. Choose key words from the text. Generally, words should fit into the chosen categories of Characters, Setting, Problem, Outcomes, and Unknown Words. It is suggested to first model the strategy with the class using a short story or picture books. This will teach the students to do it on their own.

2. Give each student a Probable Passage Worksheet (see the CD-ROM) and have them work in groups putting the words into the given categories. Words can go into only one category and a maximum of 3 words can go into the Unknown Words category, and they cannot use dictionaries to look up the word. If students disagree as to where to put a word, encourage them to give a solid reason for their decision and then let the group decide.

3. After completing the categorizing, students should complete the To discover . . . portion by asking questions they have about the words or ideas. These questions will be answered as they complete their reading.

4. Using the words and categories, students write a Gist Statement or a short summary of what they think the story will be about. Encourage them to use as many of the given words, in context, as possible.

5. As the book is read, students can refer back to their Probable Passage Worksheets to see if their predictions were right. They can also adjust words and make new predictions.

The following words and categories were chosen for *The Misfits*. Samples of categorized words, gist statements, and questions are given in Tables 5:3 and 5:4.

Table 5:3 Probable Passage Key Words

Categories	Characters, Setting, Problem, Outcomes, Unknown Words
Words	Addie, fairy, Skeezie, forum, conviction, two-party system, election, spirit, Student Council, loser, cliques, pride, democracy, teacher, DuShawn, symbol, rights, social justice, passion, freedom, no-name, moron, friends, Goodspeed, names, speech

Table 5:4 Categorized Words, Gist Statements, and Questions

Categorized Words	Gist Statements	Questions
Characters: Addie, DuShawn, Teacher, Skeezie, fairy, teacher *Setting:* election, Student Council	• A character wins the election for Student Council. There's a problem with kids calling other kids names, moron, loser, and other names. I think this may take place at school.	• Where does this take place? • How many people ran in the election? • Do the kids in the book have rights? • What does Skeezie mean? • What is a misfit?
Problem: social justice, democracy, election, pride, moron, forum, friends, loser, names, moron	• DuShawn and Goodspeed are having an election. Their best friends, Skeezie and Addie, don't know who to pick without getting anyone mad. They end up having a word fight. They lose their pride and spirit.	• What is a two-party system? • What do the characters in the book do? • What is a clique? • Do they lose their pride? • Do the people get social justice?
Outcomes: rights, freedom, pride, social justice, friend, passion, spirit		
Unknown Words: cliques, forum, passion, two-party system, Goodspeed	• Addie thinks the teacher is a loser. DuShawn thinks Skeezie is a moron because he beat him in the election. They both become friends and leave school with pride.	

During Reading Strategies to Relate Prior Knowledge to Information in the Text

When people read, doesn't it look like nothing much is happening? We talk about reading being so relaxing. Sitting back and enjoying a good book. Good readers, however, know that reading is a very active process. The mind of a good reader is constantly involved and engaged in the reading. Kyleen Beers (2003) relates the story of trying to explain to a 12th grader, Gene, what active reading means. Gene assumed that some people just "get" the reading so they are able to answer the important questions on tests and quizzes. He didn't know that good readers often reread a passage, or ask questions about what is happening. During Reading Activities help students become active readers who are engaged in the reading—not just sitting and staring at the printed page.

Dialogue Journals

Teachers have students journal all the time. We frequently have a journal topic of the day and we encourage our students to write a few paragraphs explaining that journal writing encourages fluency. Rarely graded and edited, journal writing allows students to get their thoughts and ideas down in writing, giving them something to go back to in order to reflect and learn. Rasinski & Padak (2004) use Dialogue Journals to catch both response and note-taking about a book. In the case of *The Misfits*, the entries were by two different students. Each student was given a buddy to write and respond to, and topics or questions were given to which they responded back and forth. This set up an active dialogue in the classroom and supported the risk-taking environment that had been established. Again, by doing this later in the year, the students tended to trust one another and felt confident in their writing.

Dialogue Journal Strategy

1. Assign each student a buddy journal partner. Explain that they will be writing in their own journals and then responding to their buddy's journal. If there are an odd number of students, the teacher could be a buddy as well. In addition, on days when students are absent, assign temporary buddy journal partners, or the teacher should fill in for the day.
2. As students set up their journals, fold each page in half, lengthwise, allowing the journal owner to write on one side and the buddy to write on the other.
3. As often as is necessary, assign a journal topic or a freewrite and allow 5–7 minutes for the first writing.
4. Buddies should then exchange journals and respond to the first person's writing.
5. Allow time for each buddy to read the other person's writing.

Dialogue Journals used with buddies allowed the students to not only reflect on what they had read but to respond to what others in the classroom were thinking. The dialogue was interesting and vital. When dealing with the contents of this book, it was helpful to have frequent time to write and reflect on what had happened in the book. Table 5:5 contains the journal topics for the reading of *The Misfits*. Rarely was a question asked. As can be seen, the students frequently wrote in response to something they had read in the book. *Fast-Writes* (Robb, 2000) are a way for students to quickly get down their feelings and ideas about what they have just read. When doing a Fast-Write, students should write about some passage, topic, concept, or key word for at least six to eight minutes without stopping. If they run out of things to say, they should continue writing anything until the ideas begin flowing once again.

Table 5:5 Dialogue Journal Topics for *The Misfits*

Topics
Respond to the quote on page 14, "People who are misfits because they're just who they are instead of 'fits,' who are like everybody else." Do you agree or disagree? What do you think? Why? (This quote is taken from the context of Bobby Goodspeed contemplating who are misfits and who are not.)
Choose one character to study/follow during the reading of the book. What do you think of him or her? Why?
Fast-Write (Robb, 2000) about chapter 8 in which Addie, a middle-class White girl, asks DuShawn Carter, one of three African-American students in the seventh grade, to run for class president.
Fast-Write (Robb, 2000) about chapter 10 in which The Gang of Five and DuShawn discuss race, skin color, and culture.
List all of the names you have been called over the years. Reflect on the statement, "Sticks and stones may break our bones, but names will break our spirit" (Howe, p. 142).
Journal about the signs that have been placed around the school. What have you been hearing? Seeing? What is happening in the halls of the school? (The activity supporting this journal entry will be explained further in this chapter.)
React to Bobby's speech for Student Council (see pp. 249–252).

One of the many benefits of Double Entry Buddy Journals is the interesting dialogue that occurs as a result of two students bouncing ideas off of each other. When dealing with the book *The Misfits*, students frequently expressed strong opinions about racial equality and the need for people to be themselves. The free-flow exchange allowed the students to ask questions about the content or ideas of the book and receive responses from their peers rather than from the teacher. A few examples of these Dialogue Journals are given in Table 5:6.

Table 5:6 Dialogue Journal Examples (Writing is exactly as the students wrote)

Jahmarra	Eric
Prompt: Respond to the quote on page 14, "People who are misfits because they're just who they are instead of 'fits,' who are like everybody else." Do you agree or disagree? What do you think? Why?	
I think that is true. Because people do what everyone else does. They want to fit in. And they think if someone does it it is cool for them to do it. The misfits just want to be themselves.	I think the misfits are people who are just their self. Fits are want a be's. People should just be their selfs and not a want a be. Like some people are just their self.
Anthony	Kayla
Prompt: Fast-Write about chapter 8 in which Addie, a middle-class White girl, asks DuShawn Carter, one of three African-American students in the seventh grade, to run for class president.	
What Dushawn said was wrong he did not have to make fun of everybody like that. Talking about people eyes and skin color. He didn't have no room to talk he could not make fun of nobody	You're right DuShawn should of never said what he said. And yea he could of been ugly. Now about Skeezie puting something in the locker well I think that was the guy that Addie also wanted to run and

cont.

because he was probably ugly to. And what do you think about that one boy that put something in somebody's locker?	he said no because he was already running. Well I think Skeezie was trying to get him to say yes to Addie and stop running for the person he was already running for.
Morgan	*Mychel'le*
Prompt: Fast-Write about chapter 10 in which The Gang of Five and DuShawn discuss race, skin color, and culture.	
I don't think it's right for Dushawn Carter to talk about Heather like that. Because even though he is saying what he thinks, it's still wrong to say something like that because it's racial and can hurt peoples feelings. I think this school is too racial.	I agree. DuShawne should think before speaking you never know Heather could have been there. I think it's wrong to talk that way. That had a little bit of gossip in it. I agree about the school to. The whole Paintbrush Falls town probably racial.
Josh	*Julie*
Prompt: Journal about the signs that have been placed around the school. What have you been hearing? Seeing? What is happening in the halls of the school?	
I think that it will have an effect because people in the eighth grade are looking at the signs and getting mad because they have been called those names. People in the 5th grade are doing the same thing and throwing them in the garbage can. I think it will have a bad, bad effect.	That's what I think too. I saw a sixth and eighth grader throw away signs and start talking to people about them. I don't even think a lot of my friends was talking about it. One girl was talking to her friend and they saw sissy crossed out and they went over to people and started calling them sissy.

Signal Words

As readers read, they often come upon words such as "next," "alike," or "only." Good readers recognize that those words have special meanings that alert the reader to something that is happening in the text. Signal Words (Beers, 2003) tell readers about a sequence, a similarity, or a contrast in what they are reading. These kinds of words give us information about what is happening in the text. They signal to the reader that something is coming or has happened, two things are somehow similar, or things are being contrasted. By teaching our students to be aware of these words, we give them yet another tool with which they can unlock the meanings of text.

Signal Words Strategy

1. Post three pieces of chart paper on the wall or board. Label them "Sequence," "Contrast," and "Similarities."
2. Discuss the meanings of the three words and give examples of each category.
3. As a class, brainstorm words for each category.

When doing this with the whole class, students are engaged in active problem solving as they think about words and listen to others. Students will frequently piggyback off of others' words, and the brainstorming becomes lively and creative. These lists of words can be kept up and referred to during the reading process. As the students created the lists themselves, they take ownership and pride in becoming active, independent readers. Examples of Signal Words are given in Table 5:7.

Table 5:7 Signal Words

Sequence Words	Similarity Words	Contrast Words
before, after, end, later, now, in-between, earlier, between, yester-day, tomorrow, next, first, second, soon, today, when, tonight, morn-ing, last, past, immediately, future, present, then, finally, subsequently, beginning, middle, ahead, behind, shortly, long, prior, ago	also, like, as, identical, compare, as well as, common, similarly, and, congruent, same, parallel, alike, exactly, two of a kind, categorize, because, symmetrical, just as, too, same way, for example, and	not, different, uncommon, yet, neither, opposite, only, not alike, one of a kind, but, except, how-ever, exclude, despite, although, or, unless, otherwise, regardless

Poetry Notebooks

The basis of *Poetry Alive!* (1990) is that students interpret and perform poetry. Based on these principles, small groups of students collect poetry and perform these poems on a weekly basis. Students keep their selected poems in Poetry Notebooks. These notebooks expose students to poems on a weekly and daily basis, allowing them to become not only acquainted with poetic language and format but to find poems to be yet another rich, dynamic way of building understanding of text. This entire process—planning, practicing, and performing—takes about 30 minutes per week, and the benefits far outweigh the time spent. Not only are students engaging in reciting poetry, they are involved in interpretation, problem solving, collaborative performance, and the enjoyment of hearing poetry read aloud. When reading *The Misfits*, the teacher chose poems based on the themes of tolerance and acceptance. Three of these poems were "No Difference" by Shel Silverstein (1974), "Call Backs" by Sara Holbrook (1996), and "They Only See the Outside," by Kalli Dakos (1993). Poems can be chosen on any theme from any book. Pairing poetry to prose creates a sense of continuity of theme between the two formats, as well as supporting the topic at hand. For ideas for teaching poetry performance, see Wolf's *Something is Going to Happen* (1990).

Poetry Notebook Strategy

1. At the beginning of the year, give each student a manila folder with two holes punched in the top. Use two prong holders to hold the poems in the folders. All poems to be included in the folder will have the same two holes punched.
2. Go over the *Poetry Alive!* guidelines for performance. These should be written somewhere in their notebooks:
    Everyone must participate,
    Groups can use only one prop: A chair
    Bow when you are finished.

3. At the beginning of the week, students are given the same poem to be put in their Poetry Notebook. Read the poem aloud and use this time to teach some aspect of poetry, such as allegory, alliteration, free-verse poetry, rhyming, etc.

4. Allow 8–10 minutes for planning their performance. Students can assign reading stanzas or who will act out parts of the poem while others read. Collect and put the notebooks away.

5. At the end of the week, allow students five to seven minutes to practice their performance.

6. Each group should then perform their poem for the entire class. While a number of groups are performing the same poem, the performances are never the same and tend to become more and more creative as the school year progresses.

7. Grading can be done by assigning points for participation.

Poetry Notebooks become a staple in the classroom as students begin to write or submit poems to be included for performance. By the end of the school year, it is not unusual for the students to have performed as many as 40 different poems. When compared with the learning that takes place, the weekly time commitment is minimal.

Literature Circles

Harvey Daniel's Literature Circles (2002) have become part of the everyday experience for many students. An effective tool for building comprehension as well as a structure for dynamic literature discussions, Literature Circles provide students with an avenue into becoming active, independent readers. The structure is flexible enough that they can be used and implemented in any classroom. In reading *The Misfits*, rather than assigning the usual Literature Circle jobs of discussion director, illustrator, etc., students-engaged in the process by using stacks of sticky notes on which they wrote comments, questions, interesting words, or drew pictures and placed the notes right on the page. Having learned the Literature Circle jobs in readings of other books, the students felt confident in writing discussion questions, writing interesting words, making connections to the text, summarizing important passages, or drawing pictures. Yellow sticky notes stuck out of the books like flags pointing to exciting and interesting parts of the text. Students used them as springboards for discussion and problem solving.

Literature Circle Strategy

1. Review the various Literature Circle jobs: Discussion Director, Connector, Word Master, Illustrator, Summarizer.

2. When reading the book, students should write questions, comments, words, etc. on sticky notes and place them directly on the page which they are reading.

3. Allow ample time for discussion and problem solving about characters, plot, or any other question brought up in the reading of the book.

The sticky notes helped the students in making meaning from the book. When faced with a confusing passage or idea, they would simply pull out a sticky note, write down their question, place it safely in their book, and come back to it when discussing the book. By using Literature Circles in this way, the students could busy themselves with the reading and know that all of their questions would be answered. As they also wrote down interesting passages and words, they were able to share these without the worry of interrupting others' reading, as they knew that their ideas were written down and could be shared with their classmates later. Examples of comments and questions are given in Table 5:8.

Table 5:8 Literature Circle Sticky Notes

Why is Mr. Kellerman so mean?
Haberdasherily—that is a long word!
Addie's real name is Addison.
What is conjecture?
What does Joe feel like when he finds out Addie likes Colin?
What is gorgonzola?
Why is Mr. Kellerman telling a kid his life story?
What does HellomynameisEric mean?
Mr. Kellerman is 45 years old.
Why does Mr. Kellerman live with his mom?
P.F.M.S. = Paintbrush Falls Middle School
Skeezie's real name is Schuyler Tookis.
Mr. Kellerman and Bobby have the same first name and they both lost their moms.
What is the relationship between Bobby and Mr. Kellerman now?
Why can't Addie act a little bit like Bobby?
I agree with them that everyone should stop calling people names.
How do you die of cribdeath?
I think Bobby gave a good speech.
Skeezie should use his real name (Schuyler) instead of the one he is using now.
Bobby should feel happy that he is something like his mom.
Addie should know that everything is not always fair.
Why does Mr. Kellerman listen to everyone else?
Faux-pas which is French for "screw up."
Mr. Kellerman was called names when he was in school.
Kelsey likes Bobby not Joe. DuShawn likes Addie. Addie likes Colin.

Character Bulletin Boards

As independent readers read, they can see and hear the characters as they go about their lives. The voices of the characters become part of the reading, making the experience rich, and the faces of the characters bring depth to the story. Independent readers create these voices and faces as they become acquainted with the people in the book. For whatever reason, however, dependent readers do not experience this dimension as they read. When our students have trouble bringing face and voice to the characters in a book, Character Bulletin Boards (Beers, 2003) can help. As they read and get to know the characters, these bulletin boards become places on which they can give form to the characters. When done in small groups, students spend time brainstorming and discussing the social, emotional, and physical traits of each character. These bulletin boards can be a work-in-progress as the book is read and students add information as they watch characters change and grow.

When reading the book *The Misfits*, students were divided into small groups and assigned one member of The Gang of Five—Addie Carle, Bobby Goodspeed, Skeezie Tookis, or Joe Bunch. These groups then took it upon themselves to learn as much about their character as possible, and then they created bulletin boards on which they taught the rest of the class about their character. As time went on, the bulletin boards grew with interesting facts and personal traits, and students often referred to them as they read the book. Having created faces for each of The Gang of Five, students found it easier to relate to the characters and were more engaged in the reading of the book.

Character Bulletin Board Strategy

1. Choose the main characters in the book, divide the class into small groups, and assign one character to each group.
2. Groups should spend time creating lists of physical, emotional, and social traits for their character.
3. Using the book, create a rough draft of what the character looks like. From this rough draft, create a large model of the character using construction paper. This model can be done like a puzzle, in which the students cut out each part of the person and then glue them together. Tape the model to a bulletin board and label it with the character's name.
4. On 3 in x 5 in cards, students will write the emotional and social traits of their character and place them around the character.
5. As time goes on, students can place other things around their character, such as pictures of what they like, places they visit, etc. The Gang of Five bulletin board included cards from a Report Sack activity that will be explained further in this chapter.

When creating the Gang of Five on a bulletin board, the students became very creative as they included minute details about the characters. For example, Joe Bunch had the pinky nail on one hand painted with a picture because he liked being creative. Bobby Goodspeed was a bit pudgy around the middle, as this was one of his traits for which he was frequently ridiculed. The bulletin board was bright and cheerful and became the center point for the reading of the book. Pictures of the Gang of Five bulletin board are given in Figure 5:1. See the CD-ROM for a PowerPoint presentaton on the Character Bulletin Boards.

Figure 5:1 Gang of Five Character Bulletin Boards

| Joe Bunch | Addie Carle | Bobby Goodspeed | Skeezie Tookis |

Report Sacks

When creating Report Sacks (Glasgow, 2002), students choose characters and are given, or collect, objects that reflect the traits of that character. This variation of Report Sacks is much the same, except the Report Sacks are emptied and the students are given the objects and then brainstorm how the character would use them. Then, on a 4 in x 6 in card, they create a picture of the object, write how their character would use the object, and, when using Character Bulletin Boards, place the cards around their models. When reading *The Misfits*, the groups of students were given a pencil, ruler, box of markers, tape, and a book.

Report Sack Strategy

1. Using the groups assigned for the Character Bulletin Boards, give each group the same five to six objects (markers, ruler, pencil, book, tape) that would be used by the characters in the chosen book.
2. Students should brainstorm how their character would use each object.
3. On a 4 in x 6 in card, students should draw a picture of the object and describe how their character would use it.
4. When creating Character Bulletin Boards, place the cards around the model on the board.

While each group is given the same objects, the students have to know their character well enough to know how that character would use the object. Very rarely will they use it the same way. The objects should somehow relate to the experiences and plot of the book. For example, in the case of *The Misfits*, the setting was a middle school, so common school supplies were used. The books given were chapter books, and the students were told to decide what kind of book their character would read and create a cover for that book on the card. Examples are given in Table 5:9.

Table 5:9 Report Sacks

Name of Character	Object and Use
Bobby Goodspeed	Markers—Bobby used the markers to make the no-name signs. Ruler—Used to put the line through the names they had been called. Pencil—Used to write notes to Kelsey. Book—*The Big Clock*—we think he would read animated comic books. Tape—Used the scotch tape to hang up the no-name signs.
Joe Bunch	Markers—The markers are for the yin-yang sign, also for drawing the circle around the names and lines through the names. Ruler—To measure lines and make the no-name signs. Pencil—Used to write in Joe's diary and to write on the posters. Book—*Joe's Diary*—he would write in there. Tape—Used to hang up campaign posters around school.
Addie Carle	Markers—Used for coloring signs. Ruler—Used for putting lines through the no-name signs. Pencil—Addie uses a pencil for everything, especially for taking notes at The Forum and school work. Book—*Laws and Rules*—to look up school and government rules. Tape—Uses the masking tape to help make circles around the no-name signs.
Skeezie Tookis	Markers—Used to color on his desk. Ruler—Used to stick notes through slots in lockers. Pencil—He would write a note and put it in somebody's locker. Book—He would give his book to the library or to Addie. Tape—He would use it to tape a ripped paper.

After Reading Strategies to Engage Students in Written and Oral Activities

As the teacher read the final lines of *A Bad Beginning* (2000) by Lemony Snicket, the students clapped and immediately began asking questions and talking about the book. One student asked, "What are we going to do with the book? Can we do something?" Having finished the book, they needed to do something with the story of the Baudelaire orphans. They were itching to create, imagine, or act. After reading activities do just that. They give readers the opportunity to reflect on themes or concepts, to act out scenes or become characters. Good readers need a time to discuss and share what has happened to them through the reading of the book. In addition, after reading activities solidify the book in our minds, allowing the book to become a part of who we are. Having finished reading *The Misfits*, students engaged in writing poetry and creating puzzles in which they pulled the whole story together.

Copy Change Poetry

Copy Change Poetry (Dunning & Stafford, 1992) gives beginning poets a structure to hang their words on. Students take a written poem and change the words to reflect a new and different theme. Using another person's poem often takes the fear out of writing poetry, as all the new author has to do is copy some parts and change other parts to create a new poem. When doing a copy change poem, begin by choosing a poem that reflects the theme or key concept in the book. For *The Misfits*, the picture book, *The Important Book* (1949) by Margaret Wise Brown, provided a base upon which the students created their own poetry. Each page of *The Important Book* is written as a short—but important—poem about some everyday object. The book is meant to point out the relevance and use of things we use and see each day.

For *The Misfits*, students created an Important Book about the members of the classroom. Using the format of the poetry found in *The Important Book*, students wrote poems about their journal buddies. The poems were collected, word processed, copied in bulk, and turned into a class book. Each student had a copy of the book entitled *Our Important Book*. The teacher then wrote a long poem, with one line included about the important thing about each student.

Copy Change Poetry Strategy

1. Choose a poem—in this case, *The Important Book*—that reflects the theme of the chosen book and provide each student with a copy of the poem.
2. Discuss the theme or key concepts learned from the book.
3. Discuss the process of writing Copy Change Poetry. Students can change words in the poem but should try to keep the basic format intact. If the poem rhymed, the new poem should also rhyme.
4. Each student should write an Important Book Poem about their journal buddy.
5. Collect the poems and word process them, landscape, two to a page.
6. Using the same format, write a poem with one line about the important thing about each student.
7. Have students create a cover, or create one yourself.
8. Make as many copies as necessary so each student has a copy to keep.
9. When declaring authorship, be sure to add some thanks to the author and the title of the original poem.

Creating *Our Important Book* allowed the students to reflect on the strengths of each person in the class. Through the buddy-journal process, they had become acquainted with each other by sharing thoughts and ideas. Keeping in mind the themes of tolerance and acceptance, as learned through the reading of the book, *The Misfits*, the creation of a poem about their buddy allowed them to appreciate their classmates and point out each others' strengths. Examples of pages from *Our Important Book* are given in Table 5:10.

Table 5:10 Copy Change Poetry in *Our Important Book*

Aaron	*Shawn*
The important thing about Aaron is that he is always there to make you laugh.	The important thing about Shawn is he is never lonely.
Aaron makes people laugh,	Shawn is always with someone,
He has lots of friends,	He always makes friends easily,
He tells jokes, He is friendly,	He makes good points about things,
And he is fun to be around.	He talks to all of the teachers,
But the important thing about Aaron is that he is always there to make you laugh.	And he likes to play sports.
By Mike Jones	But the important thing about Shawn is he is never lonely.
	By Alexandria Rodgers
Eric	*Jahmarra*
The important thing about Eric is he likes to skateboard.	The important thing about Jahmarra is she is too nice.
Eric is cool,	Jahmarra is cool,
He talks a lot,	She is stylish,
He always talks about BMX bikes,	She wears lots of Spongebob Squarepants,
He writes really neat,	She is smart,
And he loves to ride his skateboard.	And she has good handwriting.
But the important thing about Eric is he likes to skateboard.	But the important thing about Jahmarra is she is too nice.
By Jahmarra Warfield	By Eric Lee

Book Report Puzzles

Since the beginning of schools, students have written book reports. They usually include a summary of the book, the main characters, setting, and possibly an opinion part in which the students tell why they liked or disliked the book. The purpose is often to find out if the student has read and understood the book. While the traditional book report has many benefits, when doing project-based learning, the written book report is often seen as unnecessary when the students have been involved in active, ongoing meaning making. There are many alternatives to written book reports, including a Book Report Puzzle.

In general, children love puzzles. There is a certain excitement about finding the right piece to complete a face or part of the scenery. In addition, the making of a puzzle supports their visual/spatial intelligence in that they are involved in mental imagery and spatial reasoning as they create their puzzle (Campbell, Campbell, & Dickinson, 1996). The Book Report Puzzle entails the retelling of key elements and key concepts of the book, as well as visualization of the characters and the ability to pull the whole thing together, creating a whole.

Book Report Puzzle Strategy

1. Either purchase precut blank puzzles or use uncut corrugated cardboard that the students can cut into puzzle pieces.
2. Set the criteria for the image on the puzzle. Include the characters and the theme portrayed in either words or images. In addition, puzzles must be colorful and neat.
3. Students should create a rough draft of what the puzzle will look like. Edit for any errors.
4. Create the puzzle using only colored pencils or markers, as crayons tend to smear. If the students used uncut cardboard, draw in light pencil a puzzle design and cut out the pieces.
5. When the puzzles are finished, allow time for the students to share their puzzles and tell the story to each other.

When doing this activity with *The Misfits*, students were very creative in their portrayal of the characters and the theme. Some simply wrote out the motto of the No-Name Party, and others created images of tolerance and acceptance. Figure 5.2 shows examples of student work.

Figure 5:2 Book Report Puzzles

No-Name Signs

In order to catch the attention of the student body of Paintbrush Falls Middle School, the Gang of Five created No-Name Signs. Using a list of names that they, themselves, had been called, Addie, Bobby, Skeezie, and Joe created over 60 signs with a name and the universal sign for no—a large red circle with a slash over the name. Finding various reasons to be excused from different classes the next day, they covertly placed the signs all over the school and waited. Everybody at Paintbrush Falls Middle School was talking about the signs by the end of the day. Everybody except the Gang of Five.

In an effort to take the lessons learned from the reading of *The Misfits* beyond the classroom, the students decided to create their own No-Name Signs using names they had been called over the years. Lively conversation filled the classroom as students shared names they had been called and the feelings surrounding the name. Plans were made for the creation and placement of the signs, and the class was sworn to secrecy. For examples of the No-Name Signs, see Figure 5:3, and for a list of the names used, see Table 5:11.

Figure 5:3 Example of the No-Name Sign

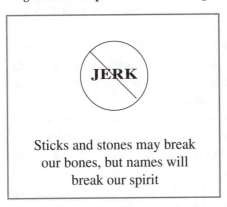

Sticks and stones may break our bones, but names will break our spirit

Table 5:11 Names Gathered by Students

Names Collected by Students for No-Name Signs			
braceface	brat	faggot	homo
metalmouth	bucktooth	numbnuts	fart machine
stupid	gay	crackhead	fat
spoiled	forehead	punk	pain
queer	monkey	know-it-all	prep
loser	wimp	geek	immature
slut	retard	fruitcake	dumbo-ears
ugly	teeth	ho	two-face
skitzo	sissy	heifer	weeble-wabble
white-honky	fag	fruitcake	turdmuffin
flunky	dumb	four-eyes	n*****
nerd	mental	jerk	whore
dork	freak	weirdo	cross-eyed

No-Name Sign Strategy

1. In their buddy journals, students should write a list of the names they have been called. Exchange journals with buddies and react to the list of names.

2. Using the individual lists, brainstorm a class list, eliminating any duplicates. If the name is a swear word, it should not be put on a sign, as profanity is not allowed in school. However, time should be spent in

discussing the feelings created when called these names. Understanding and healing can take place as the students discuss and commiserate.

3. Using a large font, word process the names so there is no distinguishable handwriting. Type the motto of the No-Name Party on the bottom of each sign: *Sticks and stones may break our bones, but names will break our spirit.*

4. Using large circles and rulers, students will create the universal sign for no on top of each word.

5. Send students out, two at a time, with hall passes, to put up the signs around the school. Be sure they cover the whole school, including the auditorium and cafeteria. Encourage them to be quiet and quick, without drawing attention to themselves.

6. As they go about their day, students should listen for comments and questions made regarding the signs. Allow time for journal writing about what they heard. In addition, discuss the effect the signs are having on the school.

As a debriefing for the entire school, I read Bobby's speech, found in chapter 16 of *The Misfits*, over the loudspeaker system. I gave a brief summary of the book and read the speech, in which Bobby expresses his feelings and thoughts about name-calling. As I left the office after reading the speech, I heard riotous applause throughout the school. Indeed, *The Misfits* had changed the school.

Related Young Adult Literature

Goobie, B. (2002). *Sticks and stones*. Victoria, BC, Canada: Orca Book Publishers.
After developing an unearned reputation as a slut, Jujube finds a novel way to take on her tormentors and help a group of girls win back their self-esteem.
Hinton, S. E. (1967). *The outsiders*. New York: Viking Press.
The struggle of three brothers to stay together after their parents' death and their quest for identity among the conflicting values of their adolescent society.
Howe, J. (2001). *The misfits*. New York: Atheneum.
Four students who do not fit in at their small-town middle school create a third party for the Student Council elections to represent all students who have ever been called names.
Konigsburg. E. L. (1996). *The view from Saturday*. New York: Atheneum.
Four students, with their own individual stories, develop a special bond and attract the attention of their teacher, a paraplegic, who chose them to represent their sixth-grade class in the Academic Bowl competition.
Snicket, L. (1999). *The bad beginning*. New York: Scholastic.
After the sudden death of their parents, the three Baudelaire children must depend on each other and their wits when it turns out that the distant relative who is appointed their guardian is determined to use any means necessary to get their fortune.
Spinelli, J. (1990). *Maniac Magee*. New York: HarperTrophy.

After his parents die, Jeffrey Lionel Magee's life becomes legendary, as he accomplishes athletic and other feats which awe his contemporaries.

Spinelli, J. (1997). *Wringer*. New York: HarperCollins.

As Palmer comes of age, he must either accept the violence of being a wringer at his town's annual Pigeon Day or find the courage to oppose it.

Tolan, S. (1996). *Welcome to the ark*. New York: Morrow Junior Books.

When four child prodigies transfer from a center for research and rehabilitation to an experimental group home, they face another way of connecting with their world.

References

Beers, K. (2003). *When kids can't read, what teachers can do: A guide for teachers, 6–12*. Portsmouth, NH: Heinemann.

Campbell, L., Campbell, B., & Dickinson, D. (1996). *Teaching and learning through multiple intelligences*. Needham Heights, MA: Simon & Schuster.

Dakos, K. (1993). *Don't read this book, whatever you do!: More poems about school*. New York: Aladdin.

Daniels, H. (2002). *Literature Circles: Voice and choice in book clubs & reading groups* (2nd ed.). Portland, ME: Stenhouse Publishers.

Dunning, S., & Stafford, W. (1992). *Getting the knack: 20 poetry writing excercises*. Urbana, IL: National Council of Teachers of English.

Glasgow, J. (Ed.). (2002). *Using young adult literature: Thematic activities based on Gardner's multiple intelligences*. Norwood, MA: Christopher-Gordon Publishers, Inc.

Holbrook, S. (1996). *The dog ate my homework*. Honesdale, PA: Boyds Mill Press.

Rasinski, T., & Padak, N. (2004). *Effective reading strategies: Teaching children who find reading difficult* (3rd ed.). Upper Saddle River, NJ: Pearson Education, Inc.

Robb, L. (2000). *Teaching reading in middle school: A strategic approach to teaching reading that improves comprehension and thinking*. New York: Scholastic.

Silverstein, S. (1974). *Where the sidewalk ends*. New York: HarperCollins.

Wise Brown, M. (1949). *The important book*. New York: HarperCollins.

Wolf, A. (1990). *Something is going to happen: Poetry performance for the classroom*. Canada: Poetry Alive! Publications.

Wood, K. (1984). Probable passages: A writing strategy. *The Reading Teacher, 37*, 496–499.

Chapter Six

Taming a Tiger: Drunk Driving and Suicide in Draper's *Tears of a Tiger*

Carolyn Suttles

Suicide is now the third leading cause of death in 15- to 24-year-olds.
—Shneidman, 1996

The average age when youth first try alcohol is 11 years for boys and 13 years for girls.

According to research by the National Institute on Alcohol Abuse and Alcoholism, adolescents who begin drinking before age 15 are four times more likely to develop alcohol dependence than those who begin drinking at age 21. It has been estimated that over 3 million teenagers are out-and-out alcoholics. Several million more have a serious drinking problem that they cannot manage on their own. The three leading causes of death for 15- to 24-year-olds are automobile crashes, homicides, and suicides—alcohol is a leading factor in all three. The death of an adolescent leaves family, friends, and community members grieving their premature loss.

According to Cunningham (1996), a consultant from Teen Age Grief, Inc., the needs of the bereaved teenager have been sorely overlooked for decades. In many grief-recovery programs, support is often available for younger children and adults, but there is a definite void in teen services. Cunningham has seen this void throughout our country. She says teenagers often give us mixed messages. They tell us that they need, and expect, our help in providing them with food and a nurturing environment but also tell us, on the other hand, that they can run their lives on their own. Because people do not always know how to respond to teens, they frequently back off, resulting in a teen who is left to grieve alone or with very limited support. Such is the case for the main character in Sharon Draper's *Tears of a Tiger* (1994).

As adults, we know that dealing with grief is difficult. We turn to family, friends, religious leaders, counselors, self-help books, seminars, etc. to try and cope with the death of a loved one. What we sometimes don't realize is that our students need the same help and strategies to cope with their feelings. This became evident to me when I began having my students write multigenre papers. Part of my requirement was that the papers had to be a snapshot of one event in their families' histories that they would want to keep. This paper was to be that permanent "picture" to be passed through the family, almost like a scrapbook of photos would be. I was amazed at how many of my students selected the death of some family member to remember. For many, this death was the first that they had to face, and their feelings were not under their control. The writings became one way of dealing with the deaths. Since I already used the novel *Tears of a Tiger* to introduce the multigenre paper, I decided to create a unit that focused not on death, but on the lives that go on after a death. These students needed to see what options they had for help. They needed to learn about coping strategies. They needed to see that dealing with death is a common experience that many could understand and empathize with. They needed to know that grieving is a normal process and not an illness to recover from quickly.

The crux of the unit centers on the characters from *Tears of a Tiger*, who are faced not only with the sudden, tragic death of a well-loved classmate due to drunk driving, but also with the suicide of a friend who is never able to come to terms with his grief and guilt. The students will also read a picture book, *I Never Knew Your Name* by Sherry Garland, examining their feelings about suicide survivors. After viewing a videotape about a drunk driver's guilt over a death he caused while driving drunk, students will write and produce a public service announcement about drinking and driving. After participating in a Reader's Theater, students will write multigenre papers celebrating the life of a family member or good friend or commemorating the final days of that person. See Table 6:1 for Reading and Writing Strategies in this Unit.

Frontloading Strategies to Instill Curiosity and Motivation to Read

Freewriting

Students are asked to take 15–20 minutes to freewrite about their earliest recollections of dealing with death. The writing could be about a great-grandparent, grandparent, family friend, etc. Most students have no problem remembering about these times, because they seem to have made an impact on them. For those who have had no experiences that they can recall, ask them to write about a time that death has affected their families. Certainly, their parents or another family member has had experiences with death that they could think about. The idea here is to simply get the students thinking about one of the themes of the unit. After the students have finished, ask if any of them would like to share a sentence or two to begin a discussion.

Where Is Grandpa?

After this discussion, hold up the children's book, *Where Is Grandpa?* by T. A. Barron (2000). Begin by asking the students to look at the front cover. Ask them to verbalize what the young boy might be feeling from the picture. Then

Table 6:1 Reading and Writing Strategies in this Unit

Strategy	Set Purpose	Prior Knowledge	Make Predictions	Critical Thinking	Asking Questions	Visualizing the Text	Making Connections	Main Idea	Compare Contrast
Freewriting	•	•	•	•	•		•	•	•
Picture book discussion	•	•	•	•	•	•	•	•	•
Vocabulary of death and mourning		•	•	•	•		•	•	•
Anticipation Guide	•	•	•	•	•		•	•	•
Significant passages	•	•	•	•	•	•	•	•	•
Music Lyric	•	•	•	•	•	•	•	•	
Who I am	•	•	•	•	•		•	•	•
Video Compare/contrast	•	•	•	•	•	•	•	•	•
"I Am" poem	•	•	•	•	•	•	•	•	•
Poem in two voices	•	•	•	•	•	•	•	•	•
Elegy	•	•	•	•	•	•	•	•	
Group discussions	•	•	•	•	•	•	•	•	•
Clothesline	•	•	•	•	•	•	•	•	•
Making it your own	•	•	•	•	•	•	•	•	•
Readers' Theater	•	•		•		•	•	•	
Multigenre Paper	•	•		•	•	•	•	•	•

read the book. Ask the students to look at the freewriting again, to see if any of the emotions that they wrote about were the same as those the boy in the story was feeling. Discuss the emotions that surface when we deal with death.

Vocabulary of Death/Mourning

Have the students make two columns on a sheet of paper. Put a heading at the top, one column labeled "good" and the other "bad." Read the list of words below (Table 6:2), asking the students to put the word in either the "good" column or the "bad" column, depending on whether the word has a positive, or good, connotation or a negative, or bad, connotation. You may not want to use the word "connotation" until after the exercise, depending on the level of the students. After having the students classify the words, discuss as a class the meaning of the word "connotation" and then the meanings of the words from the list. Ask students why they think we have come up with so many euphemisms for death and mourning. They should be able to see that society struggles with the grieving process also, so we try to either find positive, lofty words to describe it or treat it with humor or disdain.

Table 6:2 Vocabulary of Death/Mourning

Cash in	Decay	Fatality
Check out	Meet the grim reaper	Death blow
Croak	Passing	Yield
Decease	Eternal sleep	Depart this life
Demise	At peace	Sink into the grave
Depart	Crossing over	Relinquish
Drop	Wasted	Pay nature's debt
Expire	Terminal	Return to dust
Pass away	Cessation	Go to one's lasting home
Perish	Loss	Sorrow
Snuff	Passing on	Dolor
Succumb	Bereavement	Distress
Bite the dust	Grief	Lament
Breathe one's last	Mourn	Bewail
Give up the ghost	Valley of the shadow of death	Bemoan
Kick the bucket	Curtains	
Meet one's maker	Angel of death	
	Mortality	

Anticipation Guide

Before students begin reading, help them activate their prior knowledge by anticipating some of the themes and issues presented in the novel. Discuss the images on the cover jacket of the book. What will happen in this story? Prepare the Anticipation Guide, or use the one in Table 6:3. According to Tierney, Readence, & Dishner (1995), Anticipation Guides that present students with a set of generalizations related to the theme of the novel helps dependent readers in particular to construct meaning of the text before they begin reading it. Ask the students to respond to the statements according to their beliefs. Do they agree or disagree with the statements? It's important to stress that there are no right or wrong answers. This will help students explore their own thoughts about the issues and allows them to connect ideas and make predictions. The students respond first in writing, and then they are ready to discuss the responses as a class.

Table 6:3 Anticipation Guide for *Tears of a Tiger*

Directions: Read each statement and put a check mark in the "yes" column if you believe the statement and could support it, or put a check mark in the "no" column if you do not believe it and could not support it.		
Yes	**No**	**Statement**
		1. Family members, spouses, or significant others often cause someone to commit suicide.
		2. Survivors often feel anger toward the person who has died.
		3. The death of a loved one is one of the greatest causes of stress.
		4. The lack of support may hamper a survivor's healing.
		5. Not talking about death is better because no one is reminded of their feelings then.
		6. Almost everyone deals with death in the same way.
		7. Children and teens are often unprepared to deal with death.
		8. Showing concern and listening to someone who is grieving is one of the best things to do for someone in that situation.
		9. Suicide is the #2 killer in the United States for those between the ages of 15 and 24.
		10. Few suicide attempts happen with little warning.
		11. Talking about death could make someone consider suicide.
		12. People who commit suicide are weak and just don't know how to deal with life.
		13. Some people who do not have coping strategies for grief may turn to self-destructive behavior.
		14. Common stages of grief are depression, anger bargaining, and acceptance.
		15. Being depressed is just part of being a teenager.

During Reading Strategies to Point Out Relationships Among the Information

Significant Passages

Pass out a packet of small post-it notes to each student, or have them bring in a set of their own. As students are reading, have them mark the pages of passages (30 words or fewer) that seem dramatic, provocative, surprising, disturbing, etc. to them. Let them know that when they are done reading they must eliminate passages until they have only the 10 most significant passages to work with. When they have completed reading the novel, they select the 10 most important passages. Out of those 10, they will select the one "quote of the novel." They then need to write a reflective journal entry explaining why these made their top 10 and why the "quote of the novel" was selected. See Table 6:4 for an Excerpt of Jason's Reflective Journal Entry.

Table 6:4 Excerpt of Jason's Reflective Journal Entry on Significant Passages

The most important passages that I chose from *Tears of a Tiger* appear on pages 52–54. In these passages Andy tells his psychologist what happens at school. At a visit with the school guidance counselor, Andy expresses his desire to go to college and major in prelaw. The counselor responded that "someone of my athletic potential shouldn't be tryin' to make his college career too complicated." She said "Why don't you major in P.E., enjoy your college years, then maybe come back here in a few years to teach gym?" (p. 52). Not only did this counselor destroy his dreams, but Andy goes on to talk about the ways teachers expect him to be another stupid black kid. "So it's easier to pretend to be stupid than to be bothered with all that grade-grubbin' that the white kids do." (p. 52). Andy then goes on to describe the "A" he received on an advanced math test. When the teacher passed back the papers, he said, " . . . even Andy got an A this week. I must be slipping—my tests are getting too easy if even Andy can get an A on them, or maybe he cheated." (p. 53). Andy says that even some of the black teachers treat him wrong. He feels that no matter what he does, it's never good enough. Good grades would certainly please his parents, but of course, they have no idea what the consequences would be for him. If he did get good grades, he'd be like Marcus. Kids call him "curve buster" (p. 50) and everyone hates him. I think this lack of support by his parents, peers, counselor, and teachers to accomplish his goals of getting into law have a major impact on his suicide later on in the story. My quote for Andy for the book is, "No matter what I do, it's never good enough, so why bother?" (p. 53).

Music Lyric

While selecting their top 10 passages, students should also select one scene that they want to capture with a song lyric. They need to isolate the emotion of a character in the scene and select a song lyric that conveys that emotion. Students are to bring in a copy of the lyrics and explain to the class how the song reflects the emotion of the character in that scene.

Who I Am

After students have read about a quarter of the novel, they will write a poem about the main character, Andrew Jackson. The format for the poem will give them writing guidance and make them think about the main character. The first stanza should include what Andy looks like. The second stanza will include information about his skills. The third will include things Andy says, and the fourth describes his life. Finally, the fifth stanza should include why it's better for people to accept him the way he is instead of thinking he should be perfect. Reflecting on Andy to write this poem will give the students greater insight into him and will help them to understand him throughout the rest of the novel.

Dead Drunk: The Kevin Tunell Story

Watch the video, *Dead Drunk: The Kevin Tunell Story* (1992), about a teen who kills someone in a drunk-driving accident. His situation is similar to the main character's in *Tears of a Tiger*, except his memories and guilt are court-imposed. An insight into Kevin's story illuminates some of the grief and guilt that Andy feels. After watching the 30-minute video, split the students into groups and have them identify and discuss the types of conflict Andy felt (man vs. man, man vs. society, and man vs. self) and the types of conflict Kevin felt in the video. How are the two similar, and how are the two different?

Two-Voiced Poem

Before writing a two-voiced poem, the students need to really understand the characters and their conflicts. Prewriting helps them to clarify their thoughts. Begin the class by discussing conflict. We discuss internal vs. external, as well as identifying types of conflict (man vs. man, man vs. self, and man vs. nature/ society). Then, the students brainstorm and list the conflicts that are in the novel. After selecting one of the listed conflicts, I ask the students to create two "I Am" poems. If they choose a character with internal conflict, they write two "I Am" poems, one for each side of the conflict. If the conflict is between two characters, then they write one "I Am" poem for each character. Using a template for writing the "I Am" poem suggested by Suzi Me (1987), see Table 6:5 for Angela Thatcher's "I Am" Poems for Keisha and Andy.

Table 6:5 Angela's "I Am" Poems for Keisha and Andy

Keisha	Andy
I am Andy's girlfriend	I am the survivor
I wonder about Andy's thoughts	I wonder about being the center on the basketball team
I hear Andy's story	I hear the screams and the crash
I see my classmates go on with their lives	I see the flames
I am Andy's girlfriend	I want Rob back
	I am the survivor
I pretend not to be frustrated with Andy	
I feel lost in a sea of white	I pretend to be okay most of the time
I touch a snowflake falling to the ground	I feel the weight of the guilt
I worry when my friends aren't happy	I touch Keisha's arm as she holds me close
I cry when I wish Andy was the boyfriend I had before the accident	I worry about Rob being cold
I am Andy's girlfriend	I cry when I think about Rob
	I am the survivor
I understand that the world isn't perfect	
I say that everything will be ok	I understand that my drinking and driving was wrong
I dream about being carefree again	I say that I am sorry
I try to be a good friend and girlfriend	I dream about the crash
I hope Andy will be okay soon	I try to forgive myself
I am Andy's girlfriend	I hope the psychologist can help me
	I am the survivor

After the students have composed the two "I Am" poems, I ask them to perform several poems from *Joyful Noise: Poems for Two Voices* by Paul Fleischman (1988). After discussing the characteristics and format of the two-voiced poem, I ask the students to take the two characters (or one in conflict) and create a two-voiced poem. The students then get another class member to perform the poem in front of the class with them. Two-voiced poems are most effective when performed as dialogue. See Table 6:6 for a student example, written by Angela Thatcher, who chose to show the conflict between Keisha and Andy from the novel.

Table 6:6 Angela's Poem in Two Voices: "Our Relationship"

Andy and I aren't as close since The accident	Keisha and I are as tight as ever!
I always try to be Patient with him Even if I just want to Slap him	She's always listening and Being understanding I can talk to her
He just won't let go. I just don't understand why Andy Just won't try To be happy	I can't seem to let go.
I don't know how much longer I can stick it out With him.	She gets me like no one else does.
He can't let me go	We'll be together always She's my lifeline. I can't let her go.

Elegy

Read a few examples of elegies, like "Elegy" by Robert Seymour Bridges. Define elegy, "a lyric poem of mourning or lamentation for the dead." Discuss the language and imagery used in Bridges' poem. Ask students to make a list of words that people use to express sorrow. Students can use this as a word bank for composing an elegy in the voice of Andy mourning Robert Washington's death.

Have students read the elegies that they wrote while reading the novel. Look again at "Monty's Good-bye to Andy." Have a student read Monty's words. Brainstorm the feelings that are revealed on these pages. Then have students write a second elegy in Monty's voice, grieving Andy's suicide.

After Reading Strategies to Extend the Concepts in the Novel

Group Discussions

Divide students into groups of four. Within the group, have students describe how the various teens in the novel coped with Robert's death, and then with Andy's death. Then have them describe how the adults dealt with the teens' deaths. Finally, have the students compare the information. Do adults deal with death differently than teens? Finally, have the same groups discuss the deaths that they have been touched by and how they grieved. They may refer back to the freewriting they did at the beginning of the unit for ideas. The final activity for the groups is for each group to create a poster of support systems that people (adults and teens) turn to when coping with a death. The posters are then displayed around the room. An alternative activity would be to ask students to create a collage for Robert or Andy as a way of debriefing their feelings and enhancing the healing process, if they are grieving as a result of reading the book. Students should cut out words and images from magazines that remind them of the deceased and place them on a posterboard. The poster will tell the story of the character.

Character Clothesline

Give each student approximately two yards of yarn and eight clothespins. You may want to assign each student a certain character from the novel randomly or let the student select the character, but you will want to make sure that all of the main characters are selected. Tell the students to find pictures in magazines of articles or items that would give insight into their character. The item could have special significance to the character or tell us something about that person's values. After cutting out the pictures, the students should clothespin them to the yarn. Then they will write a paper explaining the significance of each item on the line. This is the prewriting for the character sketch that they will ultimately create. The items from the clothesline are central to the creation of the character sketch. It's apparent that the thinking the students must do to create the clothesline helps them to be clearer in their writing. See Table 6:7 for Lacey Gwinn's piece for the character, B. J.

Table 6:7 Prewriting for Character Sketch for the Clothesline

B. J. is a short guy and self-conscious about his height and lack of experience with girls. He does not play basketball because he is too short. His best friends are Andy, Gerald, and Robbie. He doesn't have a girlfriend because he is very shy. He does not drink like his other three friends, but is so grateful to be included that he would never try to influence them in any way. After Robbie dies he starts praying to God and going to church. He knew that dealing with the situation was beyond his experience and got the only outside help he could think of. B. J. was also a quick thinker and person of action because he had the idea to break the glass out of the windshield to try to rescue Robbie. He seems more mature than his friends in many ways even though he believes they are better than him.

Making It Your Own

This activity was submitted by Dodie Zolman, and originally appeared in NCTE's *Ideas Plus*. It makes the students think about the novel and their responses to it. In order to answer the questions, they need to reflect on the novel and its characters. These responses are written in their journals, and are graded only on depth of thinking.

Complete the following statements with a minimum of three additional sentences each, reacting to what you have read.

    a.   If I were in this story, I would/wouldn't have . . .

    b.   I really admire the character of . . .

    c.   I realized . . .

    d.   I can't really understand . . .

    e.   I did/didn't like the way . . .

    f.   The character of . . . reminds me of myself when . . .

    g.   I know the feeling of . . .

    h.   The biggest thing that the character of . . . learned in this story was . . .

    i.   The most important lesson that I, the reader, learned in this story was . . .

Readers' Theater

The Readers' Theater for this chapter, *Cheers*, is based on Draper's *Tears of a Tiger* and was written by Janie Reinart, Language Arts Consultant in Cleveland, Ohio. See the CD-ROM for this chapter. Ask students to volunteer for the various roles in the Readers' Theater. Give them time to read through their parts, so that the performance will run more fluently. Perform the Readers' Theater. When finished, discuss how the Readers' Theater brought something new to the novel. Also, discuss what the students understand better after the performance.

Multigenre Paper

Since *Tears of a Tiger* is a novel written with a multigenre approach, with various genres used as example, the students have already seen what this approach can add to a subject. Explain the elements of a multigenre paper (prologue, various genres, multiple points of view, repetend, notes page, bibliography). After determining length, number of genres, and length of genre, have the students create a rubric for assessing the paper. With a little guidance, students often determine a fair assessment tool. Read a sample multigenre paper. If none are available, some can be found in Tom Romano's (2000) *Blending Genre, Altering Style*. Students are then asked to write a multigenre paper about the death of a loved one. If students are unable to write this because they have not had to deal with a loved one dying, then they are asked to write about a family member dealing with a loved one dying. On the surface, one might think that these papers would be depressing to assess, but contrarily, they usually turn out to be a celebration of one's life through the grieving experience. What a valuable coping strategy for students to see in action. After the papers have been turned in, I have students split into groups to share their papers. I allow them to select their own groups, and students are not forced to participate if they feel the paper is too personal. I have not had a student opt out yet. The papers are personal, and yet, they are worth sharing. This, too, celebrates the life of the person who is being mourned. See the CD-ROM for Katie Illes's Multigenre Paper.

Young Adult Literature Dealing with Suicide

Garland, S. (1994). *I never knew your name.* New York: Ticknor & Fields.
Grisham, J. (1999). *The testament.* New York: Doubleday.
Guest, J. (1993). *Ordinary people.* New York: Penguin Books.
Hartnett, S. (1994). *Wilful blue.* New York: Viking.

Young Adult Literature Dealing with Death and Dying

Abelove, J. (1999). *Saying it out loud.* London: DK Ink.
Cole, B. (1997). *The facts speak for themselves.* London: Puffin.
Crutcher, C. (1986). *Running loose.* New York: Laurel Leaf.
Ferris, J. (1995). *Signs of life.* New York: Farrar, Straus, & Giroux.
Fleischman, P. (1998). *Whirligig.* New York: Henry Holt.
Fox, P. (1995). *The eagle kit: A novel.* London: Orchard Books.
Gaines, E. (1993). *A lesson before dying.* New York: Alfred A. Knopf.
Herman, J. (1998). *Deep waters.* New York: Philomel.
Ingold, J. (1996). *The window.* New York: Harcourt Brace.
Lowry, L. (1993). *The giver.* New York: Bantam Doubleday Dell.
Mahy, M. (1999). *Memory.* New York: Aladdin.
Nolan, H. (1999). *A face in every window.* New York: Harcourt Brace.
Peck, R. N. (1999). *Cowboy ghost.* New York: HarperCollins.
Pennebaker, R. (1999). *Conditions of love.* New York: Henry Holt.
Pohl, P. (1999). *I miss you, I miss you.* New York: R & S Books.
Powell, R. (1999). *Tribute to another dead rock star.* New York: Farrar, Straus, & Giroux.
Rylant, C. (1992). *Missing May.* New York: Orchard Books.
Schwandt, S. (1996). *Hold steady.* Minneapolis, MN: Free Spirit.
Springer, N. (1994). *Toughing it.* New York: Harcourt Brace.
Synder, M. (1995). *Souvenirs.* New York: Avon Flare.

References

Barron, T. A. (2000). *Where is grandpa?* Chris Soentpiet, illustrator; Patricia Gauch, (Ed.). New York: Philomel Books.
Bridges, R. S. (1895). Elegy. In E. C. Stedman (Ed.), *A Victorian Anthology, 1837–1895.* Cambridge, MA: Riverside Press.

Cunningham, L. (1996). *Grief and the adolescent*. Newhall, CA: TAG: Teen Age Grief, Inc.

Draper, S. (1994). *Tears of a tiger*. New York: Atheneum Books for Young Readers.

Fleischman, P. (1988). *Joyful noise: Poems for two voices*. New York: HarperCollins.

Harmon, B. (1992). *Dead drunk: The Kevin Tunell story.* (Videotape). New York: Ambrose Video.

Me, S. (1987). I am poem. In *The teachers & writers handbook of poetic forms*. R. Padgett (Ed.), New York: Teachers and Writers Collaborative.

Romano, T. (2000). *Blending genre, altering style: Writing multigenre papers*. Portsmouth, NH: Heinemann Boynton/Cook.

Shneidman, E. (1996). *The suicidal mind*. New York: Oxford University Press.

Tierney, R. J., Readence, J. E., & Dishner, E. K. (1995). *Reading strategies and practices: A compendium* (4th ed.). Needham Heights, MA: Allyn and Bacon.

Chapter Seven

Youth Violence in
Walter Dean Myers' *Monster*

Susan Cappetta

I n a 1999 study, The Sentencing Project, a national nonprofit organization committed to sentencing reform, found that almost "one in three (32%) black men in the age group 20–29 was either in prison, on probation, or paroled" (Mauer, p. 3). Why are young black men disproportionately victims of violent crime, as well as the most frequently indicted and convicted for these acts? There are no easy answers to this question.

Through a guided study of Walter Dean Myers' (1999) awarding-winning (Printz, Coretta Scott, and National Book Award) *Monster*, along with a problem-based learning lesson, students are better able to understand and begin to answer this difficult question. Steve Harmon, the protagonist of *Monster*, is a 16-year-old black teenager who is on trial for murder. Myers presents Steve's story from the personal, as well as societal, view by combining Steve's subjective journal entries with his more objective viewpoint presented in a screenplay. The reader must consider the varying points of view about crime, violence, and today's judicial system in order to determine whether Steve is guilty or not guilty.

The complexity of the text mirrors the complexity of the social justice issues presented in it. Students need reading strategies and the appropriate background knowledge in order to understand the societal, political, and racial sources of the problems for young black men, as well as the metacognitive skills to integrate the multiple viewpoints and genres of Myers' storytelling. Students may need additional information to understand the complexities of the racial, social, political, and cultural characteristics of Harlem in the 20th century. They will need to build their knowledge about the lives of black youth, of inner-city poverty, and of racism before reading Myers' novel. See Table 7:1 for Reading and Writing Strategies for this thematic unit on Youth Violence in Walter Dean Myers' *Monster*.

Table 6:1 Reading and Writing Strategies in this Unit

Strategy	Set Purpose	Prior Knowledge	Make Predictions	Critical Thinking Questions	Asking Questions	Visualizing the Text	Making Connections	Main Idea	Compare Contrast	Making Inferences
Setting Study		•	•	•	•		•	•		•
Short Stories			•	•	•	•	•	•	•	•
Think-Alouds		•	•	•	•	•	•	•	•	•
Metacognition			•			•		•		
Genre Study		•	•	•	•	•	•	•	•	•
Essential Questions	•	•	•	•	•	•	•	•	•	•
Audio Text	•	•	•			•	•	•	•	•
Socratic Seminar	•		•	•	•	•	•	•	•	•
Electronic Message Boards	•	•	•	•	•		•	•	•	
Photograph Interpretation	•	•	•	•	•	•	•	•	•	•
Sound Track		•	•	•		•	•	•	•	•
Problem-Based Learning	•	•	•	•	•	•	•	•	•	•
Mock Trial	•	•	•	•	•	•	•	•	•	•
Affirmative Action	•	•		•		•	•	•	•	

Frontloading Strategies to Build Students' Knowledge and Experience

Accessing Prior Knowledge

If *Monster* is taught in an interdisciplinary class, where students have traced some of the racial and social experiences of African-Americans, they will have more of these life experiences or background knowledge to bring to their reading—yet they may still need the prereading activities and sources to further enhance their appreciation of the work. Students can learn about life in Harlem, New York, in the 20th century through reading stories, vignettes, and/or poems with the same setting, characters, and themes.

Since the setting of *Monster* is Harlem, give students the opportunity to read stories from *145th Street: Short Stories* by Walter Dean Myers (2000) to appreciate the complexity, the community, and the gang violence of 145th Street in Harlem. The readers can examine some of the positive and negative aspects of the setting, while learning about an environment that can contribute to the reasons young black youth commit crimes. "Big Joe's Funeral" is a story that shows the close-knit communal environment of the neighborhood, as does the final story, "Block Party—145th Style." "Monkeyman" exposes the student to the gang culture, an important aspect of youth crime. In the book, *Hard Time: A Real Life Look at Juvenile Crime and Violence* (1996) by Bode & Mack, voices of real teenagers who have to deal with crime and violence in their lives tell their stories in first-person narratives, poems, and comic strips. From teens who have been victimized by crime to teens who have been incarcerated for crime, the stories reveal the role of violence in today's youth—its sources and its consequences. For another perspective of a 12-year-old boy who recounts his day-to-day battles in a juvenile detention center, read excerpts from *The Buffalo Tree* (1997) by Adam Rapp.

Metacognition

The text of *Monster* can be confusing for some readers, due to the shifting points of view, as well as the various genres present in the text that add layers of meaning for the reader. Students must monitor their understanding of the shifts in text and make meaning by developing their metacognitive skills. According to Keene & Zimmerman, (1997):

> "Proficient readers monitor their comprehension during reading—they
> know when the text they are reading or listening to makes sense, when
> it does not, what does not make sense, and whether the unclear por-
> tions are critical to the overall understanding of the piece" (p. 43).

While independent readers use metacognition to monitor their understanding of text, dependent readers need to develop these skills.

Introduce the concept of metacognition with the reading of Walter Dean Myers' short stories from *145th Street: Short Stories*. Show them how to monitor their understanding by modeling your reading of a short piece of text using a think-aloud (sometimes called protocol) strategy. This is a technique in which the reader reports out, or thinks aloud about what one is noticing, thinking, and doing as one reads a particular text (Wilhelm, Baker, & Dube, 2001). Think-alouds provide a rich window into making your metacognitive skills visible to students. As Margaret Meek (1983) tells us, our job as teachers is to make public those secret things that expert readers know and do.

After modeling the strategy, students are asked to do think-alouds in their groups as they continue to read one of Myers' short stories. Ask them to reflect on this strategy at the end of each reading session. While students are honing their metacognitve skills by reading these short stories using the think-aloud strategy, they are also acquiring background knowledge about the social, cultural, or racial situations that will help them fully comprehend the setting and circumstances of *Monster.*

In order to continue to develop students' metacognitive skills, try the think-aloud with the whole group as students begin to read the novel, *Monster.* Begin by reading Steve's journal out loud as the students follow along. Tell them what was going on in your mind as you read the first paragraph, and then ask a student to summarize what you just read and tell what happened in their minds when they read/heard the paragraph. Continue in this manner with different students until someone in the class has a question, is confused, or needs further clarification. Ask students to brainstorm different ways the reader can clarify their understanding. These strategies may include questioning, rereading, or making connections to one's own life or other texts.

Genre Study

Walter Dean Myers wrote the novel, *Monster,* using text in various formats that give multiple perspectives of the crime situation voiced by the narrator, Steve Harmon. The plot unfolds in a nonlinear sequence through diary entries, memos, photographs, and screenplay. Eliza Dresang (1999) explains the rationale for this change in writing style:

> "What a person might record in a diary or journal can differ substantially from what the same person might reveal in an interview. In understanding perspective, it is important for a reader to understand that firsthand accounts may different depending upon the format in which they originally appeared. One way they may differ is that the more private the means of expression, the more candid the thoughts expressed may be" (p. 53).

Students need to pay attention to these literary formats in order to make meaning of the text and understand the writer's craft.

In *Monster,* Steve Harmon narrates the story in two basic genres. When he is alone in his jail cell, he exposes the reader to his feelings—most especially his fear, isolation, and alienation from society. When he relays the facts of his upcoming trial, he writes in screenplay format. The more the student understands about point of view, shifts in narration from first person to third person, and reading the texts of the different genres, the better able the student will be to compare Steve's private internal thoughts to the actions he shares with the reader through his public retelling of his story. Though Steve's screenplay is narrated in the third person, it is still Steve's interpretation of the actions. By understanding the differences between these points of view, the reader will better be able to make the decision about Steve's innocence or guilt of the murder.

When beginning to read *Monster*, it is important to discuss the impact of each genre on the reader. After reading some journal entries and a part of the screenplay, students can begin to respond to the questions found in Table 7:2.

Table 7:2 Questions and Responses to Gain Perspective Through Different Genres of Text

Question	Student Responses
What does a reader learn from Steve's journal entry?	• His journal format makes it easier for the reader to see what it is like to "be" Steve. • The author chose the style to be different, and it makes the book multigenre. Another touch the author made was Steve's handwriting; it makes him seem more human.
Why does Steve write in journal format?	• I think Steve writes in journal form to tell his thoughts. In a journal, you can let it all come out. I think that this made Steve feel like more of a human and less of a convict. • Steve does it to back up the movie with feelings that can't be conveyed in a screenplay.
What does a reader learn from Steve's screenplay?	• I believe that the feelings he thinks others had towards him are portrayed quite evidently in the screenplay. Say he thinks his lawyer thought he was going to lose, and then he's going to show that.
Why does Steve write his story as a screenplay?	• A quote in the beginning of the book is, "Sometimes I feel like I have walked into the middle of the movie" . . . "I wish I could make sense of it." These quotes tell us that Steve is writing the book in screenplay format because he feels like his life is one big movie, and if he made a movie about his life that feels like a movie, he could make sense of his real life.

These concepts are important to understand when reading Steve's two different genres. As students bring their own experiences, thoughts, and interpretations to the text, they need to be able to identify the purpose and perspective of a private journal and a public screenplay. Helping students identify the differences in genres will help them read to understand with more clarity, depth, and analytical ability. As students read this book, they must ask themselves the ultimate question: "Is Steve guilty of a crime?" Acting like a juror in the courtroom, they must analyze and weigh evidence to determine Steve's motivations for what he does and his ultimate guilt or innocence. As Myers leaves this interpretation to the reader, one must use his own interpretations, opinions about guilt and innocence, and reaction to Steve's point of view to determine an answer to this question.

During Reading Strategies to Stimulate Discussion

Essential Questions

Essential Questions bring students beyond basic fact-gathering, and ask them to solve a problem or make a decision. According to Jacobs (1989), an essential question asks the student to ponder major issues, problems, concerns, interests, or themes that are open-ended, nonjudgmental, meaningful, and purposeful with an emotional and intellectual component, and invites an exploration of ideas. Before reading the story, ask some of these philosophical questions to the class and take a few responses to stimulate students thinking about critical issues presented in the text. Students may continue to discuss these questions throughout the reading of the book. The questions launch them into the text of *Monster*. See Table 7:3 for Sample Essential and Defining Questions.

Table 7:3 Essential and Defining Questions

Essential Questions	Defining Questions
What is guilt and what is innocence?	In what ways is Steve guilty? In what ways is he innocent?
Can one be guilty without intentionally committing a criminal act? If yes, how can one be guilty without intentionally committing an act?	If Steve intended to act as a lookout, but changed his mind before committing the act, is he guilty? If there is no definitive evidence that Steve committed a crime, can he be guilty? Is Steve guilty?
Is justice served when a convicted criminal receives a reduced sentence in exchange for information?	Was it just when Sal Zinzi and Wendell Bolden both traded information for reduced sentences?
Is it possible to overcome superficial judgments about people and their actions?	How can Steve overcome Petrocelli's and the jurors' negative impression that he is a monster?
How much is our view of ourselves influenced by the way others view us?	How do Miss O'Brien's interactions with Steve impact his views of himself as a human being?

Audio Texts Help Students Make Connections

The screenplay format in *Monster* can be enhanced when heard or read aloud. Two ways to provide the auditory experience for students would be through listening to the audiotape of the book or by organizing students to do a dramatic reading. According to Margaret Mackeyn (2001, September):

> "Perhaps the purest way of rendering words in a medium other than print is in audio texts . . . Different characters may be rendered dramatically either by the narrator or by separate actors . . . It may develop a new relationship between listener, author, and story" (p. 174).

When students begin the story by listening as they read along, they become engaged in the text, understand the roles and voices of the different characters, and can visualize the scene. A seventh-grade student, Edward, agrees as he states,

> "Since, there are different voices; it is harder to get confused. The tape
> makes it seem like you are actually there, which is good because you
> get a fuller sense of the story. Another benefit is when listening to the
> tape, you can hear the emotions of all of the characters while they talk."

The opportunity to participate in reader response theory given this relationship may be a natural next step in comprehension. Students are much better prepared to then move into a classroom reading with students assigned different roles or reading the text on their own.

Socratic Seminars

Socratic Seminars are an excellent way for students to engage in authentic discussions around a text by analyzing specific passages, providing text support to their interpretations, and speaking in small enough groups where the dialogue progresses in a natural and unhindered manner. According to Canady & Rettig (1996), "Socratic seminars return ownership for learning to students as they explore a reading, back up their opinions with textual evidence, challenge each other's views, and, most importantly, find, articulate, and develop their 'voice'" (p. 30). Ideally, a Socratic Seminar would involve six to eight students. In large classes of 25 to 30, it would be better for students to participate in fewer seminars with fewer participants than more frequent ones with 12 to 15 students in them. The benefits of the format come when students have the chance to respond to their peers, build on their ideas, and offer other perspectives without extensive wait time.

One of the unique features of a Socratic Seminar discussion is the role of the observers. When students are not discussing the text in the inner circle, they are observing their peers by recording what they say, how they say it, if they support their ideas with text, if they share talk time, and if they actively listen. Teachers may also have the observers take notes on the content of the discussion and then respond to the previous group's comments in a subsequent seminar. At the end of each seminar, the observers share their notes with the class. This keeps all students in the class actively engaged and attentive to the discussion. See Table 7:4 for Sample Socratic Seminar Questions for *Monster*. For an actual transcript of a Socratic Seminar discussion from a seventh-grade class, see Table 7:5 for Transcript of a Socratic Seminar.

Table 7:4 Sample Socratic Seminar Questions for *Monster*

1.	With support from the text, explore how Steve is learning about who he is by examining how others judge him.
2.	Discuss Steve's need to view himself through the eyes of others. Specifically, why does Miss O'Brien's smile mean so much to him? (Myers, 1999, p. 137)
3.	On page 138, Steve tells Miss O'Brien "I'm not guilty." She replies, "You should have said 'I didn't do it.'" With direct support from the text, explore the difference between not doing something and not being guilty. Make sure to consider Steve's reaction when his mother tells him, "I know you're innocent" (Myers, 1999, p. 148).
4.	As you reach the end of the book and hear Steve's verdict, determine whether or not justice is served in his case.
5.	Guilt and innocence can be defined in several ways. There is legal, as well as moral, guilt. Based on both Steve's journal entries and screenplays, determine whether Steve is guilty or innocent. Support your response with adequate text support.
6.	Will Steve commit another crime? (Walter Dean Myers answers this question on the audio tape. If you have the audio version of the tape, listen to Walter Dean Myers' introduction and discuss whether or not you agree with his thoughts.)

Table 7:5 Transcript of a Socratic Seminar

Student	Is Steve making an honest film?
Eric	Ok. Well. I'll start by saying that none of us really know whether or not he was making an honest film, because we weren't there. If he was making a movie, he could make sense of the whole situation. If he's making sense of it, it has to be true. He does make sense of his life. On page 4 he says, "I think to get used to this I will have to give up what I think is real and take up something else. I wish I could make sense of it."
Krish	I disagree. He says he'll have to give up what he thinks is real. Isn't being real being truthful? I don't think Steve is making an honest film because he said he switched around the moments a little and said it as he remembered it as he says on page 275. This would affect it because he may have said things in a meaner way than Petrocelli really said it, and he might have said things that O'Brien may never have said.
Tyler	I think it's kind of hard to tell because most of it is a screenplay and the only little bits of the truth come out in the journal entries like on page 220, when he shows what he really thinks. "Truth is truth. It's what you know to be right."
Ian	Right. I agree. It also doesn't seem like he's lying. For example, in the journal entries everything seems real to him and he's scared. That's not something he would like about himself.
Nick	Yeah. But you're talking about the journal entries. What about the screenplay?
Eric	During the whole book, the screenplay stays true to what Steve says in his journal. Steve has no reason to lie in his journal because no will ever see it besides him. So, if Steve's journal is not false, then neither is his screenplay.
Krish	I think Steve is guilty but he doesn't realize it.

cont.

Nick	On page 115 it shows that he is in the store. He says, "What did I do? Anyone can walk into a drugstore and look around." He knows he was there. He's trying to convince himself that it was okay.
Patrick	He's leaving out all the bad stuff. This is one of the things he doesn't know that he's doing. He is unsure of himself when it comes to bad things in life.
Eric	Look at page 281. He says, "That is why I take the films of myself. I want to know who I am." He's saying in movies that he will find out who he is. That's important to him, so he wouldn't lie about it.
Tyler	He changes. I think later in the book he convinces himself that he's not guilty. He writes all those monsters on the paper on page 24 in the beginning. He sort of thought he was guilty in the beginning.

The conversation continues as students debate the honesty of Steve's film. Often these dialogues will veer into different discussions. This group moved from the honesty of the film to Steve's honesty to his guilt or innocence. At the end of *Monster*, many students continue to debate his guilt or innocence, even when they have heard Walter Dean Myers admit Steve is guilty at the beginning of the audio tape.

Electronic Message Boards

Students growing up in the Digital Age are comfortable reading and writing text on a computer screen. Digital communication has become an integral part of teenagers' lives, and students who are able to apply this practice to their study of literature—both reading online and writing in a digital fashion—may be better able to demonstrate their understanding. Facile with the language of e-mail, AOL Instant Messenger (AIM), and message boards, they discuss the same questions they address in a Socratic Seminar in three types of exchange: AIM conversations, e-mail correspondence, and a class message board. The benefit of the message board is the ability for several students to respond to the same questions, as well as to each other—similar to a Socratic Seminar. The difference from the Socratic Seminar is the mode of communication. Whereas a discussion is entirely verbal, a message board encourages a student to process the information in a conversational format, but write the answer to a peer.

One difference between formal written responses to literature questions and the electronic message board is spelling and sentence structure. Students who are familiar with the shortened version of Instant Messenger writing often abbreviate and do not capitalize their writing. Teachers who are uncomfortable allowing their students to use this informal electronic language can require more formal English. See Table 7:6 for Excerpts of Discussion From Class Message Board.

Table 7:6 Excerpts of Discussion From Class Message Board

Is Steve guilty or innocent? Define his guilt. Define his innocence.
Re(1): Is Steve guilty or innocent? Define his guilt. Define his innocence. Posted on May 12, 2003 at 09:19:53 PM by [VA]IvyBat I say he's innocent because, A) He did not participate in the actual robbery or murder. B) He may not have known he was committing a crime. C) All he did was walk in and walk out.
Re(2): Is Steve guilty or innocent? Define his guilt. Define his innocence. Posted on May 13, 2003 at 04:54:08 PM by LAST WHITE BALLA (a.k.a. FAKEMAN) i completely disagree with IVYBAT. steve is partly guilty and partly innocent. i would have to say that steve is obviously guilty of committing a crime. however, steve is not guilty of the degree of which he was being tried- steve was innocent of murdering someone but guilty of stealing. i mean rut, i thought at 16 years old, a person knows if they are committing a crime.
Just adding on Posted on May 13, 2003 at 03:50:36 PM by [VA]IvyBat Guilt is a complicated thing and Steve falls under both categories of guilty and innocent. His guilt is shown with the fact that he knew he was committing a crime. He has a guilty Conscience, which is, although different, just as important as physical guilt because you feel responsible for the act.

More examples of these discussions may be found at http://www.boards2go.com/boards/board.cgi?&user=CoreCappetta.

There are several ways to create a message board for a classroom discussion. Some schools have their own Web sites with discussion-board software. If this is the case, a director of technology can help set up the site. Several companies have free message board services. Most take one through the set up step by step. A teacher may also enlist the aid of a digital expert, as many students today know more about technology than the adults in their lives. I use www.boards2go.com.

Multiple Intelligences

The multigenre style in *Monster* not only includes journal format and a screenplay, but it also includes drawings, photographs, and a musical reference to further enhance Steve's story. Students who possess strong visual/spatial intelligence (Gardner, 1983) can apply this intelligence to their verbal/linguistic understanding of the text when asked to observe and analyze the photographs and drawings throughout the book. See the CD-ROM for a collage of themes and ideas by Abbie Graham.

Visual/Spatial Intelligence

When students are asked the significance of the different pictures, they are able to apply visual learning skills to their linguistic reading ones to understand the text more deeply. An example of a student response to the significance of the photograph on page 128 is:

"Looking at the facial expression Steve has, it seems like he knows why he is there and knows what he has done. It must be scary for him to know how much trouble he is in. It brings out his human side and shows his remorse." The student is able to interpret Steve's human side from the visual photographs as well as the text.

There are more student responses to the impact of the photographs on the discussion board found at http://www.boards2go.com/boards/board.cgi?&user=CoreCappetta.

Musical Intelligence

Thomas Armstrong (2003) claims that a student who has difficulty reading using traditional methods may benefit from the aid of a focus on music. Many students possess a musical intelligence that may aid their understanding of the texts they are reading. Students can apply their musical aptitude to the understanding of the book when asked to imagine what type of music should accompany different parts of the screenplay. Steve Harmon suggests this musical component when he says, "I put strings in the background. Cellos. Violas" (Myers, 1999, p. 271). When students listen to the sound, rhythm, and lyrics of music and apply its connection to the theme and mood of a story, they will further demonstrate their increased reading comprehension. See Table 7:7 for Excerpts of Patrick's Sound track, Table 7:8 for Excerpts of Rutledge's Sound track, and Table 7:9 for Excerpts of Krish's Sound track.

Table 7:7 Excerpts of Patrick's Sound Track

For the sound track of *Monster*, I would have a lot of different varieties of music: rap, classical, patriotic, and hip-hop. I think that these together would create the mood of the ghetto, the patriotic theme of what he did to his country, and also what Steve was talking about with the "strings in the background. Cellos. Violas."	
Opening Credits	"Amazing Grace" This song would be good because it talks about how someone was bad but then he realized his bad ways and changed. This can be immediately connected with Steve because if he is guilty, maybe he can change his ways like the person in this song. By starting this song in the beginning, you get the sense of good vs. bad, and guilty vs. innocent.
Closing Credits	"The Star Spangled Banner" Once again, this song fits into the patriotic theme in this trial. In the book during the verdict, Steve moves the camera to the picture of George Washington. Does this judicial system work? If Steve is guilty, but has proven himself innocent, what does that say about the country? The judicial system is flawed, not immensely, but it is. It is Steve's right to a fair trial, but to his country it is not fair, because he has taken someone's life, and should be punished.

Table 7:8 Excerpts of Rutledge's Sound Track

Page 156	As Steve looks down on the people in the street below his jail cell, "The Flight of the Bumblebee" would play in the background, bringing out a feeling of activity and joy for the people on the streets. Then, when the camera zooms back into the jail cell and focuses on Steve's longing face the music will softly change to blues and a feeling of depression will overtake the atmosphere. The mood of the viewer and the picture will be dramatically changed as the fear in Steve's eyes slowly becomes more and more apparent. I made these selections to help the viewer relate to Steve so that in the end of the movie, the viewer is relieved at the verdict, Not Guilty, and all the more astounded when his lawyer, O'Brien, does not hug him at the end.
Pages 219–222	The song, "Let Me Rest in Pieces" by Saliva is a song about how the lead singer of Saliva lost his brother in a shooting. This scene would have voice-overs of the three cellmates talking about how they lost large parts of their lives. I chose this song because the two stories directly coincide and the slow, depressed tone of the song would directly harmonize with the atmosphere of the dark cell. The mood and meaning of the voices of the three men would be brought out and it would help the viewer relate to them and how they believe that they were cornered by "the system."

Table 7:9 Excerpts of Krish's Sound Track

I would choose rock music that is combined with "meaningful" words. I would put some rap also since many rap songs have words that go along with the story of racism and scary things, such as monsters. One band I would choose is *Linkin Park*.	
Page 98	"Papercut" is a song that relates to Steve when he is looking in the mirror at himself. It is a face that haunts him. "Papercut" relates more to the haunting part. "It's a face that I hold inside . . ." The face Steve saw of himself is so different to him, almost a stranger. Yet he sees it as an evil face, almost of a monster.

Certain activities can be completed during the reading of the book, as well as when the book is completed. A Socratic Seminar question that can be discussed at different stages of the book is whether students believe Steve Harmon is guilty or not guilty of the criminal charges he faces. Likewise, students can create the musical sound track as they read, or when they review the book upon its completion.

After Reading Strategies to Promote Problem-Based Learning

The postreading strategies for this unit engage students in active learning strategies, such as problem-based learning of social justice issues, role playing a mock trial for Steve Harmon, and debating Affirmative Action.

Problem-Based Learning

In this strategy, the problem comes first. Used somewhat widely in medical schools and to a lesser extent in other professional schools, students learn in a way that simulates actual working conditions as closely as possible. Students encounter an open-ended, ill-defined problem. In practice, this means that the first thing students are given is not a lot of information about a subject, but a realistic problem in the form of a case study. According to Fink (2003), "They [students] must learn to make a preliminary analysis, gather information or data, assess the relevance of the new information, propose a solution, and assess the quality of their tentative solution" (p. 21). A Problem-Based Learning (PBL) task allows students to research a real-life problem or issue in-depth, identify the different causes of the problem, and work together to pose solutions. When students are able to articulate a plan or solution to their particular problem, they are able to write a letter to an editor, a congressman, or a member of a committee or council already working on solutions to the same problem. Through this process, they make real-world connections and take actions that validate their learning experience.

The key to a problem-based activity is an essential question that poses a current-day, relevant issue to be resolved. These questions encourage cooperative learning amongst students, teachers, and the community, while integrating technology to enhance student understanding of the topics they study as well as the world at large, their access to technological resources, the ability to communicate with professionals in their field of research via e-mail, and the opportunity to discuss their ideas on a class message board as they collect their data and ideas.

Since students began their study of *Monster* with Essential Questions, they will already have their initial thoughts, ideas, and conceptions of the problem for young black men in the criminal justice system—the same system that indicted Steve Harmon. They will recognize some inherent flaws within this system, as well as contributing factors from society at large that have some of its roots in prejudice and discrimination toward black youth. With this initial information from their reading of *Monster*, students are ready to gather more information to further articulate the specifics of the problems, as well as create their solutions.

The Process

The following provides a framework for the problem-based learning task.

1. Provide students with one or two general articles on black youths and crime, and take notes on the different problems and issues within the topic. Web sites can be found at:

THE PROBLEMS

http://www.sentencingproject.org/pdfs/5022.pdf.
A comprehensive study from The Sentencing Project.
All students should begin with this article or one similar to it.

http://www.bradycampaign.org/facts/research/afam.asp
Statistics on gun violence in the African-American community

http://www.sistahspace.com/nommo/index8.html
Several links to the problems and solutions

2. In small groups, teach students how to research the subject and find different articles on their own.
3. Define subtopics and problems to solve as a group.
4. Propose solutions to the issues on the message board with other members of other groups.
5. In a large group forum, propose solutions and agree upon some key ones.
6. Identify editors of local newspapers, public officials, and other directors of existing nonprofit organizations working to solve the same issues.
7. Students write letters and send them to appropriate people where possible.

It is important to emphasize the enormity of the problem to students. In order for them not to become discouraged, they need to understand how many people and organizations are working to solve the problem. Oftentimes, the letters to the editor written by middle school students can be idealistic, oversimplified, or too difficult to implement, but their desire to participate in the solutions to the issues outweighs this. See Table 7:10 for A Middle School Student's Letter to the Editor.

Table 7:10 A Middle School Student's Letter to the Editor

Dear Editor,

The problems concerning black youth are serious and need to be stopped. Facts regarding these issues are alarming and disturbing. Although these disconcerting impasses are being analyzed and may are attempt to stop them, at times the efforts seem futile.

A main strategy towards halting the widespread problems for black youth is to start at the source of each problem. Seeking out this source is potentially impossible due to the fact that the problems turn into a cycle, from poverty to crime; from crime to jail; from jail to poverty, etc. Factors concerning the start of the cycle are the communities in which black youth live. The communities in which black youth tend to commit crimes and flunk out of high school are urban. As a reiteration of this fact, the musical group, To quote A Star Tribune newspaper article of January 11, 2002, "Young black men who lived in Hennepin County suburbs, however, fared better than those who lived in the city." These urban communities, often referred to as ghettos, are inclined to discourage youth from attending school, especially high school. Although problems with schooling are a reaction to the problems in communities, they are no less important than any other. To even attempt to stifle the powers of these communities is to take on the communities as a whole. One cannot expect to make a difference by working little by little. The exclusive solution to this problem is to enforce drug laws, set up community centers, and create after-school activities all at once.

Schooling or the lack thereof, is as intense a problem as communities, drugs, or even poverty for that matter. Due to the large problems in communities and discouragement from going to school, 42% of black youth have been suspended at least once, and 48% never even finish high school. Among 52% who do finish high school, only 28% finish high school in four years. As horrid of a short-term effect this problem reaps, falling into a life crime, it harvests a long-term effect that seems far worse. Many of those who drop out and live a life of crime never find jobs, or a dependable source of money, increasing the issue of poverty. The only way this can be stopped is to make school appealing to youth, with more interesting classes, more after-school activities and athletic opportunities. This will encourage teens to attend their schools by giving them incentives to go.

Problems concerning black youth cannot be stopped overnight. Even so, starting at the source of the problems will hopefully help the rest sort themselves out. Although there are possibly no practical solutions that would work all the time, it does not mean that no one should try to make a difference.

Sincerely, Rutlege

Role Playing a Mock Trial

Steve Harmon is found not guilty at the end of the book, but the reader does not witness the jury deliberation process; it is left to his imagination. With a deeper understanding of the social justice issues involved in trying an accused young black man, students can role play a mock trial. According to Fink (2003), role play "offers students an experience that has significant psychological and social, as well as intellectual, dimensions" (p. 20). The students can take on the roles of different jurors. To simulate the composition of a real-life jury, students should be given fictitious people with different genres, races, and ages, as well as different biases. By coming to the jury deliberation room with a fictional bias based on genre, race, and age, as well as geographic location and social upbringing, the complexity of the issues will be further evident to the students as they contemplate Steve's innocence or guilt. See Table 7:11 for a Fictional Jury Composition.

Table 7:11 A Fictional Jury Composition

Student	Description of fictional juror
Student A	A 22-year-old white woman whose parents were Civil Rights advocates
Student B	A 60-year-old white man who grew up in the South, with a grandfather who fought in the Civil War
Student C	A 40-year-old Korean male immigrant who owns his own grocery store
Student D	An 18-year-old black man whose brother was convicted of a crime he did not commit
Student E	A 30-year-old black woman whose son was killed in a gang war

One way to help students become familiar with this deliberation process is to show the movie *Twelve Angry Men* (1990). As they watch the movie, students are instructed to observe the biases and opinions of the jurors at the onset of the movie, and analyze the ways these jurors change as they move to reach a verdict. After the movie, it is important to discuss the impact a prior bias has on one's decision making.

To prepare for their simulated jury, students think and speak from their assigned juror's point of view in a journal entry where they answer several questions, including, "What are my attitudes about race relations in the United States? What are my attitudes towards gangs? What are my attitudes about crime and the criminal justice system?"

It is important to divide the group into an inner circle and an outer circle. The outer circle watches the deliberations in order to give them feedback after they've reached a verdict. If the group is unable to reach an agreement within a set amount of time, you can take a vote. When the first group is finished, you can have them switch places.

The group discusses the process and the role of prior opinions and biases in a jury's verdict. Social justice issues that include prejudice, discrimination, racial profiling, and racism involve the variety of points of view present in a society, as well as stereotypes and biases that have increased throughout history. One of the critical components of studying the discrimination of young black men is the history of this discrimination. This is an easier task if the course is an interdisciplinary one taught in conjunction with social studies. A course that includes the history of slavery, reconstruction, and the Civil Rights movement adds to the biases students are able to create for their individual jurors. A juror whose ancestors fought for the South in the Civil War will bring a stronger negative bias toward African-American men than a Northerner who fought for civil rights. If students do not have this history, they can brainstorm supposed opinions and prejudices based on their prior knowledge on these issues.

Creating an Opinion on Affirmative Action

The history of African-Americans past discrimination and the progression of laws and its enforcement as they struggle for civil rights can also be directly related to one's opinion on the controversial issue of Affirmative Action, defined by Dan Froomkin (1998, October) from the *Washington Post* staff: "Born of the Civil Rights movement three decades ago, Affirmative Action calls for minorities and women to be given special consideration in employment, education, and contracting decisions." After writing letters to the editors about the problems for young black men with the issues of crime and violence, students can begin to discuss the positive and negative aspects of Affirmative Action. In keeping with the focus of the problem for black youth and violence, I limited the discussion to Affirmative Action's impact on black Americans, which led to a full investigation of both sides of this controversial issue.

Many students come to the issue of Affirmative Action with preconceived notions of the benefits and challenges to these acts. Others do not fully understand the issue. Students need to research both sides of the issue before forming an opinion. There are several sources on the Internet on Affirmative Action. After locating three articles with the appropriate student reading level, have students take notes in a two-column graphic organizer for pros and cons. See Table 7:12 for Sample Graphic Organizer for Debate on Affirmative Action.

Table 7:12 Sample Graphic Organizer for Debate on Affirmative Action

Pros	Cons
• Begins to make amends for systematic past discrimination of blacks	• Can be seen as reverse discrimination
• Creates a more diverse workplace or academic environment, which is a benefit to all people	• It is attempting to correct past discrimination and injustice when there are not the same levels of discrimination and injustice in the present

After students take notes, create a full-class two-column chart on easel paper and discuss each point in detail. It is important to keep students from making their final decisions until they have all of the facts. A direct connection can be drawn to the importance a juror has to listen to all the evidence and all sides of an issue before making a decision. It is important to stress the importance of opening one's mind to listen to all arguments from their classmates, especially the ones to which they disagree. See Table 7:13 for Student Opinions of Affirmative Action.

Table 7:13 Student Opinions of Affirmative Action

For Affirmative Action:
- I am pro Affirmative Action because it helps counter the well-documented unfairness against blacks by giving them opportunities for equal employment.
- Affirmative Action is good because it gives people who are disadvantaged a chance to "life, liberty, and the pursuit of happiness." Without it, they have great potential that they cannot fulfill.

Against Affirmative Action:
- Some African-Americans do not like Affirmative Action because it means that they may have been hired or accepted into college only because they are a minority.
- Affirmative Action is not fair because it is reverse discrimination.

After collecting all the data, students can participate in several activities. They can discuss the issue in a Socratic Seminar format, where they need to support each idea with text and specifics from their reading. They can prepare for a full-class debate. It will be especially interesting to assign students to the side that does not match their personal opinion. This helps them continue to consider the other side before making a final decision. Students can debate the idea on a class message board, where they are able to test out their arguments in an informal way.

Once the teacher feels the students are versed enough in the facts and the various arguments, a persuasive essay can be assigned. Students can also be required to offer alternative solutions if they argue Affirmative Action is not a viable solution to remedying past discrimination.

Readers' Theater

The Readers' Theater for this chapter, *To Tell the Truth*, is based on Myers' *Monster* and was written by Janie Reinart, Language Arts Consultant in Cleveland, Ohio. See the CD-ROM for this chapter.

Young Adult Literature for Crime and its Consequences

Bode, J., & Mack, S. (1996). *Hard time: A real life look at juvenile crime and violence.* New York: Bantam Doubleday Dell Books for Young Readers.
Cadnum, M. (1997). *Taking it.* London: Puffin.
Cooney, C. (1999). *Burning up.* New York: Delacorte.
Cormier, R. (1997). *Tenderness.* New York: Delacorte.
Fleischman, P. (1998). *Whirligig.* New York: Henry Holt.

Grove, V. (1999). *The starplace*. New York: Putnam.

Myers, W. D. (1999). *Monster*. Illustrations by Christopher Myers. New York: HarperCollins Children's Books.

Rapp, A. (1997). *The buffalo tree*. New York: HarperCollins.

Walter, V. (1999). *Making up megaboy*. New York: Delacorte.

References

Armstrong, T. (2003). *The multiple intelligences of reading and writing*. Alexandria, VA: Association for Supervision and Curriculum Development.

Canady, R. L., & Rettig, M. D. (Ed.). (1996). *Teaching in the block: Strategies for engaging active learners*. Larchmont, NY: Education.

Dresang, E. (1999). *Radical change: Books for youth in a digital age*. New York: The H.W. Wilson Company.

Fink, D. (2003). *Creating significant learning experiences*. San Francisco: Jossey-Bass.

Froomkin, D. (1998, October). "Affirmative action under attack." *The Washington Post Company*. October 1998. Retrieved on July 23, 2003, from http://www.washingtonpost.com/wp-srv/politics/special/affirm/affirm.htm.

Gardner, H. (1983). *Frames of mind: The theory of multiple intelligences*. New York: Basic Books.

Jacobs, H. H. (1989). *Interdisciplinary curriculum: Design and implementation*. Alexandria, VA: Association for Supervision and Curriculum Development.

Keene, E., & Zimmermann, S. (1997). *Mosaic of thought: Teaching comprehension in a reader's workshop*. Portsmouth, NH: Heinemann.

Mackey, M. (2001, September). The survival of engaged reading in the internet age: New media, old media, and the book. Children's Literature in Education, 32(3), 167–187.

Mauer, M. (1999, April). The crisis of the young African-American male and the criminal justice system. *The sentencing project*. Retrieved on July 21, 2003, from http://www.sentencingproject.org/pdfs/5022.pdf.

Meek, M. (1983). *Achieving literacy: Longitudinal studies of adolescents learning to read*. London: Kegan Paul.

Myers, W. D. (2000). *145th street: Short stories*. New York: Delacorte Press.

Rose, R. (1990). *Twelve angry men* (videotape). MGM/UP Home Video, Inc.

Wilhelm, J., Baker, T., & Dube, J. (2001). *Strategic reading: Guiding students to lifelong literacy 6–12*. Portsmouth, NH: Heinemann Boynton/Cook.

Chapter Eight

From Helplessness to Resilience in Caroline B. Cooney's *The Face on the Milk Carton* Quartet

Linda J. Rice

This chapter focuses on activities applicable to any of the four books in Caroline B. Cooney's quartet, beginning with *The Face on the Milk Carton* (1990). Although the books can stand alone as individually inspiring stories showing young adults moving from various states of helplessness to resilience, reading the first book often sparks students' interest in reading the three sequels. The four books are artfully constructed to build upon one another, revealing subsequent and intricate connections that entice students to read in pursuit of "what happened next?"

The Four Books

Following is a brief synopsis of the four books in the series, offered so that, as examples of student work appear in this chapter, the teacher/reader may understand how they fit contextually.

The Face on the Milk Carton

The dress, the pigtails, the face on the milk carton—15-year-old Janie Johnson recognizes them as her own, though she does not know the name Jennie Spring, and so begins her search for the truth. A series of flashbacks, the absence of a baby picture, and Janie's own sleuthing about the attic lead her to confront her "parents" with questions that have plagued her mind. Her parents, Miranda and Frank Johnson, reveal to Janie that (to their knowledge) she is actually their granddaughter, the child of their daughter Hannah Javenson, who joined a cult called Hare Krishna. Miranda and Frank took custody of Janie and changed their last name from Javenson to Johnson to avoid being found by the cult, which Hannah refused to leave.

Although at first Janie is relieved, many unanswered questions lead her to the town library, where she finds articles about the kidnapping alluded to on the milk carton. Upon figuring out that Hannah was not her mother, but her kidnapper, Janie talks her friend Reeve into traveling from Connecticut (where she has lived her life as a Johnson) to New Jersey in hopes of finding the Springs' (her biologi-cal parents) home. Janie tells Frank and Miranda Johnson that she has found the Springs, and the Johnsons are compassionate toward what the Spring family must be feeling. After much discussion and persuasion, Janie ends up calling the Springs' home phone number. Book 1 ends with Janie on the telephone saying, "Hi. It's . . . your daughter. Me. Jennie" (p. 184).

Whatever Happened to Janie?

In book 2, Janie Johnson, who is really Jennie Spring, is reunited with the family whom she was kidnapped from 12 years prior. The sequel illuminates Janie's struggle to transition from her affluent, only-child home in Connecticut to the New Jersey home, which concentrates more on putting food for seven on the table. *Whatever Happened to Janie?* expands the tensions inherent for Janie upon having moved in with her "new" parents, Mr. and Mrs. Spring, and her four sib-lings. While the twins, Brian and Brendan, were too young to have memories of their kidnapped sister, Janie/Jennie's older sister, Jodie, is disappointed by Janie/Jennie's less-than-enthusiastic response to her newfound family. Meanwhile, Janie/Jennie's oldest brother, Stephen, holds deep resentment for the way the kidnapping has affected his upbringing, in particular his parents' overprotective tendencies.

Throughout this emotional adjustment, legal matters linger. The FBI has ques-tioned the Johnsons about Hannah's history and the Springs about Janie/Jennie's disappearance 12 years earlier in a shopping mall. The FBI is searching for Hannah, who, when/if caught, will stand trial for kidnapping.

A minor, Janie/Jennie does not have the legal right to leave the Springs even though she is feeling crowded by her new home and siblings, is unhappy at her new school where she is the object of much talk, and is missing her old life. However, out of love for her daughter, Mrs. Spring drives Janie back to Con-necticut to live with the parents she knows best. Angry with Hannah, the only person Jodie and Stephen can realistically blame their life situation on, the two siblings venture to New York City, hoping to find the kidnapper in a soup kitchen and living on the streets. In their search, Jodie and Stephen meet up with a police-man who listens to their story and convinces them that they are wasting their time. "You don't need to take revenge on Hannah Javensen," he says. "Life al-ready has." Having taken this simple wisdom to heart, Jodie and Stephen return to their family that loves them, and look forward to visiting Janie in Connecticut.

The Voice on the Radio

Book 3 is about Reeve's betrayal of Janie as he tells her story, without her permission, on the airwaves all over Boston through his college radio show. Mean-while, still in high school, Janie is horrified to learn that the yearbook staff in-tends to use her story as its center feature. Janie knows that the Johnsons, already bombarded with reporters, do not want to keep rehashing the story of how their cult-driven daughter, Hannah, stole a baby 15 years ago. Janie's other family, the

Springs, continue making efforts to be part of her life, and gradually Janie begins wanting them in her life as well.

Brian, Jodie, and Janie decide to take a road trip to Boston and surprise Reeve. When they are near the campus and tune in to the radio, they hear a "janie" (the popular name attributed to Reeve's radio stories about the girl he loves). A confrontation ensues as Jodie lambastes Reeve for his despicable actions for "five minutes of fame," and Janie only speaks to him long enough to tell him that their relationship is over.

Heartbroken and ashamed, Reeve is even more disturbed by a call he received at the station from a woman claiming to be Hannah. Though later, Reeve's sister, an attorney, investigates the cult records to find a death certificate indicating that Hannah died five years earlier. As the story ensues, Janie learns about forgiveness from Mrs. Johnson, and the book closes with Janie and Reeve, home for Thanksgiving break, pulling away from the family to talk about unfinished business (and implied reconciliation).

What Janie Found

Taking over the job of paying bills because her father, Frank Johnson, is hospitalized after a stroke, Janie finds a file marked "Paid Bills" inside, which is an envelope marked "HJ." Upon opening the envelope, Janie discovers that her father has been sending money to his daughter—Janie's kidnapper—Hannah Javensen.

Meanwhile, Janie's brother Stephen has moved from New Jersey to Colorado, where he is attending college and trying to rid himself of the hardships brought about by the kidnapping. Janie learns that the checks her dad has been sending to Hannah go to a post office box in Colorado, so she devises a plan for her, Brian, and Reeve to go and visit Stephen, with her real intention being to meet her kidnapper. The visit draws Janie and Stephen close together, and Stephen, after an emotional breakdown, releases much of the hostility and resentment he has been harboring for years as a result of the kidnapping.

On the verge of sending a note to arrange a meeting with Hannah, Janie realizes that her mother, Miranda Johnson, has already won the terrible fight for custody and putting her through additional torment (the trial of her daughter Hannah) would be unfair and unkind. Janie realizes that she has not one, but two families who love her, and that is more important than drudging up the past in a search for answers from Hannah. Following Reeve's suggestion, Janie sends not only the check Hannah would be expecting, but all of the money that is in the fund. This gesture was like "paying the ransom" and putting the kidnapping behind her. Janie ponders it this way: I've been fighting "a war with one family, war with another, war with Reeve, war with myself. I even flew out here to wage war with Hannah Javensen. It's time to sign a peace treaty" (Cooney, *What Janie Found*, p. 177).

Strategies in this Chapter

The novels that make up Caroline B. Cooney's *The Face on the Milk Carton* quartet are of great interest to reluctant and advanced readers alike. The collection is fast-paced, suspense-building, and founded upon issues of sustaining interest to young adults. Yet, as issues such as independence from parents, friendship, love, and betrayal emerge and are developed with the mature sophistication and believability that are characteristic of the most capable authors, Cooney's work maintains a reading level and vocabulary that is consistently accessible to most teen readers. As a result, the books can be read independently even by the most reluctant readers, and the need for prereading activities is minimized. With a brief contextual overview of the four books in mind, the balance of this chapter focuses on a range of writing, performance, and visual learning strategies aimed at helping students to comprehend, and more deeply understand, what they read. While some of the writing assignments are designed to give students practice with traditional types of writing (expository, narrative, persuasive), others focus on students' creative expression (character poem, tanka, triolet, and sestina). All of the writing exercises are designed to draw out students' criticial thinking abilities and consider character motives and/or issues in a deliberate manner. Other activities facilitating student understanding include focus on language: a more in-depth look at how the author crafts her prose (through two Image Grammar exercises) and research of key terms (Vocabulary Sleuthing) related to kidnapping and its investigation, cults, and radio broadcasting. Practical and performance options include a Public Awareness Announcement, Talk Show Syndicate, and Poem for Two Voices. Finally, this chapter presents several "hands on" visual learning strategies to assist students in their quest for meaning making as they read the Cooney quartet. These include a Character Brochure, Semantic Web, Symbolic Writing Frame and Collage, Four-Sectioned Pyramid, and Pop-Up Story Ticket.

Frontloading Strategies to Build and Draw on Students' Background

Writing and Sketchbook Journal Prompts

As a means of introducing some of the challenges faced by the characters of the novels, the teacher will provide students with a list of writing and "sketchbook" prompts (see Table 8:1). Students could compile their responses in a spiral-bound notebook, drawing pad, or manila folder. Because some of the prompts require students to relate their own experiences, students should be given a choice about which two or three prompts they will respond to (i.e., not all prompts may be applicable to every student).

**Table 8:1 Introductory Writing and Sketchbook Journal Prompts for Each Book
in *The Face on the Milk Carton* Quartet**

The Face on the Milk Carton

1. Tell of a time when a friend or relative was acting in an unusual manner that concerned you. How did you (or could you have) help that person? Explain the outcome.

2. Make a collage of magazine pictures, photographs, clip art, words, phrases, and/or sketches that portray some of the significant people and events that have helped to shape who you are. Include a brief written explanation of your collage.

3. What if you saw your face on a milk carton, advertising you as a "missing child"—what would your thoughts and actions be? Explain the scenario.

4. Imagine learning that a close friend of yours had been kidnapped as a child. What would your thoughts and actions be? What would you be feeling as a result of this discovery?

Whatever Happened to Janie?

1. Book 1 ended with Janie calling the Springs. Write a script of the conversation as you imagine it.

2. Imagine that Janie agrees to go and live with the Springs. Write a journal entry or convey in some visual form (drawing, collage, chart of emotions, etc.) Janie's feelings upon moving from the Johnsons to the Springs. Consider what it would be like to be introduced to your "real" parents and siblings at age 15. If you choose the visual option, include a brief written explanation of its symbolic meaning.

3. Share an incident from your life that parallels something in Janie or Reeve's life.

4. In book 1, Janie moved from fear and helplessness to courage and resilience. List examples from memory of that journey, then tell of a time you made a similar move.

The Voice on the Radio

1. Tell of a time you went on a "road trip" with friends or family. Was it planned or spontaneous? Who went with you? Where did you go? What was the outcome? You may also "tell your story" in the form of a map or drawing of key experiences on the trip.

2. Has anyone ever shared (even gossiped behind your back) about personal details of your life in a way that made you uncomfortable or angry? If so, explain the incident and your related thoughts and feelings. Did the incident change your relationship or way of seeing that person? Explain.

3. Imagine that you were going to be featured on a page of the school yearbook. Make a page in your journal that would be all about you, giving particular attention to aspects of your life that you would like to be emphasized/published. Include captions for the pictures.

4. Janie's brother Brian wants to keep his love of history a secret for fear of being labeled a "nerd." Share a time when you have wanted to keep something secret for fear of being labeled.

What Janie Found

1. Book 3 ended with a caller to Reeve's radio show who claimed to be Hannah. What if Janie had answered the phone? Compose a transcript of the conversation.

2. Janie's growth in the first three books is evident. She has changed from a selfish, resentful child to a mature, respectful young adult. Discuss a similar situation, a time of personal growth and maturity, from your own life.

3. Draw a picture (or find one from a magazine) of how you envision Hannah. Then tell where you think she is and what has happened in her life since kidnapping, then giving up, Janie.

4. By looking at the picture on the cover and reading the promotional leads on the front and back covers of book 4, make some predictions (this may be in the form of a list) of what Janie found and what decisions she must make.

Vocabulary Sleuthing

Because cults, kidnapping, and ransom may be relatively new concepts to young adults, taking time to research these and other applicable terms before reading Caroline B. Cooney's *The Face on the Milk Carton* quartet will provide students with the opportunity to approach their reading with increased clarity and understanding. Table 8:2 offers a list of terms for students to investigate. If teachers have access to a library or media center, students could spend a class session there researching the terms, either individually or in pairs; otherwise, the terms could be assigned as homework. If the teacher elects to divide the list so that each student or pair of students investigates only one or two terms, he/she should make sure to allow class time for "report outs." All students should record the definitions prior to reading each novel.

Table 8:2 Vocabulary from the Caroline B. Cooney Quartet

Book 1: *The Face on the Milk Carton* (general terminology)	Book 2: *Whatever Happened to Janie?* (focus on legal terminology)
Adolescent trauma	Brainwashing
Center for Lost and Missing Persons	Counter-Surveillance
Child Custody	Domicile
Cult	Elements of a Crime
FBI	Expungement
Guinness Book of World Records	Family Law
Hare Krishna	Fraud
Heroin	Interrogations
Identity Crisis	Felony
Kidnapping	Forensics
The New York Times	J. Edgar Hoover
	Juvenile Case
	Larceny
	Liable
	Lindbergh Kidnapping
	Minor
	Prosecute
	Protection of Children from Sexual Predators Act of 1998
	Skip Tracing
	Soup Kitchens
	Uniform Crime Reports
	U.S. Department of Justice
	Warrant

cont.

Book 3: *The Voice on the Radio* (emphasis on terms related to broadcasting)	Book 4: *What Janie Found* (general terms that students may be unfamiliar with)
Airtime	Clammy, p. 34
Audience	Brawny, p. 49
Broadcast	Robust, p. 49
Campus	Desperate, p. 60
Confession	Loathed, p. 63
Dead air	Demented, p. 66
Deejay	Geode, p. 76
Drama	Intimate, p. 82
Exploitation	Adrenaline, p. 83
Fame	Coaxed, p. 89
Plea	Travelogue, p. 89
Ratings	Kidnapette, p. 105
Shock Jock	Materialize, p. 105
Syndicated	Pretenses, p. 114
	Wheatgrass, p. 122
	Impaled, p. 124
	Catapulted, p. 163

During Reading Strategies to Apply Self-Monitoring Strategies

The Reader's Eye: Seeing the Story through Expository Writing

As a way to explain what they know and understand about their reading, students' writing of expository essays gives them an opportunity to link their personal views and life experience with the novels in Caroline B. Cooney's *Face on the Milk Carton* quartet. The teacher can design—or have the students design—a number of prompts from which students may choose. Table 8:3 offers five expository prompts for students to write about while reading *The Voice on the Radio* by Sarah, and Table 8:4 shows a sample student response by Sarah. As a guideline, each essay should be from one to two pages.

Table 8:3 Expository Writing Prompts for *The Voice on the Radio*

1.	Imagine you are Janie. What would you have done when you found out that your boyfriend was telling the entire listening audience about your deepest secret? In relation to the book and its timing, tell when and how you would have responded.
2.	What irritates you the most about Reeve's actions and attitudes? Be sure to state the problem and provide specific examples of why it bothers you. Also, provide a possible solution.
3.	What is the most important thing a person should know about having a long-distance relationship and why? Relate your personal experience and that of Janie and Reeve.

cont.

4. Imagine you were Janie's sister or brother. What advice would you give her about the kidnapping situation and/or her relationship with Reeve? Explain in detail.
5. Which character in the novel can you most relate to? Why and/or how? Be sure to give specific examples to support your response.

Table 8:4 Expository Essay (Response to Prompt #3)

Long Distance Relationships

There are a lot of things a person should know about trying to have a long-distance relationship. Some of the things a person should know include the following: do not expect everything to remain the exact same; do not panic if you do not hear from that person 20 times a day; just because you cannot get a hold of your significant other, do not assume he or she is cheating on you; be ready to make compromises and sacrifices that you may not have made if it was not a long distance relationship; and finally, realize that he or she will form other relationships with people you do not know, and you should not feel guilty for doing the same.

Out of these points one should know, I feel that the most important point to remember is not always to assume that he or she is cheating on you if you cannot get a hold of him or her. The reason that I feel this is the most important thing to remember is because not trusting the other person will just push the two of you apart and lead to a major problem. I have personally been in a long-distance relationship, and that is exactly what happened. We both always thought the other was cheating, and it eventually came between us, and we split up. You have to trust in order to keep a relationship alive, and if that trust is not there, then there is no point in staying together.

In *The Voice on the Radio*, Janie and Reeve did not have this problem. That is why their relationship worked (up until Janie found out about Reeve's radio stories). When Janie went to school on lipstick day, and she got kisses from everyone, including other guys, Reeve could have gone crazy and thought that meant that Janie was cheating on him. However, he knew that Janie was just friends with her schoolmates and did not have to worry about that. If that would have happened to me at school during my long-distance relationship, my boyfriend would have thought just the opposite. He would have thought that I was cheating on him.

In conclusion, in order for a long-distance relationship to work out, there has to be trust and no assumptions that you are being cheated on from little reasons that do not matter. The only thing that will result from this is distance coming between the two of you, as well as a good chance of breaking up.

Imaginings through Narrative Writing

Just as expository writing can provide insight into what students are noticing about a book and relating to their own lives, narrative writing can help students show what they know as they imagine and describe an added scene, situation, or scenario from the Caroline B. Cooney novel they are reading. The teacher may prepare prompts for students to respond to, or the students may write their own. The prompts in Table 8:5 are for students to choose from while reading *The Face on the Milk Carton*. Table 8:6 provides a sample student response by Roxanne Sturm. As a guideline, the essays should be from two to three pages.

Table 8:5 Narrative Writing Prompts for *The Face on the Milk Carton*

1. Describe your reaction to finding a milk carton with your picture on the back that had you listed as a "missing child." Set up the scenario and describe your thoughts and actions involving your discovery. (Think about Janie's reaction.)

2. Imagine you found out that your best friend had been kidnapped as a child. Describe the situation, your thoughts about it, and the actions you would take regarding the discovery. (Think about Reeve's position in the novel.)

3. Narrate the events of a day in Janie's life as she would record it in her diary. (Build upon the events in the book.)

4. Imagine you could meet Hannah. Describe the interactions that would take place, including things you would say and questions you would ask. Also, offer insight that shows Hannah's perspective.

5. Describe a scenario involving a reunion between Janie and the Springs. Include the thoughts and emotions involved, as well as dialogue between the characters.

Table 8:6 Narrative Essay (Response to Prompt #4)

Finally Some Answers

I stared at the ceiling as I lay in bed, one thought consuming my mind: today is the day. After so many sleepless nights filled with uncertainty, I was finally going to get some answers. Today I was going to meet Hannah Javensen, the woman that kidnapped me when I was just a small child.

I lay there, paralyzed by thoughts of uncertainty, until my mom came in to tell me breakfast was ready. I forced myself to make the journey to the bathroom. I gazed at myself in the mirror as I brushed my teeth. I looked awful; my uncontrollable red hair had morphed into the shape of an overgrown afro, and my eyes had dark bags under them due to lack of sleep. I thought to myself, get a grip Janie, this is what you wanted.

By the time I got downstairs, my mom had already begun cleaning up the kitchen. A plate with two eggs, a slice of bacon, and a piece of toast sat in front of my chair next to a tall glass of orange juice; none of it looked appealing. My mom looked up from the dishes and gave me what appeared to be a failed attempt at a smile. I took my seat at the table and pushed my food around just enough to make it appear half eaten. My dad walked into the kitchen. "It's time, Janie," he said.

He drove me to the decided location: a local park big enough for privacy, but crowded enough for help if needed. My dad made small talk during the 10 minutes it took to get there. I responded with nods and smiles, but honestly all of my focus was on the digital clock counting down the minutes I had left before meeting her. Dad parked directly behind a small gazebo. There was one person sitting in the gazebo; her back was to the parking lot. That's her, I thought to myself—there's no turning back now. Dad squeezed my hand reassuringly; "I'll be right here, Janie," he said.

I made my way up to the gazebo; everything was a blur except her shiny hair glowing in the sunlight. I was so nervous, but deep down I knew I was ready. I walked into the gazebo; she looked up, and I realized how closely she resembled my mom. We stared at each other for a moment; the awkward silence was finally broken as tears welled up in her eyes and she softly whispered, "I'm sorry." I stood there, stunned by this outward show of emotions. I somehow managed to utter, "Why?"

It all came out. She was lonely and in need of love. I was adorable and talkative, thriving in her undivided attention. She told me about our traveling adventures and how much I talked about my family. It

cont.

wasn't until the cult wanted her back that she realized the consequences of her actions. She wanted to take me back to New Jersey, but she didn't know how; that was when she decided to give me to her parents as if I were her own daughter. "It was the most selfish thing I have ever done," she admitted, tears continuously streaming down her cheeks, "if I could, I would take it all back."

I didn't talk very much; I didn't know what to say. Up to this point I had felt nothing but anger towards Hannah. I saw the hurt in her eyes and felt the pain in her voice. She wasn't an evil person; she was just a lost teenager that made a mistake. Granted, the mistake had totally changed my life, but it wasn't a bad life, just different. All this time I had hated Hannah, but now all I wanted to do was hug her. I felt the tears before I even realized I was crying. We embraced, our bodies shaking with uncontrollable sobs. Suddenly, my dad was there, holding us both in the protective way that any father holds his own children.

Hannah came home with us that night. I will never forget that initial meeting. The hate is gone, and the mystery is unraveled. I know that I made the right decision in meeting Hannah. All I have left to say is face your fears, because if you don't, you might never understand the concept of true freedom.

Poetic Interludes

As students read any of the Caroline B. Cooney novels, the teacher may ask them to write poetry as a means of expressing what they are comprehending and/ or interpreting. Students might be asked to write a poem about a particular character—perhaps from that character's viewpoint—or to focus on a theme. While the teacher may desire to leave some room for free-verse and nonstructured poems, several models are offered in this section for those desiring more specific parameters.

Character Poem

The *Character Poem* begins by introducing the character's first name. Subsequent lines reveal that character's condition, personality traits, history, interests, concerns, fears, passions, etc. The poem closes with the character's last name. Table 8:7 offers two examples from *What Janie Found* by Lindsey Tucker.

Table 8:7 Character Poems

Janie Johnson	Reeve Shields
I am Janie	I am Reeve
Kidnapped Spring, pseudo Johnson	Brother of Lizzie
Lover of Reeve	Lover of Janie
Who fear betrayal	Who has to earn trust
Who hopes to discover the truth	Who fears he has lost Janie forever
Who can't escape her life	Who looks out for his friends
Which inhibits my growth	Who gives Janie the idea to unkidnap herself
Johnson	Which sets her free
	Shields

Tanka

The *tanka* is a form of Japanese poetry that uses a specific number of lines and syllables. A tanka has five lines and a 5-7-5-7-7 syllable sequence. In this brief poetic form, students reflect on a theme or event (or a combination of both). Table 8:8 shows two sample tanka written in response to *The Voice on the Radio* by Stephanie Evans.

Table 8:8 Tanka

Brian's Secret Love	Popular Deejay
My name is Brian,	Reeve Shields, how could you?
Not Brendan, he's the athlete.	Boston knows everything.
My game is the past.	Not your secrets, mine.
Thirteen years of synchrony.	Quote, "We're here. We're yours. We're sick."
History broke the sameness.	How truthful that is, Reeve Shields.

Triolet

The *triolet* is an eight-line lyric poem with repeating lines and a specified rhyme scheme. Line 1 repeats as lines 4 and 7, making its content particularly important as it serves as a kind of refrain, reiterating a key idea. Line 2 repeats as line 8, the last line of the poem. Students always like to hear that after they've written the first two lines, therefore, there are only three more lines to write (since the others are repeated)! The triolet's rhyme scheme is abaaabab. Teachers may also find it helpful to pose a question about the book, a question that will be answered in the form of a triolet. For example, the poem in Table 8:9 was in response to this question (stemming from *What Janie Found*): "How are Brian and Reeve feeling about Janie's plan to catch Hannah?" by Emily Beard.

Table 8:9 Triolet

Growing Up

Making decisions that affect her life,
Actively changing her role in the world
Situations of family strife,
Making decisions that affect her life
She thinks of love and what can suffice
Her emotions are all swirled
Making decisions that affect her life,
Actively changing her role in the world.

Sestina

Similar to the triolet's tight-knit form, resulting from its repeated line structure, the *sestina's* repeated end words provide a web-like structure, making this
poetic form particularly useful for topics suggestive of confusion or entrapment.
The sestina is an effective form for exploring the interior struggles of a character,
the issues and dilemmas that go round and round in a person's mind but seem to
have no resolve. The sestina is among the most sophisticated and challenging
poetic forms, yet its structure also provides support so that students who "don't
do poetry" have a sense of direction about what needs to be done and where the
poem is "going."

The sestina consists of six 6-line stanzas and a final *tercet* (three-line stanza),
making the entire poem 39 lines. As students write the first stanza (six lines) of
their poem, they should make sure that the last word in every line is different.
Some consideration should also be given to the ease with which the last words
can be used repeatedly throughout the poem. For instance, words like "trap,"
"family," and "show" are relatively easy to use in a variety of ways. The end
words may also be slightly changed, so long as they share the same "root." For
instance, "trap" might become "traps," "trapped," "trapping," or "untrap;" "family" might become "families" or "family's," and "show" might become "shown,"
"showing," or "showy."

After composing the first stanza of the sestina, students have a guide for the
remainder of the poem. The next five stanzas will repeat the *same last words,* but
in a different order (see pattern below).

Stanza 1	Stanza 2	Stanza 3	Stanza 4	Stanza 5	Stanza 6
A	F	C	E	D	B
B	A	F	C	E	D
C	E	D	B	A	F
D	B	A	F	F	E
E	D	B	A	C	C
F	C	E	D	B	A

Teachers may suggest that once students have written stanza 1 and know
what the end words are, students write the end words at the right hand side of the
paper for the remaining five stanzas. This helps many students in the process of
composing by signaling where each line is going. Students should also keep in
mind that just because the word appears as the last in a line does not mean it has
to be used as the last word in a thought or sentence. For instance, the end word
may—when read in the context of two or three lines of the poem—be as a word
in the middle of a complete thought or sentence.

After the students have composed the six 6-line stanzas, they are ready to
write the final tercet. The tercet uses all six end words, arranged in three lines in
the following pattern:

> E (with B somewhere in the middle of the line)
> C (with D somewhere in the middle of the line)
> A (with F somewhere in the middle of the line).

Sarah Dreitzler's sestina (see Table 8:10) provides an example of this form as it illuminates Janie's internal turmoil over being part of two families—the Johnsons and the Springs.

Table 8:10 Sestina

I am Janie Johnson

Will you remember more than my name?
When I waltz back into your life
Unannounced, unprepared, unguarded
Not ready to adopt a new family.
Will you remember my smile?
Am I ready to enter this union?

More importantly, are my parents ready for this union?
Not my birth parents, but the people who gave me my name.
The mother and father who have spent years making me smile
Who witnessed the major events of my young life
Can you stay undaunted, leave your heart unguarded?

Better yet, can you leave me unguarded?
The little girl who broke our familial union.
And traded an ice cream sundae for her family.
I forgot my life with you. I even forgot my name.
I stopped being Jennie Spring. I was given a dual life.
A life with wonderful parents, while alive in your memory was the image of my smile.

I hope you do not expect me to smile
And enter your home with my feelings unguarded.
My parents have made my life
Our family has a strong, loving union.
I don't even remember your name.
And I certainly do not accept you as my family.

I do not feel like a part of your family.
Why do you greet me with that big, sad, smile?
Why won't you call me by my name?
I'm Janie, not Jennie. That's what happens when you leave a kid unguarded.
Don't blame me for not wanting this union.
How can you expect me to trade in my parents? To exchange my life?

I am not just an item to be passed around. I'm a person with a life.
I have dreams, and fears, and strengths reinforced by my family.
I did not choose to enter this union.
I was bought by a woman with some ice cream and a smile.
I cannot leave my real family unguarded
Or enter your home and deny my real name.

I want to spend the rest of my life with the people who know my smile
The family who would never leave me unguarded.
The family who chose to let me in their union. The family who knows my name.

Poem for Two Voices

Another type of poem that helps students to express multiple perspectives is the Poem for Two Voices. Having students perform readings from Paul Fleischman's book *Joyful Noise: Poems for Two Voices* (1998) is a fun way to introduce the "how tos" of this form. Basically, there are two readers, and lines are arranged so that the person standing on the left reads the lines listed on that side, while the person standing on the right reads the other lines. Sometimes only one person is speaking; sometimes both readers say their lines in unison; still other times, both readers speak, but their differing lines make for a cacophony of sound. As the subject for their Poem for Two Voices, students should select a character or aspect of the book that demonstrates some kind of duality, tension, or difference in opinion or perspective. Sarah Kaufman's Poem for Two Voices (see Table 8:11) reveals the interior thoughts of the two biological sisters [Jennie Spring (Janie Johnson) and Jodie Spring], who have been reunited after Janie's kidnapping and are struggling with questions of identity and sisterhood. This poem was written while reading the second book of the quartet, *Whatever Happened to Janie?*

Table 8:11 Poem for Two Voices: Who Am I?

Who Am I?	
I am Janie Johnson	
	She is Jennie Spring
She is	She is
NOT	
my sister	my sister.
	We will gossip and do each other's hair
I don't need a sister,	
I am an only child.	
This is not right.	This is not right.
I	
	She
cry every night.	cries every night.
Will	Will
I	
	she
change?	change?
I am going to the dance.	She's going to the dance.
We played video games.	We played video games.
I am still not happy.	
	She is still not happy.
I am going home.	She is home.
I am a Johnson.	She is a Spring.
Am I a Spring?	She is a Spring.

How does Cooney do that? A Look at Language Patterns through Image Grammar

Examining how authors use figurative language to create vivid, imaginative, and precise writing helps students to look at a text again, in more detail, and also, hopefully, to appreciate it. This particular lesson, inspired by Harry Noden's *Image Grammar: Using Grammatical Structures to Teach Writing* (1999), focuses on *hyperbole*, the literary technique of exaggeration. To begin, the teacher will provide students with a list of hyperboles from Caroline B. Cooney's writing. Four examples are listed in Table 8:12; the teacher may want to reserve one or two of the examples for students to find, given a chapter or page range.

Table 8:12 Hyperboles from *What Janie Found*

She thought she could probably produce enough rage to power the house. She could plug the toaster into her hand and probably burn the bread with anger (p. 8)
"Calm down," said Kathleen. "You have enough adrenaline in you, you could probably reshape the bike with your teeth" (p. 23)
Six a.m. was just as early and horrible as it sounded and Kathleen's alarm clock could have been mistaken for a chain saw (p. 129)
Brian to Stephen: "You've always been the diameter of a tire iron" (p. 162)

After students have reviewed examples from the book and talked about what makes them hyperboles, they are ready to write their own, based on scenarios from the book. Teachers should emphasize that the hyperboles students write be original, not clichéd phrases the students have already heard. Sample scenarios and student examples appear in Table 8:13 by Alden Waitt.

Table 8:13 Scenarios and Student Examples of Hyperbole

Scenario 1: Janie's confusion about her identity leaves her with an uncertain feeling.
Hyperbole: Janie knew she could float through the room, unnoticed like a ghost, and no one would ever know her.
Scenario 2: Janie's brother, Brian, has not eaten in hours and has a "hollow, screaming hunger" (p. 50). He attempts to convey how hungry he is by saying:
Hyperbole: "My stomach is growling so loud it drowns out the sound of the airplane."
Scenario 3: Stephen was awed when he first saw the Colorado topography and exclaimed:
Hyperbole: "The mountains pierce the sky and will snag airplanes and clouds."

Another strategy for linking language patterns and what students know about the Cooney novel they are reading is to create new, alternate titles for the book. For this activity, also inspired by Harry Noden's *Image Grammar,* students will need to be able to differentiate parts of speech to create "grammar combinations" that reflect something important about the novel. Working in pairs or small groups, students should begin by brainstorming a list of nouns, adjectives, and adverbs related to the novel. Next, the teacher should provide examples of each of the 12 grammar combinations by Amanda James (see Table 8:14) and ask students to write their own alternative titles. Students should share their top three titles with the class and be prepared to explain what connections they made with the text that contributed to the words they chose.

Table 8:14 Grammar Combinations and New Titles for *The Voice on the Radio*

1. Possessive-Noun: *The Caller's Last Words*
2. Adjective-Noun: *Missing Airwaves*
3. Adjective-Adjective-Noun: *The One-Word Caller*
4. Noun-and-Noun: *Playtime and Let-downs*
5. Noun-of-Noun: *The Threats of a Deejay*
6. Noun-for-Noun: *Fame for a Price*
7. Prepositional Phrase: *Back on the Air*
8. Noun-Prepositional Phrase: *Screams in the Soundproof Room*
9. Infinitive Phrase: *To Interview a Killer*
10. Adverbial Phrase: *When the Sound Track Ended*
11. The-Noun-Who: *The Announcer Who Said Too Much*
12. A Command: *Tune In or Die*

Character Brochure

Glasgow (2002) suggests that creating a Character Brochure is a valuable way for students to get into the mind of a character and for teachers to check students' understanding of what they are reading. In creating the brochure, students are to include at least five pictures or drawings and at least nine paragraphs, each with a topical header, about the character. The first paragraph of the brochure should include the name and a brief description of the character. The last paragraph should focus on the character's future and goals. The topics of the remaining seven paragraphs are up to the student; however, Glasgow suggests including heroes, personality traits, "ME: In a nutshell," favorite things, pet peeves, "Little Known Facts," and baby and childhood happenings and memories. Lauren Smith's brochure (see Figure 8:1) models the format for Brendan Spring in *Whatever Happened to Janie?*

Figure 8:1 Character Brochure

Side 1 (Brochure is printed on both sides and folded in thirds)

My Hero
My hero is Michael Jordan. He is a great basketball player and I want to be just like him. I love that he can jump so high and run so fast. Michael's got game. I want to play in the NBA and do commercials just like him. That would be a lot of fun. I am a great basketball player: probably the best player on my team. I know that if I practice hard, I can be like Mike.

My Personality
I am a pretty easygoing person, like Brian, my brother. I love sports and being with my friends. I don't like school very much, but I know that if I do well, I can get scholarships for a good college where I could play sports. I'm shy around new people, like my sister Jenny, but I like people a lot. I'm a caring person. I'm very easy to get along with. Friends are probably the most important things in my life.

The Future
In the future, I want to be a professional basketball player in the NBA. I'm already really good on my own middle school team. I'd say that I am the best player on the team (but don't tell Brian I said that). If I don't become a professional basketball player, then I'd like to be a Physical Education teacher. That way I can still play sports and I could teach others how to do well and feel good about themselves.

BRENDAN SPRING

I live in a big family in a small house. There are six (or seven) of us total in a three-bedroom house. I have an older brother, Stephan, an older sister, Jodie, another older sister, Jenny, (NOT Janie), and a twin brother, Brian.

www.kent.gov.uk/e8l/Sportsdev/ basketball.html

I'm twelve years old with my twin brother, Brian, who is also my best friend. I love to play sports (especially basketball!) and I love hanging out with friends.

www.maxpages.com/sportstrivia/
Pro_Basketball_Trivia=

Side 2 (Brochure is printed on both sides and folded in thirds)

ME: in a nutshell
I am twelve years old. My best friend is my twin brother, Brian. We do everything together. It's great. My favorite things to do are hangout with friends and play sports. My favorite sport is basketball though because I am really good at it. I get pretty good grades in school but I could do better. I can't wait to be in high school. The girls are really pretty in my sister, Jodie's class.

www.twinsworld.com/babytwins/images/
copher%20twns%20-%...

My Favorites
My best friend is my brother, Brian. We understand each other better than anyone else. My favorite sport is definitely Basketball. It is really fun and I am very good at it. My favorite food is pepperoni pizza. I could eat it all day. My favorite color is blue. It reminds me of being outside.

When I Was a Baby
My sister, Jenny, was kidnapped when I was a baby, so I don't really remember her at all. My brother Brian and I have always been close since birth because we are twins. My favorite food was peaches and his was bananas. I learned to walk before Brian and I learned to throw a ball before him too. He could talk before me though.

My Childhood
It was kind of hard growing up in the Spring house. After Jenny was kidnapped, my parents became a little paranoid of all people. None of the kids in my family were ever allowed to ride the bus and my Dad had to hold our hands when he took us to school. It was so embarrassing by the time we hit fourth grade. I remember Jenny being the topic of so many conversations and I remember my parents getting really upset when we would role our eyes when they wanted to tell another Jenny story.

www.fairyhouses.com/ letters/redhead.jpg

Little Known Facts
I really do care about Jenny and I am very happy to have her home. I get shy sometimes and I'd rather not talk to her about her kidnapping because she seems scared and I am afraid to make her cry. Sometimes she says mean things to Mom and Dad like that they are not her parents and stuff. It is rude. Jodie yells at Jenny, but I never know what to say. I usually just go out and play and forget about it.

Pet Peeves
I don't like when people chew their food with their mouths open. It is gross. I also don't like people who worry too much. It gets annoying. I like to take everything as it comes. My biggest pet peeve is girls. Why are they so weird? They have to decorate things and make themselves smell like flowers. It's so weird.

After Reading Strategies to Engage Students in Ethical Thinking

A Case for "Doing the Right Thing" (Persuasive Writing)

After students have read any of the novels from *The Face on the Milk Carton* quartet, they may analyze the characters' actions through a persuasive paper. In writing a two- to four-page paper critiquing some aspect of the novel, students will have to review the text to make their argument. Table 8:15 provides sample persuasive writing prompts, while Table 8:16 provides a sample persuasive paper.

Table 8:15 Persuasive Writing Prompts for *The Voice on the Radio*

1.	Using textual evidence, make an argument for whether or not Janie should forgive Reeve.
2.	Using textual evidence, make an argument for why Janie should or should not live with her kidnapped family, the Johnsons. Your argument should also include why or why not the Springs would be a better or worse family for Janie to live with.
3.	Create an argument on whether or not Janie did the right thing by not telling her family (the Johnsons) about Reeve telling her story on the radio.
4.	Play "devil's advocate" by creating an argument that supports Reeve's decision to tell Janie's story on the radio.

Table 8:16 shows Amanda James' response to the third persuasive prompt. Note that her response begins with narrative and expository writing (strategies practiced in the During Reading section of this chapter), building a case with plenty of background information, before delivering the persuasive response and judgment about Janie's decision not to tell her parents what Reeve had done. Amanda's persuasive essay also exemplifies a text-based response, as she includes quotes throughout.

Table 8:16 Persuasive Essay (Response to Prompt #3)

Scared of silence, Reeve began. He began talking about Janie. He started the beginning of Janie's pain. The microphone was his way of connecting to the listeners, and nothing would stop him once he began, not even after knowing how hurt Janie would be. Once he got started, he just kept going, spilling every secret Janie wished he would keep.

Janie kept on believing that Reeve was the one. "She could transfer whole hours of prom memory into her future wedding" (p. 7). What she longed for was to be with Reeve, go to school with Reeve, to marry Reeve. "There was no stopping a Reeve fantasy once it took off. Now Janie saw herself keeping house on a yacht" (p. 7).

And at a moment's time, everything fell apart. Reeve's voice echoes through the speaker as Janie, Jodie, and Brian sat astonished in the hotel room. "She, Janie, was blank; a computer disk that has not been formatted" (p. 121). She could not imagine even looking at him. To Janie, Reeve was nothing but a

cont.

liar and a sell-out. A moment of panic flashes over her, and she feels fear for the first time since the whole [discovery that she had been kidnapped] began.

After Janie went back home, the thought of Reeve and what he did only made the matter worse. By not telling the Johnsons what Reeve had done, Janie felt that she could hide from the fact that Reeve had betrayed her. She only thought about what had happened when she began searching for her family, and that was the reason that the whole thing started in the first place. The amount of pride Janie showed toward Reeve in front of her family only made things more complicated. The best thing to do was to keep [Reeve's actions] to herself, praying that her parents wouldn't find out. "Janie gave her mother another hug to buy time. That, too, was awful—using a hug to hide in. Janie ached to tell her mother about Reeve. But she put her parents first" (p. 139).

Janie definitely did the right thing by not telling her parents. Things were finally getting better in their family, and Janie knew that this would make things more chaotic. The best thing for Janie to do was to ignore what Reeve had done and get over it by herself. Janie obviously didn't feel that things would be okay with Reeve ever again, even though through all of the pain, she wanted to hear his voice again. "She could not bear the thought of discarding him. Yet he, time and again, had discarded her. But I still love him, she thought" (pp. 175–176).

Reeve was wrong for telling Janie's story, and he knew that. It still didn't stop him. It didn't stop him from hurting Janie, and that caused her to lie to the Johnsons. After things finally got settled again, there was no way that Janie could tell her parents what happened, not after all they had already been through with Hannah. It would just be too much for them emotionally. Fortunately, the story ended on a good note and had Janie and Reeve talking again, so there wasn't any point to go back and tell the Johnsons what Reeve had done on the airwaves. To Janie, it was over. "If there's any hope of any love anywhere, there had to be the change to try again" (p. 182).

Public Awareness Announcement

Knowing where to get help is an essential part of finding solutions to many of life's problems. Public Awareness Announcements on an array of issues from Smoking, Depression, and Substance Abuse to Physical Assault, HIV Testing, and Parenting have been designed to reach out through the air waves and offer assistance to those in need. With this activity, students consider an issue related to the Caroline B. Cooney novel they are reading and turn it into a Public Awareness Announcement. If desiring to expand the realm of options for this project, the teacher may invite students to choose "any" social issue they find to be of importance. Teachers may also want to support students' research effort by taking them to a library or media center. After researching their topic, students are to create a slogan to inform the public of the issue. They will then arrange the slogan with other text and graphics to make a poster (or standard 8 ½ x 11 in paper) featuring the issue of their Public Awareness Announcement. Figure 8:2 provides Stephanie's example focused on Child Safety Awareness, an issue directly related to the Cooney quartet.

Figure 8:2 Public Awareness Announcement

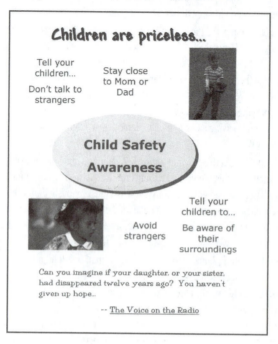

Talk Show Syndicate

Working collaboratively (groups of three to five work well), students will choose a researchable topic related to the Caroline B. Cooney novel they have been reading. Topics might include, but are not limited to: cults, kidnapping, soup kitchens, the allure of being a deejay, and/or dealing with betrayal. Students will integrate their research into their Talk Show Syndicate script, which may be videotaped or performed live in front of the class in the style of *Oprah* or *David Letterman;* students should note, however, that the tone of their talk show should suit the content and seriousness of the subject matter they are presenting. To add a layer of complexity to this assignment, students are to "think like directors." That is, they are to prepare the script with Audio notes on the right side of their paper and Video notes on the left side (see Figure 8:3) by Ben Antonini, Melisa Bushong, Lindsey Tucker, and Alden Waitt. Terms students need to know are as follows: ECU (extreme close-up), CU (close-up), MS (middle shot), WS (wide shot), and for navigating from shot to shot, CUT, DISSOLVE, PAN, Z/I (zoom in), Z/O (zoom out). Those wanting more elaborate instruction on camera shots, interview shows, and television productions should consult Rod Fairweather's (1998) *Basic Studio Directing*, a user-friendly, beginner-level media manual filled with terminology and examples.

Figure 8:3 Talk Show Syndicate Director Notes and Script

DAVID LETTERMAN INTERVIEW WITH JANIE

VIDEO	AUDIO
CU: DAVID	**DAVID**: You were kidnapped as a young child, raised by another family, and grew up believing the people you were living with were your true parents. Could you tell everyone how you found out about your history (being kidnapped)?
CUT TO WS: DAVID AND JANIE CUT TO CU: JANIE	**JANIE**: I found a picture of me as a little girl on a milk carton as a missing child. I called the number and told them it was me. Then, I flew out to meet my real family.
CUT TO WS: DAVID AND JANIE	**DAVID**: What was it like to meet your real parents/family?
CUT TO CU: JANIE CUT TO ECU: JANIE	**JANIE**: It was difficult meeting my real family because it has been so many years and I now have brothers and sisters I never knew I had. The living situation was hard to transition. My real family is working middle-class and work hard for their money. My surrogate parents are wealthy and don't think twice about buying anything. It was an adjustment to live with my real family. Plus, I went from only having parents to having brothers and sisters.
DISSOLVE TO VLS: JANIE, PSYCHIATRIST, AND FBI AGENT Z/I TO MS: JANIE	**DAVID**: The Johnson's did not know you were kidnapped right? **JANIE**: That's right. Hannah, their real daughter, kidnapped me and told her parents I was her daughter. They took me in and raised me. Hannah vanished one day and the Johnson's changed their last name and raised me as their child.
CUT TO WS: DAVID AND JANIE	**DAVID**: Did you ever try to find Hannah?
CUT TO MS: JANIE	**JANIE**: Yes! There have been many attempts, but none have been successful. She's still out there somewhere!
CUT TO MS: DAVID	**DAVID**: This must have been difficult for you to find out. What do you plan to do now?
CUT TO MS: JANIE	**JANIE**: It has been difficult. But I recently took a trip to Colorado to see my brother, Stephen, and we plan on visiting more often. I hope to be part of both families. I will live with my surrogate parents, but visit my real family often!

Page 2 of the group's "David Letterman Interview with Janie" explores Janie's resilience as another Letterman guest, Janie's counselor "Carla," talked about how Janie had transitioned from a life of lies and loneliness to a life of trust and recovery. Janie has also moved from "reexperiencing the event [and] avoidance of things associated with the [kidnapping]" to a healthier, future-oriented outlook that is promising both socially and occupationally. Page 3 shows the group's research as "Agent Laura Wilcox" is invited to the show. David asks, "What are the statistics of missing kids in the U.S.?" The camera cuts to a close-up of Laura, who answers, "There are 3,200 to 4,600 nonfamily abductions a year . . . 80%–90% of persons reported missing in 2000 were juveniles! The number of missing persons reported to law enforcement in 2000 increased 468% since 1982. There are three types of kidnappers: relative (49%), acquaintance (27%), and stranger (24%)." The show continues, and more research unfolds through the script. Then the last page of the script is a reference page documenting where the information was found (<findingmissingkids.com/shocking.htm>).

Semantic Web

Designing a *semantic web* is an effective strategy for prompting students to "see the big picture" of a story, identify an important theme from the novel, and visually develop that theme by offering supporting examples from the text. This activity could also take place during the reading of the novel, but waiting until after students have finished the novel makes this an ideal way to review essential plot elements and to see what themes students drew from their reading. The semantic web may be approached individually or in small groups; one advantage of small groups, of course, is the increased dialogue and deliberation that goes into choosing the key word and searching for text evidence to support the choice as relevant.

To begin, the students will choose a key concept, theme, essential word, or symbol from the book and write it on the center of a sheet of paper or posterboard. The word at the center of the web is most crucial because it, in effect, channels all future choices in completing the project. Next, students will link characters, ideas, and examples from the book to the key word. The web should demonstrate a conceptual understanding of links; to facilitate this, students should use shapes, colors, and/or layers in a deliberate fashion. The web should be broad enough to convey (or facilitate an oral presentation about) elements of plot from beginning to end and deep enough to illuminate a particular perspective, struggle, emotional analysis (of character), or other aspect of complexity from the book. Finally, students will include pictures and quotes. As a guideline, a well-developed semantic web consists of at least two to three layers, not counting the center word (see Figure 8:4 for an example by Maria Apostolou, Jeness Duffy, Roxanne Sturm, and Kelly Yambor, or view in color on the CD-ROM for this chapter). The center word should be significant enough thematically that at least four subdivisions stem from it; then, each of those subdivisions should have two or more supporting pieces of evidence (examples from the book, quotes, related descriptive words, etc.). If time does not exist for students to share their webs in class, teachers may find it beneficial to assign a one-page paper, where students discuss the organizational strategies they employed to develop their key concept, theme, essential word, or symbol, and why it was chosen.

In developing the theme of "Identity," as found in Caroline B. Cooney's *The Face on the Milk Carton*, the students who created the semantic web explored Janie's struggle from first seeing her face on the milk carton and feeling scared and helpless to seeking out the truth, having Reeve drive her to the Springs' house, confronting her parents with what she had learned, and ultimately choosing to call the Johnson family—the one she had been kidnapped from years earlier. Janie's move from helplessness to resilience through reflection and action is an imbedded theme throughout the quartet of novels. Other key words that students have effectively linked with this concept in developing their semantic webs are:

Belonging, Coming of Age, Disappointment, Emotional Growth, Forgiveness, Liberation, Love and Friendship, Loyalty, Relationships, Secrets, Transitions, and Trust.

Figure 8:4 Semantic Web

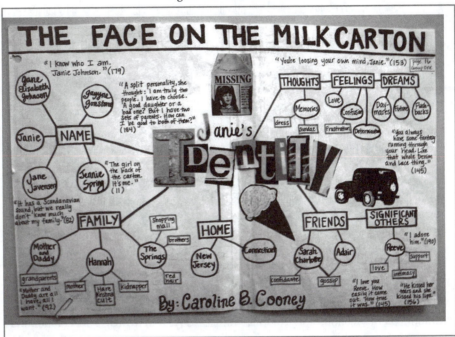

Symbolic Writing Frames and Collage

As a way to help students consider a characters in an in-depth fashion, they first complete 10 writing frames such as: "If _____ were an *object*, he or she would be _____ because _____." This writing frame was originally designed for creating images for a Coat of Arms (Olson & Schiesl, 1996), but in this activity, students will complete the writing frame and then create a collage. They will focus on one character for all 10 frames as a way of maximizing their knowledge of that character; the character's name goes in the first blank. Blanks 2 and 3 show the student's choice of *whatever is in italics* and the rationale. What follows "because" is particularly important, as this is where students demonstrate what they really know about the character and the text as a whole. Table 8:17 provides several examples for Stephen, from *What Janie Found* by Adam Remnant.

Table 8:17 Symbolic Writing Frames

1. If <u>Stephen</u> were an *object*, he would be <u>an airplane ticket</u> because <u>he escapes from his family</u>.
2. If <u>Stephen</u> were a *word*, he would be <u>distance</u> because <u>he keeps distance between himself and his family</u>.
3. If <u>Stephen</u> were an *emotion*, he would be <u>ambivalent or torn</u> because <u>he misses his family but tries to avoid them</u>.
4. If <u>Stephen</u> were a *day of the week*, he would be <u>Friday</u> because <u>he's always looking for satisfaction in the future</u>.
5. If <u>Stephen</u> were a *color*, he would be <u>gray</u> because <u>he is a confusing character with different elements</u>.
6. If <u>Stephen</u> were a *song*, he would be <u>"There is a Mountain" by Donovan</u> because <u>he goes back and forth with his feelings toward Kathleen, who he climbs mountains with</u>.
7. If <u>Stephen</u> were an *animal*, he would be a <u>wolf</u> because <u>he can get very angry and aggressive, but can also act more like a kind dog</u>.
8. If <u>Stephen</u> were a *plant*, he would be a <u>spider plant</u> because <u>he stretches himself across the country</u>.
9. If <u>Stephen</u> were a *season*, he would be <u>fall and spring</u> because <u>he leaves his family like the leaves, but will return</u>.
10. If <u>Stephen</u> were a *time of day*, he would be <u>2:00 p.m.</u> because <u>he is always stuck in the middle of Janie's past and his own future</u>.

Other suggested frames (words in italics) are: actor, animal, appliance, book, car, color, day of the week, drink, emotion, food, magazine, movie, musical instrument, plant, season, song, sport, time of day, and word. The teacher may write the basic "writing frames" on the board or prepare them in a handout for each student.

Figure 8:5 Collage

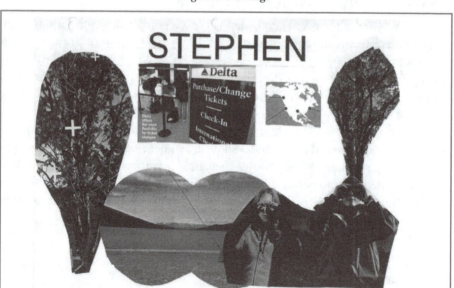

After students complete the writing frame, they are to select at least three lines and represent them visually in the form of a collage (see Figure 8:5 for an example by Adam Remnant) focused on their chosen character, then write a paper (see Table 8:18 for Adam's collage explanation) synthesizing the writing frames, collage, and text.

Table 8:18 Collage Explanation

I chose Stephen [as the focus of my Symbolic Writing Frames] because he is one of the more complex characters in *What Janie Found*. He is conflicted in many ways. He misses his family, but also tries to run away from them at the same time. I tried to illustrate this in my writing template and transfer those thoughts into my collage.

One thing that I put in my writing template was this: "If Stephen were a season, he would be fall and spring because he leaves his family like the leaves fall from the tree during autumn, but he will return to his family like the leaves do in the spring." Even though Stephen tries to run away from his family because of the problems they have had in the past with Janie's kidnapping, it is clear that Stephen still has an emotional attachment to them. When Stephen is in Colorado he sees a family restaurant, and Cooney describes his reaction: "In that moment, Stephen wanted his sister and his brothers and mother and father so fiercely it felt like a heart attack" (p. 16). I represent this in my collage by putting a tree with autumn leaves on the left and a tree with spring leaves on the right.

I also tried to represent Stephen's running away through the airport picture, which has a sign for where people buy tickets. I thought an airplane ticket was a good symbol of how Stephen escapes by putting distance between himself and his family. I also tried to show the locations pointed out [New Jersey and Colorado]. Stephen has trouble coping with his family being so confusing because of their past, and this confusion is complicated even more through different parts of the family living in different parts of the country. Finally, I included the picture of Stephen and Kathleen in order to show how he spent time with her in the mountains. I thought it was good that she had binoculars, too, because she was always peering into things, especially wanting to know details about Janie. This complicated things for Stephen because his whole reason for moving west was to put that behind him.

A close look at Adam's Collage Explanation shows that he included four concepts from his Writing Frame (fall and spring, an airplane ticket, distance, and ambivalence). Additionally, his explanation models specific references to the text and reveals the meaning and choices behind the pictures on the collage. Collectively, the Symbolic Writing Frames, Collage, and Explanation also reveal Stephen as a character who struggles from a sense of helplessness, a victim of his protective parents, to resilience, moving away, and seeing his family anew.

Four-Sectioned Pyramid

The Four-Sectioned Pyramid is a hands-on, creative way for students to show what they learned from the text. The Pyramid sections may explore themes, different characters' perspectives, conflicts and resolutions, pivotal points of plot, important settings, etc. To build the pyramid, students will need to follow these four steps: 1) Make four squares from typing paper or construction paper (approximately 8 ½ x 11 in), 2) Fold each square diagonally two times, 3) Cut one of the corners (only one!) to the center of the square, and 4) Fold one fourth of the paper under another one fourth (making a single pyramid) and attach with glue or tape. Students will repeat this process for each of the four squares of paper, then fit the sections together (back-to-back) to make a Four-Sectioned Pyramid. Once the structure is complete, students combine their knowledge of the book, logic, creativity, and organizational skill to explore important aspects of the novel.

Melisa Bushong's Four-Sectioned Pyramid (see Figure 8:6 or view in color on the CD-ROM for this chapter) explored Janie's struggles with betrayal and love through the Johnson and Spring families.

Figure 8:6 Four-Sectioned Pyramid

In Melisa's Four-Sided Pyramid, the blue section represents the Springs, showing how their world was consumed with the kidnapping of their daughter, Jennie. This brought police to the house and impacted all of the Spring children. The yellow section shows the comparative stability of the Johnson family, depicted by pictures of a bride and groom and an older couple. The pink section represents Janie's quest for love and friendship. In presenting her work, Melisa talked about Janie's romantic love for Reeve, as well as her dream of marrying and having children with him one day (depicted by the baby pictures on the pyramid), and of Janie's friendship with Sarah-Charlotte. Finally, the red square represented how Janie was betrayed. The two maps represent the homes of the Springs and Johnsons, tearing Janie apart. The word "secret" appears on a box, while a folder marked "HJ" reminds the reader of how Frank Johnson wrote checks to Hannah, his daughter who kidnapped Janie. The plane represents Janie's plan to fly west, find Hannah, and seek resolution, while the island represents Janie's desire to get away from it all. The radio, of course, depicts Reeve's betrayal of Janie, as he broadcast her story, without her knowledge, over the Boston airwaves. The centerpiece of this section consists of a broken heart and a clip art comic saying, "Is anyone out there listening?" Janie so wanted to be heard, so wanted to trust. Only after a long and intense journey, gaining strength by confronting truths, could she find trust, security, and love again.

Pop-Up Story Ticket

This hands-on activity helps students to create a visual representation of some important aspect of the story. When closed, the pop-up looks like a ticket (with a concept word); when opened, the pop-up extends words and pictures related to the particular concept. The teacher may elect to hole-punch the top of the tickets and hang them from the ceiling as mobiles. To make a Pop-Up Story Ticket, students will follow these steps: 1) Take a sheet of construction paper (preferably starting with an 11 in x 14 in construction paper cut down to 8 in x 14 in; this sizing makes the pop-up look more like a ticket) and fold it in half, 2) Crease both sides into triangles (approximately two inches in on each side) and fold them into the middle of the ticket, and 3) With the ticket open, attach pop-ups to the corner of each triangle (see Figure 8:7 or view in color on the CD-ROM for this chapter). The pop-ups must be facing toward the center of the inside of the ticket, so that they do not stick out when the ticket is closed.

With the structure complete, students decorate it, so as to explore some important aspect of their Caroline B. Cooney novel. The example in Figure 8:7 shows Melisa Bushong's portrayal of Janie's two families: the one she has grown up with and the one from which Hannah kidnapped her.

Figure 8:7 Pop-Up Story Ticket

Outside of Story Ticket	Inside (pop-up) of Story Ticket

Evident in the pictures on the inside of the ticket is the contrast between the Johnsons (left side) and the Springs (right side). Whereas the Johnson family has raised Janie as an only child in a nice home with plenty of money, the Springs have four other children and struggle to make ends meet financially. The apples and oranges represent the different lives Janie would experience living in Connecticut with the Johnsons versus New Jersey with the Springs. While tempted to place fiscal privilege and her familiarity with "only child" living ahead of getting to know a "new," less affluent family, Janie realizes that there is more to life than material worth. In presenting her Pop-Up Story Ticket, Melisa was able to explore not only the factual difference between two families, but Janie's heartfelt discovery, highlighting her movement from despair and betrayal to hope and truth. Examples of a multigenre paper and Readers' Theater as additional after reading strategies appear on the CD-ROM for this chapter.

Concluding Remarks

Throughout her quartet of novels, beginning with *The Face on the Milk Carton*, Caroline B. Cooney affirms young adults' ability to face serious challenges and triumph. Whether analyzing Brian's ability to turn his love of history from a secret to a mark of pride, Stephen's move west to "escape" family—only to realize he valued them after all, Reeve's hard lesson about not betraying a person's trust, Jodie's patience in attaining the relationship she wanted with her sister, or Janie's quest for truth, students have multiple ways to envision teen determination and victory through Cooney's novels. This is especially evident in the protagonist, Janie, who ultimately, through her painstaking effort to learn the truth, gets to know the Springs and deal with her kidnapping by paying off Hannah, and, in effect, "unkidnapping" herself, comes to the realization that she has two families whom she deeply loves.

> "My family, she thought [in reference to the Springs]. These people
> I'm just getting to know are my family. What are any answers worth
> when you can just go get a pizza with your own family instead? . . . I
> found the right thing to do [paying off Hannah]. I found the way home"
> (Cooney, *What Janie Found*, p. 164, p. 181).

Whether students read one book in the series or all four, the activities in this chapter are designed to make their understanding visible, while dealing with a vital life concept: overcoming obstacles to move from helplessness to resilience.

Young Adult Literature

Cooney, C. B. (1990). *The face on the milk carton.* New York: Bantam Doubleday Dell.

Cooney, C.B. (1993). *Whatever happened to Janie?* New York: Dell Laurel Leaf.

Cooney, C. B. (1996). *The voice on the radio.* New York: Bantam Doubleday Dell.

Cooney, C.B. (2000). *What Janie found.* New York: Dell Laurel Leaf.

References

Dixon, F. W. (1988). *Cult of crime.* Madison, WI: Demco Media.

Fairweather, R. (1998). *Basic studio directing: Media manual.* Oxford, UK: Focal Press.

FindMissingKids.com. Retrieved on March 3, 2003, from http://findmissingkids.com/shocking.htm.

Fleischman, P. (1988). *Joyful noise: Poems for two voices.* New York: HarperCollins.

Glasgow, J. (2002). *Standards-based activities with scoring rubrics: Middle and high school English. Volume 1: Performance-based portfolios.* Larchmont, NY: Eye on Education.

Goodnough, D. (2000). *Cult awareness: A hot issue.* Berkeley Heights, NJ: Enslow.

Keslo, M. J. (1988). *Abducted!* New York: Markel.

Long, D. *Kidnapped.* Retrieved on March 3, 2003, from http://duncanlong.com/science-fiction-fantasy-short-stories/kidnap.html.

Monte, D. P. (2002). *Trustworthy.* Dayton, OH: Oakwood.

Nasaw, J. (1993). *Shakedown street.* New York: Delacorte Press.

Nixon, J. L. (1999). *The kidnapping of Christina Lattimore.* New York: Bt. Bound.

Noden, H. (1999). *Image grammar:Using grammatical structures to teach writing.* Portsmouth, NH: Heinemann Boynton/Cook.

Olson, C. B., & Schiesl, S. (1996, Spring). A multiple intelligences approach to teaching multicultural literature. *Language Arts Journal of Michigan, 12*(1), 21–28.

Pascale, F. (1992). *Kidnapped by the cult (sweet valley high, no. 82).* New York: Bantam.

Patneaude, D., Micich, P., & Mathews, J. (1993). *Someone was watching.* Morton Grove, IL: Albert Whitman.

Pinkwater, J. (1987). *The disappearance of sister perfect.* New York: E. P. Dutton.

Porterfield, K. M. (1995). *Straight talk about cults.* Retrieved on March 3, 2003, from http://www.FactsonFile. com.

Roybal, L. (1994). *Billy.* Boston: Houghton Mifflin.

Sebestyan, O. (1995). *The girl in the box.* New York: Bantam Starfire.

Snyder, Z. K. (1985). *Famous Stanley kidnapping case.* New York: Yearling.

Thesman, J. (1990). *Rachel Chance.* Boston: Houghton Mifflin.

Waddell, M., & James, R. (1997). *Kidnapping of Suzy Q.* London: Chadwick.

Werlin, N. (2001). *Locked inside.* New York: Laurel Leaf.

Chapter Nine

Struggles with Poverty, Teen Pregnancy, and Workplace Harassment in Wolff's *Make Lemonade*

Linda J. Rice and Joyce Rowland

One out of four individuals (25%) under the age of 18 was living in poverty in the United States in 1996 (Center for the Study of Poverty, Columbia University)

Jolly tells LaVaughn a story about an old, blind woman and her orange. She explains that the woman was walking home with her orange to feed her starving children, when a group of boys tripped her. She fell on the ground and cut her face, and one boy helped her to her feet and handed the old woman her orange with her cane. When she returned home, she realized that the boy had replaced her orange with a lemon. Instead of getting upset, the woman used the lemon and some old, caked sugar to make lemonade for her children (Wolff, pp. 171–173). *Make Lemonade* (1993) by Virginia Wolff is about fighting for what you want. All characters in this novel are striving to be something better, to accomplish whatever their goals may be. Both Jolly and LaVaughn worked hard to make the most of what they had, and they did it together. Even Jeremy looks forward to tomorrow, always hoping that his lemon plant will grow. This book concentrates on learning life lessons, coming of age, finding friendship, remaining loyal, overcoming problems, dealing with emotions, making sacrifices, and parenting. The moral of the story is simple and complex at the same time: When life hands you lemons, you've got to make lemonade! (Excerpts are woven from student papers by Brenna Clark, Sarah Keenan, and Melissa Hargett.)

While the issue of poverty remains a social concern for American legislators and citizens, individuals living in poverty still have to cope with their lives and find ways to survive. In *Make Lemonade*, the author addresses the issue by removing the racial and geographic indicators from her novel so that she can focus on the individual choices of her characters and the power of relationships. LaVaughn, the 14-year-old protagonist, is determined to go to college—even though no one in her family ever has—as a way of escaping the poverty of her neighborhood. As such, she accepts a babysitting job with Jolly, a teen mother of two young children. Abused as a child, Jolly lived in a box under the freeway. The children's fathers abandoned her. She has been beaten for trying to escape gang life, is sexually harassed at work, and then fired from her low-paying job. LaVaughn sympathizes with Jolly and the children, and ends up babysitting for free until she realizes that both of them need to make better personal choices in order to succeed. Jolly must become more self-reliant, and LaVaughn must find a way to make money to go to college. Through the strong bond of friendship, the girls help each other make responsible decisions and find the resources needed to improve their quality of life. While using this novel as a basis to discuss the problems of poverty that many teens face, we also wanted to be able to help our students become positive thinkers and decision makers about their own situations. In short, when life gives our students lemons, we want them to be able to "make lemonade."

Make Lemonade provides many themes from which the reader can draw lessons. Themes of poverty struggles, teenage pregnancy, parenting choices, sexual harassment in the workplace, and the importance of education are at the forefront of this novel. Another benefit of this book is that while its simplistic, conversational wording is easily read by low-level readers, its poetic style adds a beauty and flow that makes it appealing to advanced readers as well. Although students' reading of the book alone may not provide sufficient understanding for full-fledged discussion, the carefully planned reading strategies presented in this chapter are sure to generate students' interest and enhance their comprehension. As Lois T. Stover (2003) points out in her article, "'Mind the Gap:' Building Bridges between Adolescent Readers and Texts," the teacher's role is to stimulate the students to make connections to their own lives and experiences, or to "'mind the gap' between their world and that of the literary works we present" by building bridges (p. 83). The following suggestions for prereading, during reading, and postreading activities provide a foundation that will facilitate open discussion of these issues and establish a clearer understanding of the book as it relates to each student's life. See Table 9:1 for Reading and Writing Strategies for *Make Lemonade*.

Table 9:1 Reading and Writing Strategies in *Making Lemonade*

Strategy	Set Purpose	Prior Knowledge	Make Predictions	Critical Thinking	Asking Questions	Visualizing the Text	Making Connections	Main Idea	Compare Contrast
Setting the Mood	•	•	•	•				•	•
Making Lemonade	•	•		•	•	•	•	•	•
Tea Party	•	•	•	•	•	•	•	•	•
Writing the Story		•	•	•	•	•	•	•	•
Workplace Harassment		•	•	•	•	•	•	•	•
Guest Speaker	•	•	•	•	•	•	•	•	•
Choices and Consequences	•		•				•	•	•
Coffee House Poetry Slam	•	•	•	•	•	•	•	•	•
Poem in Two Voices	•	•	•	•	•	•	•	•	
Survey of Social Issues	•	•	•	•	•	•	•	•	•
Letter to Author	•	•	•	•	•	•	•	•	•
Readers Theater	•	•	•	•	•	•	•	•	•
Timeline	•	•	•	•	•	•	•	•	
Discussion Grid	•	•	•	•	•	•	•	•	•
Response Paper	•	•	•	•	•	•	•	•	•

Frontloading Strategies to Establish a Purpose in Learning

Setting the Mood with Dr. Seuss

This focus activity begins as the teacher asks the students to have paper and pencil on their desks and introduces Dr. Seuss' book, *Oh, the Places You'll Go* (1990), asking students to listen to the story not as children, but as young adults ready to go out into the world. Before reading the book aloud, the teacher instructs the class to be prepared to write down at least three lines, or partial lines, that seem interesting or that catch their attention upon hearing.

The teacher should provide a strong, animated reading of the book and take time to show the pictures to the students. Upon completion, ask the students to consider the lines they wrote down while responding to the following questions in a one-page journal entry:

- Why would your English teacher be reading you this book, an elementary book?
- What message do you think Dr. Seuss was trying to give to you, a middle or high school student?

Rather than grading this assignment, the teacher should collect the papers and read through them, highlighting one sentence that stands out from each paper, for example: "The future is a good place, though it takes some doing to get there;" "It's about adventure and fun and the challenges we will face on the way to being successful;" "Things can be wild and crazy, totally exciting, full of color and people; when you work hard, it pays." The next day, the teacher should begin the class by reading through all the one-liners without revealing the authors. The resulting exposé is a positive way to begin a class as students listen attentively to hear what the teacher pulled from their written reflections. This activity is an effective means of helping students to think about their own future, and how they may even go about making dreams become realities through goal setting. This parallels the vision of LaVaughn, the protagonist students will soon be introduced to in *Make Lemonade*.

Making Lemonade

In preparation for this prereading activity, the teacher will need to obtain the following items: 8 lemons, at least 4 cups of sugar, 2 pitchers, 2 lemon juicers, cups (2 for each student in the class), and potting soil. The teacher should slice one or two of the lemons into small bits, allow each student to taste one of the bits, and record on the board words and phrases that the students use to describe their tasting experience. After sprinkling sugar on the lemons, the teacher asks the students to taste the lemons, and again records their descriptive phrases. The teacher or a student will squeeze the remaining lemon halves onto the lemon juicer to make lemonade. The recipe requires 3 whole lemons and 1$\frac{1}{4}$ cup of sugar for 2 quarts of lemonade. As students drink the lemonade, they are to write a free-verse poem (see Table 9:2 for an example) to share with the class. After writing their poems, students can rinse the seeds off and plant them in the potting soil that has been put in cups, making sure to water lightly. In closing, the teacher facilitates a discussion with the students about whether or not the seeds will grow.

Table 9:2 Example of Free-Verse Poem (while drinking lemonade)

Making and Drinking Lemonade
By Tiwanda Johnson

Tipped on both ends and cut in two
Light juice and pulp over the squeezer

Yellow and bright
Yellow and smooth
A ripe lemon is sour—
and sweet?

My mouth starts to water
Before the juice falls

Juice touching my tongue
My lips pucker in

Little seeds
So white and soft
Oh, how you make a lemon so juicy!

Scoops of sugar
White, fine, and granular
Oh, how you make a lemon so sweet!

Yellow and bright
Yellow and smooth
With a little help from sugar
You are sour <u>and</u> sweet!

Tea Party

The "Tea Party" activity is used to frontload meaning when introducing the novel. This activity is based upon the ideas of Sue Perona, South Coast Writing Project and the University of California—Santa Barbara, described by Kylene Beers in *When Kids Can't Read, What Teachers Can Do* (2003).

In this activity, all students are given a different snippet of lines (from early chapters in the book) from which they try to piece together the setting, characters, point of view, tone, and conflicts of the book. Xerox the first chapter and cut into Tea Party Snippets from *Make Lemonade*; each student will need one snippet. The teacher will then explain to the students that at a tea party, people mingle and visit, rather than just sit in one spot. While visiting with one another, students' goals are to find out anything they can about the book. The mingling in the class should begin in groups of two or three. Next, the groups of two or three should merge into groups of four to six. This merging should continue until the class is basically in one big group. That is when the teacher knows the open house is over and then asks the students to be seated.

Use the board or overhead to write down information that the students have discovered. The teacher, as discussion leader, should ask for information on setting, recording the students' answers. Then, do the same for characters, point of view, tone, and conflicts. By this time, the students have enough knowledge—and hopefully enough curiosity—to begin reading.

Writing the Story (Predictions about *Make Lemonade*)

According to research done by Denner & McGinley (1992) of the University of Michigan, the most effective way to get students to comprehend and remember what they have read is to have them actually write their own story based upon their own predictions of what will happen next after having read a portion of it. With that in mind, have the students read only to the end of chapter 10 (24 pages) in *Make Lemonade*. Then, ask them to write their own stories, based on what they know so far.

While some students predict that LaVaughn's mother makes her quit the babysitting job, leaving Jolly without assistance and befalling a tragedy for her and her children, others believe that the father of Jolly's children comes back and wants to be involved in the childrens' lives—some even predicting that the two marry, find "good jobs," and make a comfortable life for the kids. Still others, already showing some insight into the way social services work, predict that Children's Services are called about Jolly's home, see the filth of it, and take Jilly and Jeremy away. Most story endings are not without hope, however, as students tend to write about Jolly "cleaning up her act" and finishing school, so she can obtain a job and "get her kids back." Other predictions revolve around Jolly and LaVaughn developing a close friendship and going to college together.

Students should share their stories in class—either by reading aloud to the whole class or as divided into small groups. Asking students to consider their cause and effect thinking and to analyze why they think the story will have a particular outcome offers insight into what they comprehend, notice, and find to be important as they read. In addition to reviewing what they know about the text, the time of sharing and related discussion provides an opportunity for students to creatively extend their thinking. Sometimes, students' predictions are informed by their own life experience or that of friends, relatives, acquaintances, and/or other books they have read and/or films they have seen. Teachers may choose to make this a point of emphasis during discussion to demonstrate how past experience informs our ability to make predictions. In closing, the teacher should ask the students to keep their stories in mind as they read *Make Lemonade* and compare their predictions with the outcome of Wolff's novel.

During Reading Strategies to Understand Complex Social Issues

Workplace Harassment (Research Activity)

Following the reading of chapter 25 (Part I), ask students to do some research on sexual harassment in the workplace. If the school has a computer blocking service, students will need to look up "harassment in the workplace" rather than sexual harassment. Each student should bring to class one Internet article and one book or magazine article about sexual harassment in the workplace. Among their findings, students might present the definition of sexual harassment, forms of sexual harassment, the differences between Quid Pro Quo Harassment and a Hostile Work Environment, relevant court cases, and disturbing statistics surrounding this problem. While a number of basic terms and facts may be found on sites advertising the services of any of the myriad of discrimination attorneys (which are some of the first to appear when conducting a basic Internet search of the topic), more in-depth information—and court rulings—will appear by encouraging students to read articles from online law reviews. An easy way to find these articles is to go to www.askjeeves.com and type in "law reviews." When the professional links appear onscreen (from Duke, Florida State, Georgetown, New York University, Stanford, University of Akron, and many others), click on the site, then type "sexual harassment" in the "search" box. Specific articles will appear that explore definitions and link historic court rulings with contemporary issues related to the subject. After students have surveyed some of the information about harassment in the workplace, have them verbally express two things they learned from their research. Logically, discussion and points of clarification may follow.

Guest from Children's Services Agency

Invite a guest speaker from the county Children's Services Agency. Ask the students to come prepared with three questions each for the agency worker, and then allow time for students to ask questions. In advance, explain to the workers that they should be prepared to speak about when and why children are removed from their home, how welfare works, and how long a person can be on welfare.

Jolly and LaVaughn's Choices and Consequences (Flowchart Analysis)

Provide students with one or both of the choice and consequence flowcharts shown in this section in Figure 9:1. Students may work collaboratively on this assignment and should describe at least three repercussions resulting from each possible plan of action for Jolly and/or LaVaughn in her/their given dilemma(s). After completing the flowchart, students should determine the best course of action, based on the evidence or list of "consequences/repercussions" they compiled. If desired, students may reproduce the flowchart on a sheet of posterboard or overhead transparency to facilitate "report outs" to the class. In addition to responding to the "choice and consequence" scenarios proposed here, students may elect to identify others from the text. Furthermore, teachers should encourage students to apply this analytic process to their own lives when faced with important decisions and/or personal dilemmas.

Figure 9:1 Jolly's Choices After Losing Her Job

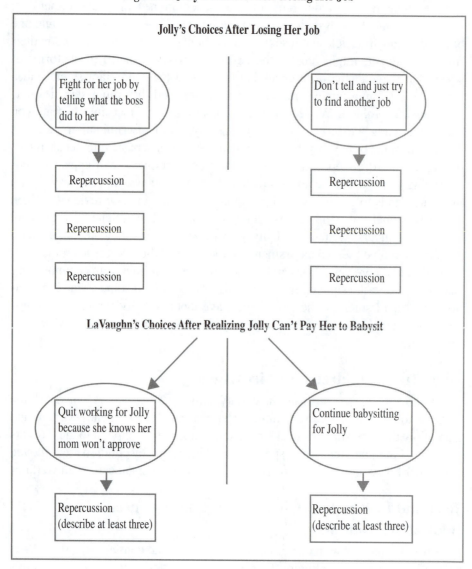

Survey of Social Issues

Working with a partner, students are to decide on a question they would like to find an answer to concerning the public's opinion on one of the social issues discussed in this book (poverty, teen pregnancy, workplace harassment, parenting choices, welfare). Collaboratively, the pair will create 10 questions designed to lead them to the answer to their question. Students are to type their questions into a survey, using a combination of yes/no, Likert scale, and short answer formats. The students will decide on a target audience (such as teenagers, adults, males, females, etc.) and survey at least 25 people who represent it. Students are to compile their answers and draw conclusions from the information gathered. Next, they will graph their information on posterboard and write up a report, explaining what they wanted to find out, what questions they included on their survey, who their audience included, what the results of the survey were, and what conclusions they drew from their results. Finally, students present this information to the class.

Coffeehouse Poetry Slam

Ask students to write a "Found Poem," an "If I Were LaVaughn" or "If I Were Jolly" poem, or a "Poem in Two Voices." Another option would be to ask students to write another chapter for the book. They should write another episode for Jolly or LaVaughn that fits in between the existing chapters or occurs after the final chapter of the book.

To write a Found Poem, ask students to find their favorite chapter in *Make Lemonade*. Ask them to copy favorite lines or images on different sticky notes. Then ask students to arrange them in an order that makes a point or creates an image. They may add transitional words or phrases. Ask students to share their poems at the Coffeehouse Poetry Slam.

An "If I Were" poem begins with those words and reveals what the writers would do if they were that character. Ask students to choose a character and then find an incident in the book that shows the character in a crisis or faced with a problem to solve. Ask them to write a poem that tells what they would do if they were in the same situation. Share the poems at the Coffeehouse Poetry Slam. See Table 9:3 for Carly Canzonetta's "If I Were Jolly" poem.

Table 9:3 "If I were Jolly" Poem

If I Were Jolly
by Carly Canzonetta

If I were Jolly
What would I do?
I'd call up a lawyer
And then I'd sue!

It's not just the job
That would be at stake.
My own sense of pride's
What he'd tried to take.

I'd fight and I'd claw
Till I found a way
To make that ex-boss of mine
Finally pay.

If he'd done it to me
You know there'd been others.
Evil men like him
Cause unwed mothers.

He needs to be stopped
Before it's too late!
Surely the law will protect
Women from this fate!

A "Poem in Two Voices" features two voices talking, usually one at a time, but overlapping in wording as the voice moves from one character to the other. To give students practice in this type of poetry, students may read and/or perform several poems from Fleischman's *Joyful Noise: Poems for Two Voices* (1988). When writing the poem in two voices, students must consider which lines should be said together as a chorus, which lines should be said together as cacophony, and which lines should be said separately. Students will need help in formatting the lines to show the orchestration. See Table 9:4 for excerpts from Carrie Christman's "When Life Gives You Lemons . . . Make Lemonade," a poem in two voices. When all the poems have been written and revised, host a coffee-house-type classroom where students can share their poetry while fellow students show appreciation for their work.

Table 9:4 A Poem in Two Voices

When Life Gives You Lemons . . . Make Lemonade
By Carrie Christman

My name is LaVaughn I am fourteen years old.	My name is Jolly I am seventeen years old.
I have many hopes and dreams for my future.	I have many hopes and dreams for my future. I have two children, Jeremy and Jilly.
I need a job. A job will pay for college.	I need a babysitter to keep my job. My job pays for the diapers . . . the food . . . the heat.
She needs a babysitter . . . I need a job "I have to ask my mom." "You don't live in reality."	"I can't do it alone" " . . . . Mom?" . . . . reality is baby puke, no electricity, no warm water.
	Reality is my babies only got one thing in the whole world and that's me.
I am going to get out of here. I will go to college. I have a burden. I have no father.	I am never going to get out of here. I have many burdens. Too many to count. I can't find another job.
What about welfare? All you have are excuses	. . . . WELFARE!!! will take my babies.
All you do is try and find someone to blame	You think you are so perfect Your textbooks are your bibles You always go to your classes You always pass your tests
	None of that can keep you from getting pregnant when some guy gets you down where he wants you
I have many hopes and dreams for my future. I take classes To go to college. I am clinging with everything I got.	I'm not good enough for you! I am clinging with everything I got. My son needs glasses
Who can you blame now? Your son?	My son How-could-you?
He's more expensive now More breakable He's more on your mind all the time.	He's on my mind all the time.
Take hold, Take hold, Take hold . . . You'll make it	I've done the dishes all the way I cleaned the countertops I've done my homework
	I can make it

After Reading Strategies to Reflect on the Meaning of the Novel

Story Portrait

The Story Portrait is an activity that requires students to focus on the main point of a book and to represent their understanding in a one-page graphic design that resembles a picture or portrait (Glasgow, 2002, pp. 183–184). See Figure 9:2 for a sample Story Portrait by Erin Hitti. The first step is to draw a border or frame around the "portrait" based on a significant or important idea from the book. The border may consist of words, pictures, or both. Inside the border, in the "portrait" area, students are to draw a symbol for the main idea or message of *Make Lemonade*. This symbol will represent the student's interpretation of the story. After generating the symbol that represents the "big idea" of the story, students will consider a related theme from *Make Lemonade* and write it in a phrase or sentence within the frame. Next, students are to find a quote that blends the symbol and the theme statement together in the framework of the portrait they are "painting" and write the quote somewhere on the portrait to complete the picture. Finally, students will write a one- to two-page justification (see Table 9:5 for Erin Hitti's paper) of what they included in the story portrait and why. As an after reading activity, the paper should be written in a way that demonstrates that students have read the entire novel, therefore making connections among the various components of the Story Portrait, and *Make Lemonade* as a whole.

Figure 9:2 Story Portrait

Table 9:5 Explanation of Story Portrait

In creating my story portrait, I considered many important ideas that played into the general theme. I concluded that the theme of *Make Lemonade* by Virginia Wolff was that "Hard work and self-motivation help us achieve our goals." The quote I used to demonstrate this idea reads, "I was going to get out someday not very long in the future. It would be college for Verna LaVaughn and a good job and not any despair like I saw in these surroundings here" (Wolff, p. 65). I used these two components in my story portrait because I felt that they best exemplify the continuous theme of goal setting (college) and the realization that the goal can be reached through hard work and self-motivation.

From the beginning of the story, LaVaughn already knew what Jolly came to understand later. LaVaughn realized that in order to change her life, she would have to take responsibility for herself and make it happen. Only through focusing on her goal of someday going to college and understanding that it would take hard work and diligence to achieve that goal, could LaVaughn succeed. Unlike Jolly, who waited for billionaires to send her money in the mail and blamed all her problems on the fact that no one told her how to handle things, LaVaughn takes control of her own life. Instead of waiting for something to happen, LaVaughn takes responsibility for herself and makes it happen.

As Jolly starts to "take hold" as LaVaughn's mother would say, she becomes more determined to become a good mother for Jeremy and Jilly and starts to set goals for herself. Gradually, after much prodding by LaVaughn, Jolly's house becomes cleaner, she takes on more classes through the Mom's Up program, and she needs LaVaughn's help with the kids less and less. Ultimately, LaVaughn teaches Jolly that she can't just sit around and wait for her life to change; she has to do it herself, and that takes work. Although Jolly is discouraged and intimidated by the challenges that becoming a student entails, she perseveres, and her efforts are finally rewarded when she uses the skills she learned in school to save Jilly's life. At this point, Jolly sees that through hard work and an education she can not only change her own life, but the lives of her children as well.

Letter to Author

Writing a letter gives students an opportunity to consider what they really value about a book they've read and express appreciation to its author. When a book leaves students with lingering questions, the letter also provides them with an avenue to seek answers from the author. While not all students will elect to actually send their letters to Virginia Euwer Wolff, the letters will help the teacher to see what mattered to students about *Make Lemonade*. In assisting students with formulating their letters, the teacher may suggest that students reflect on how they felt about the book and why; what characters particularly impacted them; the nature of the problems the characters faced; who and/or what they identified with the most from the book; their favorite part of the book, and/or any unresolved issues or questions they would like to address with the author. The letter should be written in a formal and respectful style, as though it will actually be sent to Ms. Wolff, and be approximately one to two pages. Table 9:6, Kristina Scott's letter to Virginia Euwer Wolff, addresses several of the suggested topics for reflection and poignantly gives insight into the student's own life. The third paragraph of Kristin's letter reveals part of the appeal of *Make Lemonade*—it paints a positive vision for young people, even in the midst of poverty, to be determined, persevere, and achieve.

Table 9:6 Letter to the Author

Ms. Wolff,

I was happy to read your novel *Make Lemonade* because I feel that it deals with real issues that teens deal with today. Often we discredit the maturity level of our youth. We put them in a category with younger children and act as though they are not old enough or ready to read about real issues. Yet they are the ones dealing with these issues every day. One in four girls is molested or has been in the past; that means that a lot of young girls are being touched and don't know who to talk to or how to deal with it. Bringing up the tough subjects in your novel is a brave undertaking.

I also like the way you addressed Jolly's pregnancy. Often we blame children for the things they have to deal with when really it is just what has been dealt to them. Jolly just seems to have been in the wrong places at the wrong time. She has had no guidance, so she does not know how to deal with the issues that confront her. You never blatantly state that she was raped, but we understand that it has not been her choice to get pregnant. We see her struggle and how she is really trying to do well but just does not know how.

LaVaughn is so focused. I like how you have put a desire and a will in her to attend college. I also come from a poor background, and I am one of the first to attend a four-year college. Neither of my parents went to college. They have never pressured me, but I knew it was something I wanted to do. I just did not know how. LaVaughn is determined and she finds out what she has to do to go. I think more young people need to know that there is a way. Often we just don't realize the help that is out there. In today's society, anyone is able to attend college.

My favorite part of your book is when Jolly realizes that she can make it. Even though the odds are stacked against her, she will be able to persevere. After school she will probably be able to get a job and pay rent. She starts to take better care of her children and study. All of these things she would have probably done before if she had known how. She just needed some direction.

Thank you for your time.

Sincerely,

Kristina Scott

Timeline

Creating a timeline as a post reading activity helps students to review the crucial events of a story and analyze how authors construct and develop various aspects of a novel, such as characters, plot, setting, and conflict. Upon completing a timeline, students often discover details of a story they did not previously recognize or had remembered (or comprehended) inaccurately. In this way, a timeline clarifies and deepens students' understanding. The advantage of constructing a timeline after reading a book, instead of during, is that students already have the "big picture" in mind, especially if the teacher has facilitated discussion and other activities by which themes are explored. With the "big picture" outlook, students are able to create a timeline that surpasses the standard linear structure and includes symbolic elements that have the effect of showing more of the story and more of the students' critical and creative thinking.

As a general guideline, the teacher should ask the students to create a timeline by which they will convey their understanding of the pivotal events (at least 15) from *Make Lemonade*. The "events" should be supported by quotes from, and pictures related to, the text, causing students to review details and take a second look at the author's use of language and structure. Most importantly, to encourage critical and creative thinking, the teacher should ask the students to go beyond the traditional "line" format and employ a layout strategy that emphasizes either the story's structure or meaning (ex: lemon tree, road map, plot pyramid, winding river, mountain climbing expedition, etc.). Kim Boedigheimer arranged her timeline (Figure 9:3) as a board game with lemons, sugar cubes, pitchers, and water drops (the components of lemonade), symbols she used to categorize the types of events (difficulties, positive happenings, points of understanding, and moments of purification) in Wolff's novel.

Upon completing the visual component of the timeline, students should write a paper (one to two pages) in which they describe their particular layout strategy and how it reflected either the story's structure or meaning. The paper should also include a discussion on how "translating" *Make Lemonade* into a timeline (including pictures and quotes) affected what students were able to "see" in the work, or what became emphasized as a result of this way of "seeing" the literature. Kim's paper (Table 9:7) provides an example of this.

Figure 9:3 Timeline

Table 9:7 Written Response about Timeline

I chose to make my timeline a board game for two reasons: 1) There are many events in the novel over which Jolly had no control, much like rolling dice in a board game, and 2) Jolly missed the period in her childhood where she would have been carefree and able to enjoy frivolous activities such as playing board games. I made Jolly's path purple as a representation of her bruised and dark path, and LaVaughn's path pink not only to symbolize innocence but also to contrast the depth in the purple color.

The *Make Lemonade* board game is played in the following way. The board includes four different symbols: lemons, sugar cubes, pitchers, and water drops. The spaces decorated with lemons contain those events in the novel that were difficult for the characters (e.g., "Sexually harassed and fired"), and the sugar cube spaces represent events that were positive (e.g., "Teach Jeremy numbers"). The spaces with pitchers are moments when, like taking individual elements of fruit and sugar and combining them to make one product, the character was able to assess the individual events and understand them in a larger context (e.g., "Realize Jeremy's mortality"). Finally, the spaces with water drops represent the moment of purification in the novel—the moment when a character purified her past by recognizing the adversity she had faced and overcoming it by choosing to move forward toward a better life (e.g., "Join a babysitting pool"). The goal of the game is to gather enough lemons, sugar cubes, pitchers, and water drops to make a glass of lemonade. Part of the purpose of the game, then, is to show the player that it is just as important to gather lemons as it is to obtain sugar cubes (i.e., it was important for LaVaughn and Jolly to have gone through trials. Though their suffering seemed unfair, it taught them valuable lessons).

By dividing my board into various "lemon" and "sugar" moments, I was forced to question whether some moments could not be both. For example, "Jilly chokes" was a horrible "lemon" moment for Jolly but a "pitcher" moment for LaVaughn, who realized Jolly's true significance at that time. I saw that it is not always easy, or appropriate, to categorize an event as fundamentally positive or negative. The timeline also required me to correlate events in the novel. For example, I find it interesting that Jilly's activities are closely connected to Jolly's. Jilly is upset when Jolly is beaten (Wolff, p. 54); Jilly crawls when Jolly collects her strength and confronts LaVaughn (Wolff, p. 137), and Jilly walks when Jolly finally understands that her living condition is not her fault (Wolff , p. 173). Jilly appears to be the power of Jolly, the part of Jolly that demands to be heard, and I think it is an interesting contradiction that such strength should come from a harmless baby. With the requirement of quotes in the timeline, I was able to appreciate the language of the novel all over again. Wolff is truly gifted with her voice. I hope that my quotations convey her mastery of syntax and elegance in phrasing.

Story Discussion Grid and Response Paper

A means of examining the internal workings of characters, the structure of the Story Discussion Grid helps students to analyze characters through comparison and contrast. The Story Discussion Grid, developed by Yarick (1995, p. 13), can be completed individually in preparation for class discussion or done collaboratively to generate discussion in small groups. Additionally, teachers may use this activity to focus students' attention on how authors develop characters whose actions and relationships are believable. This project may be completed on a sheet of posterboard or on the computer (see Figure 9:4), using the Table-Insert-Table feature on Microsoft Works or a comparable program. To begin, students will choose five characters from *Make Lemonade*. Next, students will create a grid with six columns and five rows (or vice versa). In the example provided (Figure 9:4), Stephanie Evans organized her columns by character and her rows with the required information for the assignment. The rows are to be labeled as follows: 1) Character, 2) Four Words Describing Character, 3) Character Feels, 4) Character Needs, and 5) Character Fears. Holistically, the completed chart facilitates students' discussion of the novel and assists them in reviewing the text to support what they have included on the grid. An added guideline to keep students looking back to the text is to require them to include quotes—one in each row for the protagonist and at least two for each other character, though students may choose the rows (i.e., they do not have to provide a quote in every row for the supporting characters). Students should also include a symbol to represent each character and additional pictures as desired. This encourages students to think symbolically and creatively, while also making the Discussion Grid more visually appealing.

Figure 9:4 Discussion Grid

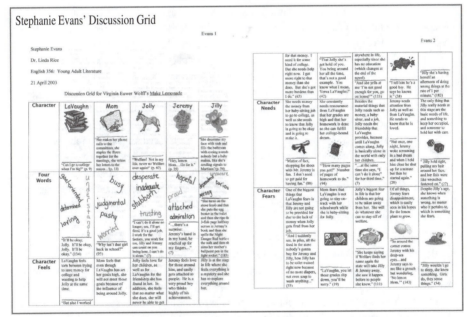

Next, considering the information gathered on their Discussion Grid and the book as a whole, students respond to a series of questions, in an essay of one to three pages, to position themselves as readers who identify with, and even critique, characters and their changes. This process also serves as an analytical and personal review as students consider their own views and connect their own lives with aspects of *Make Lemonade*. Table 9:8 provides an example of Stephanie Evans' response to these questions from Milner & Milner (2003, p. 131).

1. Which character chiefly engages your interest? Why?
2. If a character changes, why and how does the character change? Or did you change your attitude toward a character not because the character changes but because you came to know the character better?
3. How has the author caused you to sympathize with certain characters, and how does your response contribute to your judgment of the conflict?

Table 9:8 Response Paper

As I was reading Virginia Euwer Wolff's *Make Lemonade*, one of the main characters that immediately engaged my interest was LaVaughn. Being only 14, she was already setting goals in her life that she wanted to accomplish, and she was willing to work towards those goals, such as making money (one goal) to go to college (her ultimate goal). Oftentimes, in literature and in reality, people that young do not even think that far ahead in their future. They live day to day, doing what they choose to do for that day and that day only. LaVaughn lived for tomorrow. She wanted to go somewhere in life and was not going to settle for putting things off for tomorrow or the next day. She formulated a plan and stuck to it. I feel that that in itself said a lot for her character and personality. LaVaughn was a hard worker, and even though at times she became caught up in her job, she had good intentions both in her schoolwork and in her life as a babysitter and friend to Jolly.

In addition to La Vaughn's overall characteristics as an individual, another reason that her character engaged my interest is because of the parallels that I see between her life and my own personal life. In high school and still in college, I have always set goals for myself as well as strategies to meet my goals. Even though neither one of my parents went to college, I always had the goal to go to college and graduate with a degree. Since my parents were divorced and neither one could afford to pay for the cost of college, I knew I would have to come up with a way to make it through college on my own. I worked hard to keep my grades high, similar to LaVaughn, which paid off when I graduated Valedictorian of my class and was awarded several scholarships. In addition, I began working at Arcadia Nursing Center when I was 16 (and still work there today) to help raise additional money I would need, just as LaVaughn began working to save her own money. Another parallel that exists is the nature of our mothers. LaVaughn's mother is a single mother who was always pushing LaVaughn to get things done and stay on top of things, always worried about her daughter, and always very busy with work. This describes my own mother almost exactly. My mom was *always* pushing me to work harder in school, play better in sports, stay on top of things in life, and constantly worried about these things. I understand now that it is because she wants me to do and have the things in life that she could not, but when I was growing up, that was something I did not understand. When I was yelled at for getting an "A-" instead of an "A" I thought it was just because I did not make her proud enough, but now I understand.

My attitude towards Jolly changed throughout the novel as I got to know her better. At first, I was disgusted with her in a way because of the stereotype that I often give teenage mothers who have kids that are always dirty and messy, live in a home that is filthy, and where the mother takes advantage of the babysitter. This was the way that I saw Jolly at the beginning of the book. However, it was the little things here and there that made me change my mind about her. For example, when the bits and pieces of her personal life were revealed, such as with her own family, life on the streets, and how she got pregnant, I began to see things in a different light. I started to see Jolly not as the stereotype of teenage mothers, but as the victim of a terrible life. Another aspect that really changed my opinion was how at times, Jolly's love for her children was revealed in those touching moments, such as when Jolly would pick Jilly up and just hug her tight and talk quietly in her ear. To me, that really showed a motherly love and affection. I feel that this change of opinion was due in large part to the way Wolff wrote the story, leading the sympathy to build, rather than just laying it all out from the beginning. Wolff slowly wrote in Jolly's personal life, breaking it up throughout the novel with bits and pieces scattered throughout the various scenes and chapters. She could have given the entire background of Jolly's life in the first introduction of her character, but chose to present her in this manner instead, which I feel was very effective. By changing my opinion of her character, I was able to see the conflict more sympathetically, and see that Jolly really was trying to make a difference and do the best for her children, where at first I felt that they were being neglected. Having this different attitude towards the characters at the end of the book gave me a satisfying feeling at its ending, rather than feeling bitter towards this teenage mother stereotype that I originally had.

Stephanie's second paragraph is particularly powerful in demonstrating a student's ability to convey understanding on a very personal level, thus emphasizing the link between self-reflection and literary comprehension. And, through its emphasis on how her view of Jolly changed, Stephanie's third paragraph shows the impact of going back to the text to see how Wolff developed that character. Evident is Stephanie's careful text analysis and deliberate consideration of her stance as a reader, who, impacted emotionally by *Make Lemonade,* replaced stereotypical notions with sympathetic understanding.

Readers' Theater

Writing a Readers' Theater begins with students' choosing a perspective or dilemma from *Make Lemonade* that they would like to emphasize in a dramatic form. By selecting lines from the text—and limited use of a narrator's voice (lines added by the student for transitions and/or to improve the flow of the script)—students create a Readers' Theater script of one to three pages. On the CD-ROM for this chapter there is an example of the format, and students should make sure to cite page numbers from the novel after each line taken from the text. In order to make this an effective review of *Make Lemonade* as a whole (and not just a limited conflict or confrontation spanning a few pages or chapters), teachers should ask students to make sure their script has sufficient breadth to make evident their understanding of the theme as it emerges and develops throughout the book.

Effective Habits for Teens

This exercise begins as students read an excerpt from Sean Covey's *The Seven Habits of Highly Effective Teens* (1998). After reading chapter 1, "Get in the Habit," pages 3–9, students form small groups to discuss the validity of each of the seven habits that this author offers. Then, individually, students will compose a self-analysis paper in which they discuss whether or not they have each of the habits suggested by this author. This analysis should be supported by specific examples from the students' actions exemplifying (or not) each trait. Students may again meet in small groups to share their self-reflection papers. After the groups have had their second round of sharing, students should individually read from page 220 (beginning with the next to the last paragraph) to the end of the chapter. Finally (for homework), all the students are to write a paper (one and a half to three pages) discussing whether they think they are a highly effective teen, based on the criteria offered by the author.

Additional Ideas for Final Projects Utilizing Students' Multiple Intelligences

In addition to the postreading activities already explained in this chapter, teachers may find the following project options inspiring to students. Students may choose from the list an activity of interest to them, complete it, and present it to the class. Students might also enjoy proposing their own project options.

This range of options adds a great deal of variety to presentation possibilities, while also allowing students the opportunity to capitalize on their own Multiple Intelligence profile and/or strengths.

Verbal/Linguistic

1. Write a letter of recommendation for LaVaughn who is applying for a college scholarship. Emphasize her good qualities, and why you believe she would be successful in college.
2. Write the closing remarks (a speech) that Jolly's lawyer (if she had one) would make in the court case of Jolly vs. her boss, whom she is accusing of the sexual harassment which cost her her job.
3. Write a multigenre research paper on one of the social issues in *Make Lemonade*. See Carrie Christman's example on the CD-ROM.

Musical/Rhythmic

1. Write and perform a "blues" song based on the plight of Jolly.
2. Choose song clips to represent characters in the story. Give an oral explanation as to what the clips are and why they represent the characters, and at what point in the story it represents them.

Logical/Mathematical

1. Make a comparative study of the cost of a college education. Use at least five colleges, and chart your results. Be sure to break it down into Tuition (yearly), Room, Board, Books, and Transportation.
2. Create and fill out a college application for LaVaughn. It should include a short essay on "Why I Would Be an Asset to (Name of College)."

Bodily/Kinesthetic

1. Create and write out the rules to three games that someone like LaVaughn could use to play with a 4-year-old like Jeremy. Demonstrate them with/for the class.
2. Demonstrate for the class CPR techniques along with the Heimlich Maneuver.

Visual/Spatial

1. Make puppets and put on a puppet show that would entertain children ages 2–4, such as Jilly and Jeremy.
2. Create a visual depicting the following:
   If the characters in the story were animals, what would they be, and why. Your reasoning may be in paragraph or poetic form.

Interpersonal

1. Jolly was determined not to go on welfare. Make a questionnaire of at least five questions concerning how people feel about our welfare system, and survey at least 25 students and 25 adults with it. Make a chart and write an explanation of what you found out.
2. Interview at least 10 classmates to find out what type of mother figure they have, and ask their opinion as to how important having a supportive mother is. Then, based on your study, write out your opinion as to the effect (positive or negative) of having a strong mother figure. You may bring your personal

experience into your paper, and you should bring LaVaughn and her mother into it as well.

Intrapersonal

1. Write 10 entries in Jolly's diary which might have been written within the time frame of the book.
2. Imagine what either LaVaughn or Jolly will be doing 15 years from now. Write a detailed explanation of what her life will be like.

Young Adult Novels about Pregnant and Parenting Teens

Anonymous. (1998). *Annie's baby: Diary of a pregnant teenager*. New York: Mass Market Paperback.

Cole, S. (1996). *What kind of love?* New York: Mass Market Paperback.

Dessen, S. (1998). *Someone like you*. New York: Viking/Penguin.

Doherty, B. (1992). *Dear nobody*. New York: Orchard Books.

Eyerly, J. (1987). *Someone to love me*. New York: JP Lippincott.

Fienberg, A. (2000). *Borrowed light*. New York: Delacorte Press.

Grant, C. D. (1998). *The white horse*. New York: Simon & Schuster.

Hobbs, V. (1996). *Get it while it's hot. Or not*. New York: Orchard Books.

Johnson, L. H. (1982). *Just like ice cream*. Wheaton, IL: Tyndale House Publishers.

Kaye, G. (1992). *Someone else's baby*. New York: Hyperion Books for Children.

Lantz, F. (1997). *Someone to love*. New York: Avon Books, Inc.

Letts, B. (2000). *Where the heart is*. New York: Warner Books.

Pennebaker, R. (1996). *Don't think twice*. New York: Henry Holt.

Reynolds, M. (1994). *Too soon for Jeff*. Buena Park, CA: Morning Glory Press.

Ripslinger, J. (1994). *Triangle*. New York: Harcourt Brace.

Sapphire. (1996). *Push*. New York: Alfred A. Knopf.

Wolff, V. E. (1993). *Make lemonade*. New York: Scholastic.

Wolff, V. E. (2002). *True believer*. New York: Scholastic.

References

Beers, K. (2003). *When kids can't read, what teachers can do: A guide for teachers, 6–12*. Portsmouth, NH: Heinemann.

Byers, A. (2000). *Teens and pregnancy: A hot issue*. Berkeley Heights, NJ: Enslow Publishers, Inc.

Covey, S. (1998). *The seven habits of highly effective teens*. New York: Fireside.

Denner, P. R. & McGinley, W. J. (1992). Effects of prereading activities on junior high students' recall. *Journal of Educational Research, 86*, 11–19.

Englander, A. (1997). *Dear diary, I'm pregnant*. New York: Annick Press.

Fleischman, P. (1988). *Joyful noise: Poems for two voices*. New York: HarperCollins.

Glasgow, J. (2002). *Using young adult literature: Thematic activities based on*

Gardner's multiple intelligences. Norwood, MA: Christopher-Gordon Publishers, Inc.

Kreiner, A. (1997). *In control: Learning to say no to sexual pressure*. New York: The Rosen Publishing Group, Inc.

Leone, B. (Ed.). (1999). *Poverty: Opposing viewpoints*. San Diego, CA: Greenhaven Press, Inc.

Lerman, E. (1997). *Teen moms: The pain and the promise*. Buena Park, CA: Morning Glory Press.

Miller, B. (1997). *Teenage pregnancy and poverty: The economic realities*. New York: The Rosen Publishing Group, Inc.

Milner, J. O., & Milner, L. F. M. (2003). *Bridging English: Third edition*. Upper Saddle River, NJ: Prentice Hall.

Seuss, Dr. (1990). *Oh, the places you'll go!* New York: Random House.

Stover, L. T. (2003, March). Mind the gap: Building bridges between adolescent readers and texts. *English Journal, 92*(4), 77–83.

Trapani, M. (1997). *Listen up! Teenage mothers speak out*. New York: The Rosen Publishing Group, Inc.

Trapani, M. (1997). *Reality check: Teenage fathers speak out*. New York: The Rosen Publishing Group, Inc.

Wolff, V. E. (1993). *Make lemonade*. New York: Scholastic.

Wolff, V. E. (2002). *True believer*. New York: Scholastic.

Yarick, S. J. (1995). *The write course: A writing course for community college freshmen*. Ottawa, KS: The Writing Conference, Inc.

Chapter Ten

From Fiction to Fact: Using Anderson's *Speak* to Teach about Rape and Other Body Issues

Colleen A. Ruggieri

> **RAPE:** Forced sexual intercourse including both psychological coercion as well as physical force. Forced sexual intercourse means penetration by the offender(s).
> —U.S. Department of Justice Bureau of Justice Statistics

"A bird doesn't sing because it has an answer, it sings because it has a song."
                    —Maya Angelou, I Know Why the Caged Bird Sings

According to the United States Department of Justice, a woman is raped in this country every two minutes. A National Violence Against Women Survey found that rape is a crime committed primarily against young people. In fact, of the women who reported being raped at some time in their lives, 21.6% were younger than age 12, 32.4% were ages 12 to 17, 29% were ages 18 to 24, and 16.6% were over 25 years old (Tjaden & Thoennes, 1998). For educators, these statistics are startling, in that they imply that at least 54% of rape victims were under the age of 18 at the time they were sexually assaulted.

Though many instructors may never know about the rape of one of their students, it's highly likely that there will be a victim sitting in nearly every classroom during the course of a teaching career. I first encountered such an experience 10 years ago when I heard a few girls talking about another student in my English class. These girls, along with the rest of the high school, were talking about Amy, a girl with a vivacious personality and a pretty smile. She had a free-spirited style that reminded me of a beachcomber; she was a girl with sandy brown hair that was sometimes braided into little strips that framed her face. She wore toe rings before it was trendy to do so. In terms of Amy's presence in my classroom, she earned average grades—but always seemed to present the most creative and artistic views on literature and life. It was a jolt to my system to hear that such a kind-spirited girl had become a victim.

Amy's assault occurred on a seemingly typical Friday night in my suburban town. Like many other students in the area, Amy and her friends were getting ready to "party" that weekend. She and her friends were trying to step things up and to score some marijuana, and they set out to buy their weed. Unfortunately, drugs weren't the only things Amy got that night. In addition to the dime bag that the girls had been so anxious to purchase, Amy received an unwanted advance from a male at the drug house. By the end of her visit, she and her friends were scurrying to the car, trying to figure out what to do now that one of them had been raped.

This event led to wide discussion and debate among every clique in the high school. The subject was not openly discussed with faculty, but most teachers who listened in the halls and between classes knew what students were saying. Some of the teenagers blamed Amy for being "so stupid." Others just looked away when the subject was mentioned. Eventually, accounts of other girls being forced into sex while they were at parties began to surface during these talks among peer groups. One account told of a senior boy tossing a girl out of his jeep after she refused to "give a little" during their date. She was forced to call her parents from a dark parking lot in a shopping center two miles from her home. When I left school that year, I vowed never to forget what happened to Amy and the other girls who had ultimately chosen to silently endure acts of violence. I searched for a literary connection to this social justice issue, and a few years ago a great book was published that provides the perfect segue.

Speak (1999), by Laurie Halse Anderson, provides educators with not only a wonderfully entertaining and award-winning book to use with students, but also a springboard for discussion and learning that helps to transform classroom experiences into meaningful, real-world applications that focus on creating a better understanding of the many issues surrounding the violent crime of rape. The book focuses on a female protagonist, Melinda Owens, who attends a party the summer before her freshman year. After consuming alcohol, she is approached and attacked by a popular senior boy. The rich storyline, well-developed characters and dialogue lend themselves to meaningful discussion and learning opportunities. Writing assignments can further enrich students' growth, especially if they provide students with direct connections to their reading.

Frontloading Strategies to Emphasize the Impact of Rape

Prior to reading the novel, examine the cover illustration. Ask the class to make predictions as to what the story might be about, based on the cover of the book and the title. Also, consider telling the students that the book is about a girl who went to a high school party and was raped. Ask them to make predictions about what the book focuses on in telling this girl's story.

Activate prior knowledge/schema by asking students to talk about what they know about the dangers of high school partying, the issues surrounding rape, and its consequences.

As a class, develop a purpose for reading. Encourage students to develop two or three predictions or questions before reading. For example, "This is a story about a girl who was raped. Will she speak out about it, based on the title?", and

"Though we might not know anyone who has been raped, we've all heard about this type of assault. What are some things that you would like to know more about by reading this girl's story?"

During Reading Strategies for Dealing with Women's Issues

In conjunction with the reading of the novel, students will research several additional issues surrounding the rape that occurs in the book, including: cliques, teen drinking, cutting, depression, and sexual harassment. Reading response journals will be written throughout the study of the book, and the unit will culminate in a multigenre writing assignment.

Response Journals

During the reading process, students should be given opportunities to practice their writing and analysis skills through response journals. These journals should not merely summarize the text; instead, they should record the reader's feelings, associations, and opinions of the characters, plot, and issues evolving in the novel. This will allow learners to freely consider the many issues surrounding the rape storyline in the book. Students may freewrite responses throughout the reading process. For instructors desiring stronger structure, prompts such as the following might be used:

- On page 4 of the novel, the protagonist states: "We fall into clans: Jocks, Country Clubbers, Idiot Savants, Cheerleaders, Human Waste, Eurotrash, Future Fascists of America, Big Hair Chix, the Marthas, Suffering Artists, Thespians, Goths, Shredders. I am clanless." She goes on to note that her clan, the "Plain Janes," has splintered and been absorbed by other cliques. Write a response in which you discuss cliques in your own school, how cliques impact socialization, how friendships change, or why cliques develop in the first place.
- Humor based on irony is used throughout the book. Find examples of this, and explain how using humor might help Melinda to cope with her situation.
- Throughout the book, Melinda describes events of The Martha Club. How does this particular group encourage conformity? In what ways do you conform to others' expectations? Is conformity always a negative thing, or can it ever be positive?
- On page 24 of the novel, it is noted that Melinda has not been submitting homework assignments. How can you explain her downward spiral academically? Can emotional hardships sometimes affect intellectual progress?
- On page 64 of the novel, Mr. Freeman, the art teacher, provides Melinda with words of praise and encouragement. How can art serve as a vehicle for expression? Is Mr. Freeman a good teacher—why or why not?

- On page 72 of the novel, Melinda describes the night of the rape. If she had chosen to tell her parents that night, how might she have approached them? Do you think they would have understood—or would they have blamed her? Would her parents have blamed themselves?
- Examine the "Top 10" lists on pages 5 and 148. Is irony being implied here? Could these lists be considered applicable for any high school? Why or why not?
- On page 164 of the novel, Melinda explains her situation through a variety of talk shows. What reflection is this on our culture? What is the relevance of her watching *Mr. Rogers' Neighborhood?*
- Throughout the novel, Melissa chose to hide in the closet. What explanation could be given for this behavior? Why do people find the need to hide—or get away from others?
- Explain the connection between casual "partying" and what happened to Melinda. Do you feel that the events portrayed in the novel are realistic? Why or why not?
- Explain an allusion used in the book. You might select *The Scarlet Letter*, Maya Angelou, or Picasso. Is the allusion thought-provoking? Why or why not?
- Analyze some of the symbols used in the book—most notably, the subject of Melinda's art project.
- Describe how the cover is an artistic representation of the story.
- Based on your research, what would you have done to help Melinda if you were her friend?

Research-Based Discussion

Throughout the book, Melinda behaves in ways that exhibit her shame and guilt about what happened to her—which is typical of many rape victims. Her refusal to talk, along with her lip-biting and cutting indicate her need to express her anger and pain. In order for students to appreciate the issues of social justice surrounding this book, they should research several topics while reading the novel. You might also find it helpful to review Title VII of the Civil Rights Act of 1964.

Have students complete online research about the following topics and questions. Students should examine Web sites for validity, document the address and content, and find passages in the novel that coincide with the information they've discovered. Use this documentation to facilitate discussions about the following topics:

1. What is the definition of rape? What are some of the emotional side effects a victim might exhibit? How do Melinda's words and behavior indicate that she has not fully recovered from her attack?
2. What are the signs of clinical depression? What should be done to help a person suffering from this problem? Is Melinda depressed? How do you know?

3. Cutting and self-mutilation are becoming more and more common among today's teenagers. Why do individuals perform such acts on themselves? What does Melinda do in regard to this topic that would concern you?

4. What is a clique? Are they present in every school? What are the benefits of these groups? The negatives? How is Melinda impacted by cliques in her school?

5. Many psychologists have found validity in using art for therapy. What does this involve? How does Melinda's art teacher seem to do this with her? What type of project benefits her? Do you think that Melinda is healed, in part, through art class?

6. In addition to suffering through an attack, Melinda must also deal with sexual harassment from her attacker. How is sexual harassment defined? Does it occur regularly in society? In your school? How does Melinda deal with this?

Prior to researching, students should understand the importance of evaluating Internet resources. For example, entering "rape" into a search engine will net more that 8 million entries. These Web sites include everything from personal poetry pages to government agencies with documented facts. Have students document the Web sites they've visited, and provide commentary regarding textual passages that demonstrate Melinda's symptoms. (See Table 10:1 for a Sample Student Worksheet and Table 10:2 for Fact Sheets for Teacher-Led Research-Based Discussions.) The University of California—Berkeley Library offers the following guidelines in examining Web sites during the research process:

A. *Read the URL* (Uniform Resource Locator) carefully. This is the unique address of any Web document.

B. *Is it somebody's personal page?* Personal pages are not necessarily "bad," but you need to investigate the author very carefully. For personal pages, there is no publisher or domain owner vouching for the information in the page.

C. *What type of domain does it come from?* (i.e., educational, nonprofit, commercial, government, etc.) Is the domain appropriate for the content?
- Government sites: look for .gov, .mil, .us, or other country code
- Educational sites: look for .edu
- Nonprofit organizations: look for .org
- If from a foreign country, look at the country code and read the page to be sure who published it.

D. *Is it published by an entity that makes sense?* Who "published" the page?
- In general, the publisher is the agency or person operating the computer from which the document is issued.
- The server is usually named in first portion of the address (between *http://* and the first/).
- Have you heard of this entity before?
- Does it correspond to the name of the site? Should it?
- You can rely more on information that is published by the source: Look

for *New York Times* news from www.nytimes.com. Look for health information from any of the agencies of the National Institute of Health on sites with *nih* somewhere in the domain name.

Table 10:1 Sample Student Worksheet for Facilitating Research and Discussion

Topic	Web sites	Quote/Passage
cliques	http://abcnews.go.com/sections/living/DailyNews/group_identity011128.html	"We fall into clans" (p. 4). "What do you want to join?" (p. 23)
depression	http://www.nimh.nih.gov/publicat/depressionmenu.cfm	"When I wake up in the morning, my jaws are clenched..." (p. 50).
		"You are the most depressed person I've ever met" (p. 105).
cutting	http://my.webmd.com/content/article/12/1689_50857	"I open up a paper clip and scratch it across the inside of my left wrist" (p. 87).
rape	http://www.clevelandclinic.org/health/health-info/docs/0600/0613.asp?index=4538	"I didn't call the cops to break up the party... because some guy raped me" (p. 183).
sexual harassment	http://teenadvice.about.com/library/weekly/qanda/blsexharassschool.htm	"You're not going to scream. You didn't scream before. You liked it" (p. 194).
art therapy	http://www.arttherapy.org/resources/research/online_articles.htm	"Art is about making mistakes and learning from them" (p. 122)."Make it bend—trees are flexible so they don't snap" (p. 153).

Table 10:2 Additional Fact Sheets for Teacher-Led Researched-Based Discussions

How does RAPE harm the victim?	Any of the following unwanted behavior may constitute SEXUAL HARASSMENT:	Symptoms of Depression
Physical harm: • Broken bones, bruises, cuts, and other injuries from violent acts • Injuries to the genitals and/or anus • Being exposed to diseases that can be passed on during sex, including AIDS, herpes, gonorrhea, and syphilis • Unwanted pregnancy **Emotional harm:** Even though the attack is not your fault, you may feel:	• leering • wolf whistles • discussion of one's partner's sexual inadequacies • sexual innuendo • comments about women's bodies • "accidentally" brushing sexual parts of the body • lewd & threatening letters • tales of sexual exploitation • graphic descriptions of pornography • pressure for dates	• Persistent sad, anxious, or "empty" mood • Feelings of hopelessness, pessimism • Feelings of guilt, worthlessness, helplessness • Loss of interest or pleasure in hobbies and activities that were once enjoyed, including sex • Decreased energy, fatigue, being "slowed down" • Difficulty concentrating, remembering, making decisions • Insomnia, early-morning awakening, or oversleeping

cont.

• Ashamed • Embarrassed • Guilty • Worthless **You may also have problems with:** • Fear • Depression • Anger • Trust • Attraction to men (if the attacker was a man) • Consensual sex later in life (inability to enjoy sex without intrusive recollections of the abuse) • Flashbacks (reliving the rape in your mind) • Nightmares • Falling and staying asleep **Compiled from the Cleveland Clinic Health Information System**	• sexually explicit gestures • unwelcome touching and hugging • sexual sneak attacks, (e.g., grabbing breasts or buttocks) • sabotaging women's work • sexist and insulting graffiti • demanding, "Hey, baby, give me a smile" • inappropriate invitations (e.g., hot tub) • sexist jokes and cartoons Compiled by Martha Langelan in Back Off! How To Confront And Stop Sexual Harassment and Harassers	• Appetite and/or weight loss, or overeating and weight gain • Thoughts of death or suicide; suicide attempts • Restlessness, irritability • Persistent physical symptoms that do not respond to treatment, such as headaches, digestive disorders, and chronic pain **Compiled from the National Institute of Mental Health**

After Reading Strategy to Represent the Novel and Its Implications

Multigenre Writing Assignments

After reading and discussing *Speak* in class, students will write a paper that consists of a series of pieces that prove their understanding and appreciation of the novel and its implications for living. Students may be asked to include everything from expository, persuasive, and narrative writing to poetry. Artistic pieces may also be considered for inclusion in the paper. Though more topic-centered than Tom Romano would advise in his book, *Blending Genre, Altering Style: Writing Multigenre Papers* (2000), this type of writing assignment provides an alternative assessment opportunity that gives students interesting ways to demonstrate the issues of social justice surrounding rape. The following is a suggested list of writing assignments, along with some student examples. (See the CD-ROM for this chapter for multigenre research papers: *From the Life of a Queen-Sized Beauty* by Lindsay Rayner; *Rape* by Sarah Marty; *Rape* by Amber Hunter; *Cut* by Sarah McCarthy; *Cut* Brochure by Sarah McCarthy.)

1. A letter to the editor of a newspaper writing to persuade people to learn more about rape, depression, sexual harassment, or cutting.
2. An explanation of how to convince a person who stereotypes others to see the difference between preconceived ideas and reality.

3. A list of steps explaining the process "How to Avoid Compromising Situations." (See Table 10:3 for Ryan Sylvestri's advice.)

Table 10:3 "How to Avoid Getting into a Compromising Situation"

1.	Always do what you are told, when you are told.
2.	Think before you speak.
3.	Be open-minded so as not to offend other people and their beliefs.
4.	Never instigate an argument just to make someone mad.
5.	Avoid flouting or showing off.
6.	Don't talk back, especially to higher authority (i.e., teachers, principals, parents).
7.	Don't bring up sore subjects from the past.
8.	Don't make fun/tease anyone, even if it is in good fun.
9.	Always tell the truth and never go back on your word.
10.	Avoid situations that could potentially lead to compromising situations.

4. A letter from another literary character to Melinda. In the letter, address her situation and provide advice. (See Table 10:4 for a class letter from Hester Prynne to Melinda.)

Table 10:4 Letter from a Literary Character

Dear Melinda,

I have read about your situation and I am writing to show my empathy. I know what it feels like to be persecuted by your peers and to deal with public humiliation. Like you, I have also suffered. However, I am here to tell you that although you are going through a rough time right now, it will make you stronger in the end.

First of all, always remember that what has happened to you was not your fault. You were a helpless victim—a young girl forced to do something against her will. Although I became pregnant through my own actions, my relationship with Arthur Dimmesdale may have never happened if I had been able to marry a man I loved when I was a young girl. Instead, my marriage was to a deformed older man, for whom I never felt any true love. I have no doubt that my life might have been much different if I would not have been forced into a joyless marriage.

I understand your need to keep a secret; I did not tell anyone the identity of my beloved. Instead, I endured the harsh looks and criticism of the Puritans. However, unlike the society in which I am living, you have people around you who can provide you with help. I would strongly encourage you to speak to Mr. Freeman, and to use your art as therapy.

Next, I appreciate your need to get away from it all and hide in the closet. I lived on the outskirts of my village, somewhat removed from daily interactions of my community. Please remember, though, that the truth will set you free—and the longer you wait, the more you will torture yourself.

I hope that you will think about these things, Melinda. Just as I endured the Puritans, you can endure the cliques in your school and the awful act of violence which you experienced. Stand up for yourself, and be the strong woman you were meant to be. The letter on your chest should not be "V" for victim. Instead, it should be "S" for survivor!

Sincerely,

Hester Prynne,

The Scarlet Letter

5. An original poem which captures an issue covered in the book. It may be rhymed or free verse, but it must be a minimum of 12 lines. You may write multiple, shorter poems to meet this requirement (i.e., three haiku). The poem should include at least two literary techniques (i.e., alliteration, assonance, onomatopoeia) to create rhythm and sound. (See Table 10:5 for Jen Petrella's original poem, "Cliques.")

Table 10:5 "Cliques"

> Staring into the crowd
> Cruel smiles
> Evil jeers
> Never really knowing how to belong
>
> With all their cookie cutter figures
> Empty thoughts
> Lack of character
> Hardly ever thinking for themselves
>
> Ruining others' lives
> Ruthless rumors
> Dirty lies
> To them the truth is much harder to find
>
> But behind plastic smiles,
> Wavy blonde hair,
> Bronzed muscles
> Is a crying child who has felt too much pain
> to ever change.

6. A copy change poem of Emily Dickinson's, "This is my letter to the world." (See Table 10:6 for a Copy Change Poem by Marie Elizabeth Dohar.)

Table 10:6 Copy Change Poem/Emily Dickinson

> This is my letter to the World—
> That I write without expectation of reply.
> Written with fate guiding my heart,
> In a world as confused as I.
>
> Too busy to listen—
> To stop and understand—
> To respect another's feelings buried deep within.

cont.

A heart too cold to change—
Too full of anger
Hurts
In its haste to move through life.

What is love—a feeling that you only read about?
And hate—is this the way I feel about you?
Who are you to decide where to draw the line?
I spend all my time
Searching for an answer—only to find no reply,
For my heart too is hurting—and I am praying not to cry.

World, don't you understand?
How can you be so cruel?
Though these tears make us real,
This chaos and confusion ceases to heal
A world in dire need of
An open heart
And listening ear.

7. A narrative in which you examine a hardship you encountered in life and how you dealt with it.
8. A journal response to a current newspaper article about a topic discussed in the novel. Include the article with your paper.
9. A journal response to a Maya Angelou quote.
10. A memo to the principal in which you explain concerns about an issue occurring in your school that was also a problem in *Speak*.
11. A survey on the subject of depression or sexual harassment. Give the survey to a large group of people in the school, and include the results. Write an analysis of your findings.
12. A 30-second PSA (public service announcement) about an issue discussed in the book.
13. A mask, using pictures or words that symbolically represent Melinda's character. (See the CD-ROM for color copies, Figure 10:1 for Brooke Katzman's The Tree, and Figure 10:2 for Mirror and Its Faces by Kristin Johnson.)
14. A book cover or piece of art that provides readers with insights into the novel. (See the CD-ROM for color copy and Figure 10:3 for Kim Kanter's Tree Collage.)

Figure 10:1 The Tree

Figure 10:2 The Mirror and Its Faces

Figure 10:3 Tree Collage

In examining the overall benefits of using Young Adult literature such as *Speak*, it is evident, as Dr. Virginia Monseau (1996) notes that:

> "Response to literature does give us clues to the psychological devel-
> opment of young adults. Paying close attention to this response, whether
> in an extracurricular activity or in our own classrooms, can only ben-
> efit us as we try to instill a love of literature in our students—and inject
> new life into teaching" (p. 56).

While we could lecture to our students and merely spoon-feed them the facts about rape and the surrounding issues of this violent act, allowing them to re-search and respond through writing will indeed allow them to make much more personal connections to the works they've studied. One of the most startling as-pects of crimes such as rape is how many incidents go unreported. Though edu-cators can't prevent violent crimes from occurring, we can empower our students by allowing them to read books such as *Speak*, and to develop their ideas within the nurturing environment of the high school classroom. Hopefully, they will find their voices and speak out about the issues which threaten social justice.

Young Adult Literature for Assault and Abuse

Assault

Draper, S. (2002). *Darkness before dawn*. New York: Simon & Schuster.
Flinn, A. (2001). *Breathing underwater*. New York: HarperCollins.
Marsden, J. (1996). *Letters from the inside*. New York: Laurel Leaf.
Mazer, N. F. (1993). *Out of control*. New York: Avon Flare.
Plummer, L. (2000). *A dance for three*. New York: Random House.
Sebestyen, O. (1988). *The girl in the box*. New York: Dell Laurel Leaf.
Sebold, A. (2002). *The lovely bones*. New York: Little Brown and Company.

Child Abuse

Crutcher. C. (1993). *Staying fat for Sarah Byrnes*. New York: Bantam Doubleday.
Crutcher, C. (2001). *Whale talk*. New York: Greenwillow.
De Vries, A. (1998). *Bruises*. Arden, NC: Front Street/Lemniscaat.
Gibbons, K. (1997). *Ellen Foster*. New York: Random House.
Klass, D. (2001). *You don't know me*. New York: Farrar, Straus, & Giroux.
Marsden, J. (1995). *So much to tell you*. New York: Fawcett Books.
Mazer, N. F. (1997). *When she was good*. New York: Arthur A. Levine Books.
McNamee, G. (2000). *Hate you*. New York: Laurel Leaf.
Voigt, C. (1994). *When she hollers*. New York: Scholastic.

Self-Abuse

Brooks, B. (1999). *Vanishing*. New York: HarperCollins.
Frank, L. (1995). *I am an artichoke*. New York: Holiday House.
Hanauer, C. (1996). *My sister's bones*. New York: Delacorte Press.

McCormick, P. (2000). *Cut*. Asheville, NC: Front Street Press.
Newman, L. (1994). *Fat chance*. New York: Putnam and Grosset.

References

Anderson, L. H. (1999). *Speak*. New York: Farrar, Straus, & Giroux.

Angelou, M. (1997). *I know why the caged bird sings*. New York: Bantam Books.

Civil Rights Act of 1964. PL 88–352. 88th Congress, H. R. 7152. 02 July 1964.

Cleveland Clinic Health Information Center. *Rate and date Rape*. Retrieved on August 21, 2002, from http://www.clevelandclinic.org/health/health-info/docs/0600/0613.asp?index=4538.

Langelan, M. (1993). *Back off!: How to confront and stop sexual harassment and harassers*. New York: Simon & Schuster Adult Publishing Group.

Monseau, V. (1996). *Responding to young adult literature*. Portsmouth, NH: Heinemann Boynton/Cook.

National Institute of Mental Health. *Depression*. Retrieved on September 2000, from http://www.nimh.nih.gov/publicat/depression.cfm#intro.

Romano, T. (2000). *Blending genre, altering style: Writing multigenre papers*. Portsmouth, NH: Heinemann Boynton/Cook.

Tjaden, P., & Thoennes, N. (1998). *Prevalence, incidence and consequences of violence against women: Findings from the national violence against women survey*. Washington, DC: National Institute of Justice, Office of Justice Programs, U.S. Deptartment of Justice.

University of California Berkeley Library. *Evaluating web pages: Techniques to apply and questions to ask*. Retrieved on September 12, 2003, from http://www.lib.berkeley.edu/TeachingLib/Guides/Internet/Evaluate.html.

United States Department of Justice. *An analysis of data on rape and sexual assault*. Washington, DC: U.S. Department of Justice Bureau of Justice Statistics. Retrieved on August 21, 2002, from http://www.ojp.usdoj.gov/bjs/pub/pdf/soo.pdf and http://www.ojp.usdoj.gov/bjs/glance/rape.htm.

Chapter Eleven

Confronting the Bully in Young Adult Literature

Jacqueline N. Glasgow

Tiny, jagged hunks of mortar were being hurled at me from all sides. My hands over my face, I tried to run home, but the assault was too relentless. "Please stop," I pleaded. My knuckles and wrists were swollen and bloody. Red welts covered my skin. I didn't know what was worse, the physical or the emotional agony.

—Jodee Blanco

This is the opening quote in Jodee Blanco's *Please Stop Laughing at Me... One Woman's Inspirational Story* (2003). This memoir chronicles in detail her feelings of depression and how difficult it was for her to face her cruel classmates on a daily basis from elementary through high school. Her experience with school bullies occurred in a variety of settings from private schools to religious ones. While her well-intended parents were sympathetic and supportive, their advice to ignore her tormentors and see a psychiatrist only led to more persecution. Even though Jodee was lonely and desperate to belong to the popular crowd, she refused to pass through the initiation rights they required: She could not demean her teachers, nor submit to sexual advances at a boy/girl party. Because she desired to join the popular crowd, but had difficulty with the hazing requirements, she both provoked and prolonged the conflict. Furthermore, she befriended other social outcasts, such as deaf students, and tended to stick up for the underdogs. As Jodee says, being different and moral was a "social death warrant" (p. 159). She does feel, however, that those painful years gave her the strength to become a successful adult. Currently, she teaches publishing at New York University and the University of Chicago.

This moving and ultimately inspiring story was the focal point for my classes and staff development workshops I conducted this year. Blanco's book takes an unflinching look at what it means to be a social outcast, and exposes how bullying is often ignored and misunderstood in schools. It is a painful read, but it does illuminate the harsh realities and long-term consequences of bullying. It is an all too often part of the way young people interact in our society. When bullying is ignored or downplayed, students suffer ongoing torment and harassment. Failing to deal with bullying endangers the safety of all students by allowing a hostile environment to interfere with learning. Blanco's book offers an opportunity to explore this social issue and find effective means to deal with it, so as to make a difference in the lives of teens—both the aggressors and their victims.

Did You Know?

Most teachers consider themselves to be caring, tolerant persons with strong classroom management and intervention skills. However, according to the research of Pepler & Craig (2000, p. 10):

- 42% of bullies and 46% of victims report that they have talked to teachers about the problem.
- 71% of teachers and 25% of students say that teachers almost always intervene.
- Actual observations indicate that teachers intervene in 14% of classroom episodes and only 4% of playground episodes of bullying.

In other words, this research points to the fact that teachers are generally *unaware* of the extent of bullying and victimization problems.

Many of our children experience problems of bullying and victimization. According to Pepler & Craig (2000), for the majority (70%–80%) the problems are minor and transitory. With minor intervention and support, these children's problems will improve. For some (10%–15%), experiences of bullying and victimization may be more serious and enduring. These children are the ones who would benefit from schoolwide intervention programs. Of course, for a small proportion of children (5%–10%), the problems of bullying and/or victimization, such as in Jodee Blanco's case, are serious and require comprehensive intervention to support their adaptive development to move them onto a positive pathway.

In this unit, students will be asked to examine their understanding and beliefs about bullying, reflect on Jodee Blanco's experiences, and then turn to Young Adult literature to analyze protagonists who bully/are bullied through Literature Circles. The texts for this section include:

- Ayers, Katherine (2003). *Macaroni Boy*. New York: Delacorte Press.
- Coleman, Michael 1998). *Weirdo's War*. New York: Orchard Books.
- Lipsyte, Robert. (1977/1991). *One Fat Summer*. New York: HarperTrophy.
- O'Dell, Kathleen (2003). *Agnes Parker: Girl in Progress*. New York: Dial Books.
- Rapp, Adam (1997). *The Buffalo Tree*. New York: HarperCollins.
- Spinelli, Jerry (2000). *Stargirl*. New York: Alfred A. Knopf.

See the bibliography of Young Adult literature at the end of this chapter for other suggested novels on bullying.

Frontloading Strategies to Develop Understanding of Bullying

In order to help students examine their understanding of bullying, ask them to complete the following Anticipation Guide, found in Table 11:1, before reading Blanco's book, and then return to it after reading the book and note any changes in thoughts or beliefs.

Table 11:1 Anticipation Guide: What Do I Believe about Bullying?

In the space provided indicate whether you agree (A), disagree (D), or are unsure (U) of the truth in the following statements:		
Before Reading		**After Reading**
	1. Bullying is the same thing as fighting.	1.
	2. Boys usually bully more than girls.	2.
	3. Telling someone you have been bullied usually makes things worse for you.	3.
	4. Most bullying by boys is physical.	4.
	5. Some children who have been severely bullied have taken their own lives.	5.
	6. Calling people names can be bullying.	6.
	7. Girls are more likely than boys to bully people by deliberately excluding them.	7.
	8. You can always stop a person from bullying you by hitting back.	8.
	9. Sometimes when you are being teased it will stop if you ignore it.	9.
	10. What schools do can never stop bullying.	10.

After discussing students' beliefs about the above statements, ask them to reflect on their own experiences of bullying or being bullied. Initially, my students were reluctant to admit publically that they had personally been involved in bullying. They more connected with teasing, exclusion, or being "picked on," so I asked them each to contribute to a class list poem by responding to the following prompt:

When I am picked on, I _____

But maybe I should _____.

See Table 11:2 for the Class Poem: When I am Picked On

Table 11:2 Class Poem: When I am Picked On

When I am picked on
     I feel sad,
     I pout,
     I become introspective and quiet
But maybe I should just ignore it.

When I am picked on
     I take it personally
     I don't know what to say
     I get real upset
But maybe I could just walk away.

When I am picked on
     I try to pretend it doesn't bother me.
     I avoid,
     I ignore and withdraw,
But maybe I should hang with friends who like me for me.

When I am picked on
     I want to run away,
     I retreat to my friends,
     I feel helpless,
But maybe I could stick up for myself.

When I am bullied
     I cry,
     i'm mean,
     I'm depressed,
But maybe I could learn how to handle the situation.

When I'm bullied
     I feel worthless and upset,
     I act in kind,
     I hate myself for being too weak and stupid to stop it
But maybe I could suck it up and stand up to my bully.

When I am bullied
     I scream and shout back,
     I fight back,
     I get real angry,
But maybe I could get help and learn to confront my bully and back her off.

(Google Images)

Semantic Word Maps

According to Vacca & Vacca (1999), *semantic word maps* depict spatial relationships among words and concepts. Ask a small group of students to draw on their prior knowledge of a concept by brainstorming words related to "bullying." If sticky notes are available, ask students to put each word or phrase on a sticky note so that they can be moved around easily for the next part. After students have exhausted the brainstorming, ask them to group the words into logical categories and label each cluster of words. With this information, ask students to create semantic maps showing the relationship among the words, and share their constructions in class discussion. Then, holding up Blanco's book, ask students to predict what they think the book will be about. See Table 11:3 for Karrie Krouse's Semantic Word Map for Bullying.

Table 11:3 Semantic Map for Bullying

VERBAL
Insults
Name-calling
Rumors
Unfair criticism
Anonymous phone call and e-mails
Teasing
Laughing or whispering about person
Intimidation

PHYSICAL
Hitting or striking
Throwing things
Using a weapon
Stealing or hiding belongings
Group assault
Sexual harassment
Extortion
Assault

BULLYING

GESTURAL
Threatening gestures
Obscene gestures
Menacing stares
Shunning
Ignoring
Pointing

Character Quotes

According to Wilhelm, Baker, & Dube (2001), another good way to prepare students to read a novel is to provide them with a number of quotes that reveal important issues or personality traits for a character in the story. From the inferences they make, students can then formulate descriptions of the characters and make predictions about the character and the character's relationship with others. By discussing preselected important quotes and passages, students can make generalizations about the character and the central issues presented in the text. They can also predict what the character's problem might be and relate it to similar issues faced by students in their school.

After selecting four to six quotes for each character, give each group a set of quotes for a particular character. Ask students to read the quotes and brainstorm as many characteristics of the character as they can. Then, ask students to predict what the character is like, what issues the character may have, and what connections they might have with the character. Ask them to make generalizations about what might happen to the character in the story. Then, ask the groups to report their generalizations and predictions. After the groups have reported, ask them to think about ways the characters might interact with each other. What do the characters have in common? How might they interact with each other? After this discussion, students are ready to read the text and affirm/refute their predictions and generalizations. See Table 11:4 for Character Quotes for Jodee Blanco. Look at the quotes and imagine what kinds of generalizations and predictions students might make about Jodee's personality, motivations, and school life.

Table 11:4 Character Quotes for Jodee Blanco

"My hands are sweating. My head is fuzzy and confused. I'm biting my lip and it's starting to bleed. And look at my hair! They always made fun of my hair because it was so wavy and almost impossible to control. Tonight, it's wilder than ever. *Oh, God, I can't do this*" (p. 4).
"Determined to make a positive impression, I wear my Vanderbilt designer jeans. They are so tight that I can barely breathe. My grandmother is right when she says beauty is pain. My mom has even bought me a pair of baby pink Candies ... How I adore these shoes! ... All the popular girls are wearing them. If you want to be accepted, you wear Candies, and when I have them on, I feel beautiful and grown-up" (p. 7).
"My hands sweat. My legs threaten to go out from under me. I pray for a fire drill, anything to get me out of this dilemma. A person should experience a nervous reaction if she is worried about failing, not because she's scared of succeeding. Taking a deep breath, I look out across the room, and begin [an impromptu speech in Public Speaking]" (p. 12).
"I asked Sister Rose if I could volunteer as an assistant for the deaf program during my lunch hour. She immediately arranged it for me. Every day, I played with these remarkable kids, and helped Sister Clara teach them how to read lips. I would talk to them, and they would try to decipher what I was saying. I doted on Marianne. She seemed so alone in the world. Even some of the other deaf children shunned her" (p. 26).
"Lying on the pavement, curled up in a ball, listening to them laugh at me, all I could think of was how I was going to explain what happened to me when I arrived home. My jacket and pants were ripped and filthy. My hair was full of gravel and spit. My arms were scratched and bruised. I remained there in the fetal position, rocking back and forth until the bell rang and I heard my tormentors leave" (p. 67).
"I dreaded my parents finding out that I was a social failure again, so every afternoon when I got back from school, I carefully hid any evidence of abuse. I applied makeup to my arms and legs so my mom couldn't see the bruises where I'd been punched or kicked. I soaked the bloodstains and mud off my clothes in the tub before she got home. If I had to cry, I turned on the stereo so no one could hear me" (p. 69).

During Reading Strategies to Explore
the Consequences of Bullying

Double-Entry Journals

According to Vacca & Vacca (1999), a *double-entry journal* is a versatile adaptation of the response journal. It allows students to record dual entries that are conceptually related. In doing so, students juxtapose their thoughts and feelings in reaction to the prompts provided by the teacher or passages students select for a particular entry. To create a two-column format for the double-entry journal, have students divide sheets of notebook paper in half lengthwise. In the left-hand column of the journal, prompt students to select a significant quote or passage from the text that interests them or evokes a strong response. In this column, they write the quote and document with the page number. In the right-hand column, the students record their reactions, interpretations, and responses to the text segments they have selected. See Table 11:5 for Nora Noble's Sample Double-Entry Journal.

Essay of Significant Passages and Most Important Quote

After having students complete 10 of these double-entry journals each on a different quote, ask them to write an essay that incorporates the 10 quotes that they feel are significant in describing Jodee's adolescent experiences with victimization. Why did Jodee have such a hard time making and keeping friends? How did she learn to overcome her tormentors? What are the keys to understanding Jodee's personality? As students think about these issues, ask them to narrow their choice of quotes down to the one most important quote of the novel. In their paper, students need to discuss their rationale for choosing the quotes and justify the meaning behind the one quote of the novel. See the CD-ROM for Liesl Carey's essay for Blanco's *Please Stop Laughing at Me*.

Table 11:5 Nora Noble's Sample Double-Entry Journal

Short Quote or Passage from the text that interests you or evokes a strong response.	Record your reactions, interpretations, and responses to the text segments you have selected.
"When I walk into the house, I go to the kitchen and open the drawer where we keep the butcher knives. I pull out the largest knife ... I tighten my grip on the knife and begin cutting my face. I am screaming, 'Mommy, make it all stop'" (p. 164).	This passage seems to be Jodee's breaking point after so much hurt and pain. I wanted to cry as I read this, knowing that I could never face what she did. Jodee's desperation at this point in the novel is quite apparent, and I really felt what she was going through. The fact that she was so numb from the constant pain she felt that she was driven to cause herself more pain is difficult to swallow. I have gone through rough periods in my life, but never to this point. This episode made me think of a good friend of mine.
	I have a friend who recently admitted to me that she cuts herself, and until I read this passage I did not completely understand how she could do something like that to herself. Why would she want to?

cont.

> Now I understand a little better. After reading about all of the pain Jodee faces, I feel like I have gone through it with her. I can sense how this constant hurt can lead to desensitization. My friend, too, was bullied in the sixth grade, and she even transferred schools because of it. I could see the changes in her when this was going on in her life, but I just thought she was unhappy and depressed. It kills me to think about what she was going through might be similar to Jodee's struggle. I believe Jodee's story is so influential that everyone should read it. We all know that bullying is mean, but I never understood how damaging it could be until now.

Paint the Personality Behind the Clothes

In *Image Grammar* (1999), Harry Noden suggests a during reading strategy that asks students to use their imaginations and write about the personality they envision behind outfits of clothes provided by the teacher (p. 40). To begin this activity, hang two sets of clothes: one for a woman and one for a man in the corner of the room. Ask the class to imagine what type of individuals wore these clothes. Have them picture their personalities, occupations, and social lives. Did they know each other? Were they friends, enemies, or just acquaintances? After brainstorming aloud or silently, students should write a description or a story about one, or both, imaginary individuals. See Table 11:6 for Paint the Personality Behind the Clothes by Brienne Manley and a photo in color on the CD-ROM for this chapter.

Table 11:6 Paint the Personality Behind the Clothes

The female is Jodee in the time of her worst despair. She confronted Mr. Warren, the principal, asking him to give Steve a detention for socking her so hard in the chest that it knocked the wind out of her. His reply to her was, "I could give him a detention . . . But don't you think it would be better if you and Steve worked out your problem between the two of you without school intervention? If I give him a detention, you're only going to be labeled a tattletale. In the real world, we must learn to fight our own battles" (Blanco, p. 70). Jodee felt more alone than ever. She felt like she had nowhere to turn. School authorities had failed her. She couldn't go to her parents for help, because they were threatening to take her to the psychiatrist's office. Her friends treated her like a freak. She was constantly missing school with strep throat and stomach aches. That night when she couldn't sleep and longed to end her life, she prayed to God (the male in the clothes). "Dear God, please forgive me for asking you this, but rather than let someone who loves life get cancer, let me have cancer instead. There are so many little kids sick with leukemia. Please, take the sickness away from one of them and give it to me. I don't want to be here anymore" (p. 71). The scene ends with Jodee crying great sobs of despair.

Unsent Letters

This activity, designed by Vacca & Vacca (1999), establishes a role-play situation in which students are asked to write letters in response to the novel they are reading. The activity requires the use of imagination, and often demands that students engage in interpretive and evaluative thinking. It also allows students to respond informally to emotionally charged passages by talking back to the character in letter format. In this case, ask students to write to a character in the book that could help stop the bullying. Who could make a difference? Peers? Parents? Teachers? Counselors? Administrators? Police? See Table 11:7 for an Unsent Letter to A.J. by Valerie Leopard.

Table 11:7 Unsent Letter to Nadia

Dear Nadia,

I just can't believe what you said to me, "Jodee, you're too serious. Yeah, we teased you. So what? It's not like you're the first person to be made fun of at this school" (p. 236). How could you possibly say that after what you and Mark and a bunch of other jerks did to me that day after gym last semester? You played dodge ball with my bra and then flushed it down the toilet along with my silk blouse uttering endless verbal assaults. I had to wear my cotton gym top to class. Everyone could see the deformity of my breasts. You call that teasing? Well, I call it ultimate humiliation and torture. To you, I'm just another innocent victim to terrorize. I lived in fear of death just walking from class to class. You have no idea how much pain you inflicted with your little jokes and pranks. You are callous and unrelenting. You take pleasure in hurting others outside your popular group. You live in total denial of the pain you cause others. I hate you with a passion! Jodee Blanco

Literature Circles to Extend Knowledge about Bully Awareness

After students have finished reading Blanco's *Stop Laughing at Me*, divide them into groups of three to five and have them choose a book for their group to read, discuss, and share with the class. While continuing to discuss the consequences of bullying, these books provide insight into the motivation and personality of the characters who bully. For this project, book choices included: *Catalyst* by Anderson (2002), *Macaroni Boy* by Ayers (2003), *Weirdo's War* by Coleman, *One Fat Summer* by Lipsyte (1991), *Agnes Parker: Girl in Progress* by O'Dell (2003), *The Buffalo Boy* by Rapp (1997), and *Stargirl* by Spinelli (2000). See the annotated bibliography of current Young Adult fiction that features a bully protagonist/antagonist at the end of this chapter as additional options for Literature Circles. The following strategies are highlights of Literature Circle tasks from the various books mentioned above.

Bully Awareness Chart

Ask students to keep a Bully Awareness Chart for the book they are reading. They should keep track of the scenes in the book that depict bullying or victim-

ization and try to discover the motivations behind the characters for either bullying or submitting to bullying. See Table 11:8 for an example of a Bully Awareness Chart for *Agnes Parker . . . Girl in Progress* by O'Dell. As Agnes starts school
in the sixth grade, she finds herself stuck with a scary teacher, gets into a fight
with her best friend, tangles with a longtime bully, and meets a wonderful new
classmate and neighbor.

Table 11:8 Bully Awareness Chart for *Agnes Parker . . . Girl in Progress*

Page #	Bully	Victim	Behavior (Quote)	Motivation to Bully	Response of Victim
p. 10	Neidermeyer	Agnes	"Ka-thwap! Agnes feels a rubbery smack against her head accompanied by a deep echoing bong! She wobbles and almost falls off her bike. It's a dodge ball, and Agnes takes it flat on the ear."	Making people mad is funny!	Anger, but does nothing in retaliation
p. 19	Neidermeyer	Agnes	"So, Gagness, didja have a nice quiet summer? Build a lot of things out of Popsicle sticks? Oh, and how's the sock collection coming?" Ooooooo, sounds fun!"	Squeals with delight!	Considers pulling her ponytail, but refrains
p. 21	Neidermeyer	Agnes	At lunch Agnes learns that Neidermeyer has convinced Brian and his friends to take turns sneaking up behind her and whispering "Squanto!" in her ear (the are making fun of her English assignment)	Name-calling— uses friends to tease Agnes	Resigns herself to the teasing, "Oh rats. And it's only the first day [of school]."

When students have finished reading the book and completing the Bully
Awareness Chart, ask them to write a paper discussing the experiences and the
changes made. For example, in the beginning of the story, Agnes seems helpless
against her bully and looks to her friend, Prejean, to step in between her and the
bully. As time goes on, Agnes becomes more self-confident as she befriends her
new neighbor, Joe. Of course, this relationship with Joe not only poses a threat to
Prejean, but also to Peggy Neidermeyer, who also has a crush on the new boy,
making Agnes an even bigger target for her nemesis. Agnes finally gets sick and
tired of putting up with Neidermeyer's jokes and threats, and manages to embar-
rass her publicly during the class presentation—in front of all the parents. As
Agnes develops self-esteem, she learns not only to stand up against her bully, but
to value true friendship and not take her friends for granted.

School Bully Awareness Log

In order to continue the discussion of bully awareness from books to real life, ask students to keep a School Bully Awareness Log for a week during this unit. They should write down the date, location/time, student(s) involved, behaviors, motivations, and consequences they observe when they notice bullying behaviors. They should look for any antisocial acts that harm another person, whether verbal, physical, or gestural. At the end of the week, ask students to pick one of the incidents and write a letter persuading the bully(s) to stop. They should provide reasons why this type of behavior is harmful, what effect it can have on others, and how they have been affected by it. See Table 11:9 for an example of a Persuasive Letter to a Bully by Nora Noble.

Table 11:9 Letter to a Bully

Dear Bully,

I am writing this letter because I am concerned about a situation that I have been witnessing lately. Often, I see you making fun of a girl in our class, Sara, by teasing her and drawing attention to what she is wearing, what she is doing, or what she is saying. I want you to know that this does not only make *her* uncomfortable, it makes *me* uncomfortable.

I know you probably think that how you treat Sara only makes you look cool, and that no one around you would ever think less of you; however, I happen to know that no one, excluding your group of friends, thinks it is funny or cool at all. In fact, we really hate the way you treat her. We like you, and we like Sara, so it concerns us that either of you should feel upset.

It may alarm you to know that what you do to Sara is called bullying. You might think that what you are doing is just playful or that Sara needs to be less sensitive and to stand up for herself, but when someone feels vulnerable, that is not easy to do. What is worse, Sara might not show it, but this bullying might be affecting her quite a bit. In fact, bullying can cause someone to have very low self-esteem, to become depressed, or even to develop problems such as suicidal tendencies, cutting, or eating disorders.

The point of this letter is not to hurt your feelings, but to remind you to consider others. I know I should have spoken up before, but I did not want to call attention to you in front of the class the way you do Sara. Also, in all honesty, it is not always easy to speak up or go against the crowd. I hope that you will take this to heart, as I just do not like to see people teasing or making fun of others. What I always consider is: How would I feel if I were in their place? And, this is not always easy to do, but if you try, you might see how hurtful your actions can be.

I know you are a good person who means well, and I am confident that you will make the right choice the next time you see Sara. Hopefully, you can find a way to apologize, whether it is by saying "hello" or starting a conversation . . . but, like my mother always said, "If you don't have anything nice to say, don't say anything at all."

Sincerely,
A Concerned Classmate

Bully Buster Brochure

In order to create a Bully Buster Brochure, students will need to research types of bullying, identify characteristics of bullies and their victims, and discover ways to prevent bullying. Provide students with Internet access and point them to Web sites such as: www.bullying.org, www.childline.org.uk, www.naspcenter.org/factsheet/bullying_fs.html, and www.nobully.org.ck. Students can complete this project individually or collaboratively with a partner. You may need to teach students how to document Web sites if they don't already know proper forms. Ask students to collect the following information for their brochures:

1. A definition of bullying
2. Different forms of bullying
3. Characteristics of bullies
4. Characteristics of victims
5. Advice for bullies and victims
6. Ways of preventing bullying

After students have collected the above information, give them options for creating the brochure. The brochure might be created with software such as Print Shop or Microsoft Publisher, or it might be created by hand with construction paper. Students should look for appropriate graphics to enhance the presentation of their information. Students should be invited to present their brochures to the class and then post them in conspicuous places, such as display windows in the school. See Table 11:10 for a Sample Bully Buster Brochure (inside the trifold with no graphics) by Valerie Leopard. See the CD-ROM for a complete Brochure.

Table 11:10 Sample Bully Buster Brochure

WHAT IS BULLYING?
BULLYING is "when people deliberately hurt, harass, or intimidate someone else" (www.childline.org).

Some ways people bully are:
- Calling them names
- Teasing them
- Pushing or attacking them
- Taking away possessions
- Spreading rumors
- Ignoring them
- Forcing them to hand over money
- Insulting them due to religion or race

WHY DO PEOPLE BULLY?
"They see it as a way of being popular, or making themselves tough and in charge. Some bullies do it to get attention or things, or to make other people afraid of them. Others might be jealous of the person they are bullying" (www.nobully.org).

WHAT CAN YOU DO?
- GET HELP! No one deserves to be bullied!
- Talk to a friend, someone at school, a parent, or someone you trust.
- Tell whoever you talk to what is happening and how it is making you feel.
- Find out the school's guidelines on bullying.
- Call Childline on 0 800 1111 to speak to an adult who is there to listen and help you find a solution.
- Keep a record of what happens to you (www.childine.org.uk).

IF YOU WITNESS BULLYING
- Don't ignore what happens.
- Let the person who's being bullied know you've seen what's going on and are concerned.
- Report the incident.

After Reading Strategies to Create an Antibullying Campaign

For the culminating project of this unit, students are invited to create a zine that demonstrated their knowledge, feelings, and research about bullying and antibullying. A zine is an independently created and published personal magazine. Students are invited to write informally and personally about bullying, using the strong voice of their own or of the protagonist of the book they've read. Since the topic of bullying evokes such strong emotional responses, the zine is a fitting outlet for this kind of writing and research. According to Britton, OSC (1977), expressive writing is the foundation for all other types of writing teachers want students to be able to do. Zine writing provides an outlet for improving expressive writing. The format for zines can be a brochure in Microsoft Publisher or a brochure created by folding paper in half and using a cut and paste method, depending on what level of technology is desired for this project. For more discussion of zine writing and the zine-assessment rubric, see chapter 4 of this volume.

For this culminating activity, students have two options. One option is to create a zine for the protagonist of the book they read during Literature Circles. Another option is to create a zine focused on a bully-prevention theme. Students can take several different approaches to the assignment. For instance, one student focused on self-esteem issues in her zine. Another student took the position of the outsider/outcast. (See the CD-ROM for Alden Waitt's zine, *On the Outside*.) Others wrote from the protagonist's point of view, such as Mike Costa in Ayer's *Macaroni Boy* (see zine by Greg Booth for *Macaroni Boy*), Stargirl Carawy in Spinelli's *Stargirl*, or Agnes Parker in *Agnes Parker. . . Girl in Progress*. (See the CD-ROM for Brienne Manley's Zine for Agnes Parker.) The requirement is to write nine zine pieces that express their opinions, incorporate research, and captures the reader's attention. In addition, they need to have a cover and inviting title, a letter to the reader, a notes page (gives the inspiration for their pieces), and references used in the research. See Table 11:11 for a Zine Assignment for Bully Unit.

Table 11:11 Zine Assignment for Bully Unit

Compose nine original pieces from the following suggested list:	
Cover with catchy title	Book/Movie Review
Table of Contents	Editorial or Letter to the Editor
Introduction to readers	Horoscopes, Cartoons, or Helpful Hints
Advice column	Sports or jokes
Poetry	Advertisement or Art Submissions
Do's and Don'ts for Parents	Song lyrics or music review
Interview or Top #10s	Notes page
Myths about Bullying	Bibliography

Erica Ann Hollars wrote her zine based on Laurie Halse Anderson's novel, *Catalyst* (2002). *Catalyst* is the story of 18-year-old Kate, who finds herself losing control in her senior year as she faces difficult neighbors, the possibility that she may not be accepted by the college of her choice, and an unexpected death. Erica's purpose in writing the zine was to capture the angst of Kate Malone, the protagonist in this novel. Using Kate as the author of the zine, Erica's goal was to illuminate the difficulties Kate faced in her teenage life—such as her problematic relationships with her nemesis, Teri Litch, her seemingly uncaring father, and her boyfriend. Erica worked on keeping the character's voices as true as possible, so the topics in the zine are closely related to the events that occur in Anderson's book. Erica attributes her zine writing style to the countless teen magazines she has read throughout her own adolescence. See Table 11:10 for the Zine Table of Contents for Erica's zine, *Journey: A Girl's Guide to Making it Through The Senior Year* to get the gist of her entries. See the CD-Rom for Erica Hollar's zine in its entirety.

Table 11:12 Zine Table of Contents for Journey:
A Girl's Guide to Making it Through The Senior Year

Introduction: Find out more about this month's edition of *Journey*

Letters to the Editor: Kate responds to all your questions and comments

Helpful Hints: How to Score BIG on the SATs—Kate shares her secrets for success

Real Life: Teenage Moms

Embarrassing Moments: Time for another laugh!

Q & A: Answer to your burning questions about Kate Malone

Feature Story: Why Every Student Needs a Safety!

Sports Star: Long-Distance runner: Tips for keeping up with the race

Poetry Corner: Kate shares her favorite poems

How to Ditch Your Boyfriend Before College—Find out how to get over him and concentrate on yourself

Horoscopes: Fun!

Notes: My inspiration for each piece

References: References I used in my research

Nora Noble's zine also focused on the ideas and themes in Anderson's *Catalyst*. Her purpose was to provide insight into the psyche of people who encounter bullying and take a look at what it means to be a bully. Nora's example demonstrates that although Kate and Teri are on opposite sides of the bully-victim relationship, they are both lonely and alienated from family and friends. When they are thrown together, these rivals must learn to understand each other. Nora wanted to tell the stories of not only the characters in the novel, but also others around us that people may or may not notice who are suffering the pain caused by bullying. She writes about the sorrow in her own heart as she considers what makes us human. Highlights of Nora's zine include "The Top 10 Ways to Manage Your Anger," "Quiz: What Exactly is a Bully?" "Unseen Bruises: A Photograph of the

Scars that are Never Seen, but that Never Heal," and an Interview with a girl that resorts to cutting herself as a way to cope with her pain. See the CD-ROM for the complete zine by Nora Noble. See Table 11:13 for Nora Noble's Poetry Corner: Lines of Anxiety and Lines of Anger.

Table 11:13 Poetry Corner: Lines of Anxiety and Lines of Anger

Shame hides inside me
and my vision shakes with tears
I wonder if they know me,
I am prey, sitting, waiting for attack,
and I fee the hate—
I will . . . every day I do,

but I won't let them know.
Is it something that I am?
What I deserve?
And hating . . .
myself
more and more each day,
I am dying inside
And never cease
asking myself
why?

Anger boils inside me
and my vision shakes with rage,
I seek out the vulnerable,
I find the look so familiar . . .
and I attack
Don't say a word,
I violate you and you learn
it isn't you, exactly
who is less deserving?
You're strong, resilient—
You'll shake it off, move on.
Yes, you'll wonder why,
and only I will know
at least, I think
I might,
but why?

Lauren Gura wrote her zine from the perspective of Bobby Marks, protagonist in Lipsyte's *One Fat Summer* (1999). Bobby Marks hates the summertime because he can't hide under heavy clothing. Then he gets a job mowing the lawn of Dr. Kahn's estate, and it isn't long before Bobby finds out how terrifying and dangerous it is to step on a bully's turf. In her zine, Lauren has included advertisements for husky clothes sizes for Bobby and a nose job for Joanie. She has an excellent joke page and an interview with a professional bodyguard who some call a professional bully, but who is a sumo wrestler on the side. Other features of her zine include cartoons, movie reviews, and true stories. The advice column, *Ask Bobby*, gave Lauren an opportunity to ask thoughtful questions and to incorporate her research in the expert responses. Here are the questions for the column, *Ask Bobby*:

1. What is your secret to losing weight? Do you recommend an exercise plan?
2. Is it okay to fight back when bullies attack?
3. I can't stop bullying a certain kid that rides my bus. My friends would all make fun of me if they knew I wasn't cool. What should I do?
4. How did you get the confidence to stand up to your bully at Rumson Lake?
5. Ever since I got the lead in the class play and Sandra Sullivan didn't, she got all her friends to flame me via e-mail and Web sites calling me horrible names. What should I do?

See the CD-ROM for the complete zine by Lauren Gura.

Research by Josh Cunningham (pseudonym) was very personal. His purpose was simple, "I want to know how to make it stop." Josh suffered through years of torture because he was identified as an easy target by his peers and, for some reason, never decides to find a way to end it. He remembers all the times teachers and other adults witnessed the abuse, but neglected to do anything about it. He knows the feeling of helplessness and hopelessness firsthand. Cunningham's research questions included: Why does bullying still exist? What are the consequences (long- and short-term effects) of bullying? What has been done to stop the practice of bullying?, and What do adults have to say about bullying as a practice? See Table 11:14 for Josh's Introduction to the Reader.

Table 11:14 Introduction to the Reader

I know the pain that bullying experiences bring to those who have the unfortunate experience of being the victims of bullies, because I have been one my entire life. I remember my parents bribing me with toys and other gifts if I would just stand up for myself and beat the snot out of the next kid that picked on me—I never did that. In all my years as a student I suffered from verbal, physical, emotional, and sexual abuse from my peers. I spent most of my energy plotting how to get safely to and from school, how to avoid the hallway to avoid slurs and shoves, and how to cut gym class to escape getting beaten up. It took me years and years to understand that I did not deserve the abuse and even then I did not understand how to stop it. From this I know the long reaching effects of bullying behavior, the ideas that people have that it's all in childhood fun and that it can even be good for a child's character. I know from being a victim that any adult that rationalizes these events in such a way is at best sadly misguided and at worst a primary player in the destruction of a person's innocence. Please read this zine with an open mind and be willing to take action when bullying occurs.

An excerpt from Josh's self-reflection paper at the end of the project serves as a closing for this chapter, in that it shows the impact this study has had on at least one of my students:

In conclusion, I found this project to be one of the most important things that I have worked on in my undergraduate work to date. It helped me to take a good hard look at one of the primary threats that faces many of our students every day. From the information that I have gathered, I hope that I will be able to make a difference in the lives of my students, that I might help them realize that there is something fundamentally wrong with watching people take pleasure in hurting others and doing nothing to stop it. Furthermore, I realize that it really does take more than just one teacher working to create a change and provide a safe environment for students to learn. We must all take a good look at our children and their behavior and one way or another help them to become better people. Teachers must realize they have a very real responsibility to their students that extends far beyond helping them to learn a topic. As teachers, we are entrusted to help our students become good, humane citizens that can give something back to this world. This project has shown me that we all still have a lot of work to do.

We do have a lot of work to do, but this project has made a profound difference in many lives. Young Adult literature has been pivotal in opening minds to conscious awareness of the consequences of tolerating bullying in our midst. It is not a trivial matter. Now, may we harness this awareness into preventative programs, where bullying is no longer tolerated and students are safe in our schools.

Bullies in Young Adult Literature

Anderson, L. H. (1999). *Speak*. New York: Farrar, Straus, & Giroux.

Anderson, L. H. (2002). *Catalyst*. New York: Viking Childrens Books.

Ayers, K. (2003). *Macaroni boy*. New York: Delacorte Press.

Blanco, J. (2003). *Please stop laughing at me . . . one woman's inspirational story*. Avon, MA: Adams Media Corporation.

Bloor, E. (1997). *Tangerine*. San Diego, CA: Harcourt.

Blume, J. (1974*). Blubber*. Scarsdale, NY: Bradbury Press.

Coleman, M. (1998). *Weirdo's war.* New York: Orchard Books.

Cormier, R. (1974/1997). *Chocolate war*. New York: Laurel Leaf.

Crutcher, C. (1995). *Ironman*. New York: Greenwillow.

Crutcher, C. (2001). *Whale talk*. New York: Greenwillow.

Curtis, C. P. (1995). *The Watsons go to Birmingham—1963*. New York: Delacorte Press.

Draper, S. (2003). *The battle of Jericho*. New York: Antheneum.

Flake, S. G. (2000). *The skin I'm in*. New York: Jump At The Sun.

Flinn, A. (2001). *Breathing underwater*. New York: HarperCollins.

Flinn, A. (2002). *Breaking point*. New York: HarperCollins.

Friesen, G. (2000). *Men of stone*. Toronto, ON: Kids Can Press.

Gallo, D. (Ed.). (2001). *On the fringe*. New York: Dial.

Giles, G. (2002). *Shattering glass*. Brookfield, CT: Roaring Book Press.

Goobie, B. (2002). *Sticks and stones*. Victoria, BC Canada: Orca Book Publishers.

Herman, J. (1998). *Deep waters*. New York: Philomel.

Hiaasen, C. (2002). *Hoot*. New York: Alfred A. Knopf.

Howe, J. (2001). *The misfits*. New York: Atheneum.

Koja, K. (2003). *Buddha boy*. New York: Frances Foster Books.

Koss, A. G. (2000). *The girls*. New York: Dial Books.

Lekich, J. (2003). *The losers' club*. Toronto, ON Canada: Annick Press.

Lipsyte, R. (1977/1991). *One fat summer*. New York: HarperTrophy.

Mayfield, S. (2002). *Drowning Anna*. New York: Hyperion.

Mazer, N. (1993). *Out of control*. New York: Avon Books.

O'Dell, K. (2003). *Agnes Parker. . . Girl in progress*. New York: Deal Books.

Plum-Ucci, C. (2000). *The body of Christopher Creed*. San Diego, CA: Harcourt.

Plum-Ucci, C. (2002). *What happened to Lani Carver*. San Diego, CA: Harcourt.

Rapp, A. (1997). *The buffalo tree*. New York: HarperCollins.

Romain, T. (1997). *Bullies are a pain in the brain*. Minneapolis, MN: Free Spirit Publishing.

Sachar, L. (1998). *Holes*. New York: Farrar, Straus, & Giroux.

Spinelli, J. (1990). *Maniac Magee*. New York: HarperTrophy.

Spinelli, J. (1996). *Crash*. New York: Dell Yearling.

Spinelli, J. (2000). *Stargirl*. New York: Alfred A. Knopf.

References

Britton, J., Burgess, T., Martin, N., McLeod, A., & Rosen, H. (1977). *The development of writing abilities (11–18)*. London: Macmillan Education, LTD.

Noden, H. (1999). *Image grammar: Using grammatical structures to teach writing*. Portsmouth, NH: Heinemann Boynton/Cook.

Pepler, D., & Craig, W. (2000, April) *Making a difference in bullying. Report #60*. LaMarsh Centre for Research on Violence and Conflict Resolution. New York University

Vacca, R., & Vacca, J. (1999). *Content area reading: Literacy and learning across the curriculum*. New York: Longman.

Wilhelm, J., Baker, T., & Dube, J. (2001). *Strategic reading: Guiding students to lifelong literacy 6–12*. Portsmouth, NH: Heinemann Boynton/Cook.

Bibliography

Children's Literature and Picture Books

Bunting, E. (1998). *So far from the sea.* Illustrated by C. K. Soenpiet. New York: Clarion Books.

Coerr, E. (1977). *Sadako and the thousand paper cranes.* Illustrated by Ronald Himler. New York: Dell Yearling.

Kodama, T. (1992). *Shin's tricycle.* Illustrations by Noriyuki Ando. New York: Walker and Company.

Maruki, T. (1982). *Hiroshima no pika.* Boston: Lothrup.

Mochizuki, K. (1993). *Baseball saved us.* Illustrated by Dom Lee. New York: Lee and Low Books, Inc.

Shigekawa, M. (1993). *Blue jay in the desert.* Illustrated by Isao Kikuchi. Chicago: Polychrome Publishing Corporation.

Uchida, Y. (1976, 1993). *The bracelet.* New York: The Putnam & Grosset Group.

Young Adult Literature

Abelove, J. (1999). *Saying it out loud.* London: DK Ink.

Anderson, L. H. (1999). *Speak.* New York: Farrar, Straus, & Giroux.

Anderson, L. H. (2002). *Catalyst.* New York: Viking Childrens Books.

Anonymous (1998). *Annie's baby: Diary of a pregnant teenager.* New York: Mass Market Paperback.

Armor, J., & Wright, P. (1988). *Manzanar.* New York: Times Books.

Ayers, K. (2003). *Macaroni boy.* New York: Delacorte Press.

Banim, L. (1993). *American dreams.* London: Silver Moon Press.

Bartoletti, S. C. (1996). *Growing up in coal country.* Boston: Houghton Mifflin Company.

Blanco, J. (2003). *Please stop laughing at me . . . one woman's inspirational story.* Avon, MA: Adams Media Corporation.

Bloor, E. (1997). *Tangerine.* San Diego, CA: Harcourt.

Blume, J. (1974). *Blubber.* Scarsdale, NY: Bradbury Press.

Bode, J., & Mack, S. (1996). *Hard time: A real life look at juvenile crime and violence.* New York: Bantam Doubleday Dell Books for Young Readers.

Brooks, B. (1999). *Vanishing.* New York: HarperCollins.

Bullard, S. (1994). *Free at last: A history of the Civil Rights Movement and those who died in the struggle.* New York: Oxford University Press Childrens.

Cadnum, M. (1997). *Taking it.* London: Puffin.

Carlson, N. S. (1958). *The family under the bridge.* New York: HarperTrophy.

Caudill, R. (1966). *Did You carry the flag today, Charley?* Illustrated by Nancy Grossman. Austin, TX: Holt, Rinehart, & Winston.

Cole, B. (1997). *The facts speak for themselves.* London: Puffin.

Cole, S. (1996). *What kind of love?* New York: Mass Market Paperback.

Coleman, M. (1998). *Weirdo's war.* New York: Orchard Books.

Collier, J. L. (2001). *Chipper.* New York: Marshall Cavendish.

Cooney, C. B. (1990). *The face on the milk carton.* New York: Bantam Doubleday Dell.

Cooney, C. B. (1993). *Whatever happened to Janie?* New York: Dell Laurel Leaf.

Cooney, C. B. (1996). *The voice on the radio.* New York: Bantam Doubleday Dell.

Cooney, C. B. (1999). *Burning up.* New York: Delacorte Press.

Cooney, C. B. (2000). *What Janie found.* New York: Dell Laurel Leaf.

Cooper, M. L. (2000). *Fighting for honor: Japanese-Americans and World War II.* New York: Houghton Mifflin Company.

Cooper, M. L. (2003). *Remembering Manzanar: Life in a Japanese relocation camp.* New York: Clarion Books.

Cormier, R. (1974, 1997). *Chocolate war.* New York: Laurel Leaf.

Cormier, R. (1997). *Tenderness.* New York: Delacorte Press.

Cornelissen, C. (1998). *Soft rain: A story of the Cherokee trail of tears.* New York: Delacorte Press.

Crutcher, C. (1986). *Running loose.* New York: Laurel Leaf.

Crutcher. C. (1993). *Staying fat for Sarah Byrnes.* New York: Bantam Doubleday.

Crutcher, C. (1995). *Ironman.* New York: Greenwillow.

Crutcher, C. (2001). *Whale talk.* New York: Greenwillow.

Curtis, C. P. (1995). *The Watsons go to Birmingham—1963.* New York: Delacorte Press.

Dadey, D. (2002). *Whistler's hollow.* New York: Bloomsbury Children's Books.

Daniel, R. (1993). *Prisoners without trial: Japanese-Americans in World War II.* New York: Hill & Wang.

Davidson, M. (1999). *I have a dream: The story of Martin Luther King.* New York: Bt. Bound.

Davis, D. (1982). *Behind barbed wire: The imprisonment of Japanese-Americans during World War II.* New York: E. P. Dutton, Inc.

Davis, O. (1995). *Just like Martin.* London: Puffin.

DeFelice, C. (1999). *Nowhere to call home.* New York: HarperTrophy.

Dessen, S. (1998). *Someone like you.* New York: Viking/Penguin.

De Vries, A. (1998). *Bruises.* Arden, NC: Front Street/Lemniscaat.

Doherty, B. (1992). *Dear nobody.* New York: Orchard Books.

Draper, S. (2002). *Darkness before dawn.* New York: Simon & Schuster.

Draper, S. (2003). *The battle of Jericho.* New York: Anteneum.

Drinnon, R. (1987). *Keeper of concentration camps: Dillon S. Myer and American racism.* Berkeley, CA: University of California Press.

Ellis, D. (1999). *Looking for X.* Toronto, ON, Canada: Groundwood Books.

Eyerly, J. (1987). *Someone to love me.* New York: JP Lippincott.

Fenner, C. (1998). *The king of dragons.* New York: Margaret K. McElderry Books.

Ferris, J. (1995). *Signs of life.* New York: Farrar, Straus, & Giroux.

Fienberg, A. (2000). *Borrowed light*. New York: Delacorte Press.

Fleischman, P. (1988). *Whirligig*. New York: Henry Holt.

Flinn, A. (2001). *Breathing underwater*. New York: HarperCollins.

Flinn, A. (2002). *Breathing point*. New York: HarperCollins.

Fox, P. (1991). *Monkey island*. London: Orchard Books.

Fox, P. (1995). *The eagle kit: A novel*. London: Orchard Books.

Frank, L. (1995). *I am an artichoke*. New York: Holiday House.

Friesen, G. (2000). *Men of stone*. Toronto, ON, Canada: Kids Can Press.

Gaines, E. (1993). *A lesson before dying*. New York: Alfred A. Knopf.

Gallo, D. (Ed.). (2001). *On the fringe*. New York: Dial.

Garland, S. (1994). *I never knew your name*. New York: Ticknor & Fields.

Gibbons, K. (1997). *Ellen Foster*. New York: Random House.

Giles, G. (2002). *Shattering glass*. Brookfield, CT: Roaring Book Press.

Glenn, M. (2000). *Split-images: A story in poems*. New York: HarperCollins.

Goobie, B. (2002). *Sticks and stones*. Victoria, BC, Canada: Orca Book Publishers.

Grant, C. D. (1998). *The white horse*. New York: Simon & Schuster.

Grisham, J. (1999). *The testament*. New York: Doubleday.

Grove, V. (1990). *The fastest friend in the west*. New York: G. P. Putnam's Sons.

Grove, V. (1999). *The starplace*. New York: Putnam.

Guest, J. (1993). *Ordinary people*. New York: Penguin Books.

Guterson, D. (1994). *Snow falling on cedars*. San Diego, CA: Harcourt Brace.

Hahn, M. D. (1988). *December stillness*. New York: Avon Books.

Hamanaka, S. (1990). *Journey: Japanese-Americans, racism, and renewal*. London: Orchard Books/Franklin Watts.

Hamilton, V. (1974). *M. C. Higgins, the great*. New York: Aladdin Paperbacks.

Hamilton, V. (1990). *Cousins*. New York: Scholastic.

Hamilton, V. (1998). *Second cousins*. New York: Scholastic.

Hanauer, C. (1996). *My sister's bones*. New York: Delacorte Press.

Hartnett, S. (1994). *Wilful blue*. New York: Viking.

Haskins, J. (1997). *Bayard Rustin: Behind the scenes of the Civil Rights Movement*. New York: Hyperion.

Herman, J. (1998). *Deep waters*. New York: Philomel.

Hesse, K. (1998). *Just juice*. New York: Scholastic.

Hiaasen, C. (2002). *Hoot*. New York: Alfred A. Knopf.

Hinton, S. E. (1967). *The outsiders*. New York: Viking Press.

Hobbs, V. (1996). *Get it while it's hot. Or not*. New York: Orchard Books.

Houston, G. (1994). *Mountain valor*. New York: Putnam & Grosset Group.

Houston, J. W., & Houston, J. D. (1990). *Farewell to Manzanar*. New York: Bantam.

Howe, J. (2001). *The misfits*. New York: Atheneum.

Hughes, D. (1989). *Family pose*. New York: Atheneum.

Inada, L. F. (1997). *Drawing the line*. Minneapolis, MN: Coffee House Press.

Inada, L. F. (Ed.). (2000). *Only what we could carry: The Japanese-American internment experience*. Berkeley, CA: Heyday Books.

Ingold, J. (1996). *The window*. New York: Harcourt Brace.

Irwin, H. (1987). *Kim/Kimi.* New York: M. K. McElderry Books.

Johnson, L. H. (1982). *Just like ice cream.* Wheaton, IL: Tyndale House Publishers.

Johnson, L. L. (2002). *Soul moon soup.* Asheville, NC: Front Street Press.

Kaye, G. (1992). *Someone else's baby.* New York: Hyperion Books for Children.

Kessler, L. (1994). *Stubborn twig: Three generations in the life of a Japanese-American family.* New York: Plume.

Klass, D. (2001). *You don't know me.* New York: Farrar, Straus, & Giroux.

Koja, K. (2003). *Buddha boy.* New York: Francis Foster Books.

Konigsburg. E. L. (1996). *The view from Saturday.* New York: Atheneum.

Koss, A. G. (2000). *The girls.* New York: Dial.

Krisher, T. (1994). *Spite fences.* New York: Delacorte Press.

Lantz, F. (1997). *Someone to love.* New York: Avon Books, Inc.

Lekich, J. (2003). *The losers' club.* Toronto, ON, Canada: Annik Press.

Letts, B. (1998). *Where the heart is.* Victoria, Australia: Warner Books.

Levine, E. (1995). *A fence away from freedom: Japanese-Americans and World War II.* New York: Putnam's Sons.

Levine, E. (2000). *Freedom's children: Young Civil Rights activists tell their own stories.* London: Puffin.

Lipsyte, R. (1991). *One fat summer.* New York: HarperTrophy.

Lowry, L. (1987). *Rabble Starkey.* New York: Bantam Doubleday Dell.

Lowry, L. (1993). *The giver.* New York: Bantam Doubleday Dell.

Lyon, G. E. (1997). *With a hammer for my heart.* New York: Avon Books, Inc.

Lyon, G. E. (1999). *Borrowed children.* Lexington, KY: The University Press of Kentucky.

Mahy, M. (1999). *Memory.* New York: Aladdin.

Marsden, J. (1996). *Letters from the inside.* New York: Laurel Leaf.

Marsden, J. (1995). *So much to tell you.* New York: Fawcett Books.

Mayfield, S. (2000). *Drowning Anna.* New York: Hyperion

Masaoka, M. (1987). *They call me Moses Masaoka.* New York: William Morrow.

Mazer, N. F. (1993). *Out of control.* New York: Avon Flare.

Mazer, N. F. (1997). *When she was good.* New York: Arthur A. Levine Books.

McCormick, P. (2000). *Cut.* Asheville, NC: Front Street Press.

McDonald, M. (1993). *The bridge to nowhere.* London: Orchard Books.

McNamee, G. (2000). *Hate you.* New York: Laurel Leaf.

Means, F. C. (1992). *The moved-outers.* New York: Walker and Company.

Miklowitz, G. (1985). *The war between the classes.* New York: Delacorte Press.

Myers, W. D. (1999). *Monster.* Illustrations by Christopher Myers. New York: HarperCollins Children's Books.

Nakano, J., & Kay, N. (Eds.). (1983). *Poets behind barbed wire.* Honolulu, HI: Bamboo Ridge Press.

Namioka, L. (1994). *April and the dragon lady.* San Diego, CA: Harcourt Brace.

Naylor, P. R. (1991). *Shiloh.* New York: Atheneum Books for Young Readers.

Naylor, P. R. (1996). *Shiloh season.* New York: Atheneum Books for Young Readers.

Naylor, P. R. (1997). *Saving Shiloh.* New York: Atheneum Books for Young Readers.

Nelson, T. (1992). *The beggars' ride.* London: Orchard Books.

Newman, L. (1994). *Fat chance*. New York: Putnam and Grosset.

Nolan, H. (1999). *A face in every window*. New York: Harcourt Brace.

O'Dell, K. (2003). *Agnes Parker: Girl in progress*. New York: Dial Books.

Oldham, J. (1996). *Found*. London: Orchard Books.

Oughton, J. (1995). *Music from a place called half moon*. Boston: Houghton Mifflin.

Paterson, K. (1985). *Come sing, Jimmy Jo*. London: Puffin Books.

Paulsen, G. (1987). *The crossing*. London: Orchard Books.

Peck, R. N. (1999). *Cowboy ghost*. New York: HarperCollins.

Pennebaker, R. (1996). *Don't think twice*. New York: Henry Holt.

Pennebaker, R. (1999). *Conditions of love*. New York: Henry Holt.

Plummer, L. (2000). *A dance for three*. New York: Random House.

Plum-Ucci, C. (2000). *The body of Christopher Creed*. San Diego, CA: Harcourt/Brace.

Plum-Ucci, C. (2002). *What happened to Lani Carver.* San Diego, CA: Harcourt/Brace.

Pohl, P. (1999). *I miss you, I miss you*. New York: R & S Books.

Powell, R. (1999). *Tribute to another dead rock star*. New York: Farrar, Straus, & Giroux.

Rapp, A. (1997). *The buffalo tree*. New York: HarperCollins.

Reynolds, M. (1994). *Too soon for Jeff.* Buena Park, CA: Morning Glory Press.

Ripslinger, J. (1994). *Triangle*. New York: Harcourt Brace.

Romain, T. (1997). *Bullies are a pain in the brain*. Minniapolis, MN: Free Spirit Publishing.

Rylant, C. (1992). *Missing May*. London: Orchard Books.

Sachar, L. (1998). *Holes*. New York: Farrar, Straus, & Giroux.

Salisbury, G. (1994). *Under the blood-red sun*. New York: Delacorte Press.

Sapphire. (1996). *Push*. New York: Alfred A. Knopf.

Schwandt, S. (1996). *Hold steady*. Minneapolis, MN: Free Spirit Publishing.

Sebestyen, O. (1988). *The girl in the box*. New York: Dell Laurel Leaf.

Sebold, A. (2002). *The lovely bones*. New York: Little Brown and Company.

Slavin, M. (1992). *Moon bridge*. New York: Scholastic.

Smith, P. (1995). *Democracy on trial: The Japanese-American evacuation and relocation in World War II*. New York: Simon & Schuster.

Snicket, L. (1999). *The bad beginning*. New York: Scholastic.

Snyder, M. (1995). *Souvenirs*. New York: Avon Flare.

Snyder, Z. K. (1997). *The gypsy game*. New York: Delacorte Press.

Sone, M. (1979). *Nisei daughter*. Seattle, WA: University of Washington Press.

Spinelli, J. (1990). *Maniac Magee*. New York: HarperTrophy.

Spinelli, J. (1996). *Crash*. New York: Dell Yearling.

Spinelli, J. (1997). *Wringer*. New York: HarperCollins.

Spinelli, J. (2000). *Stargirl*. New York: Alfred A. Knopf.

Springer, N. (1994). *Toughing it*. New York: Harcourt Brace.

Stanley, J. (1994). *I am an American: A true story of Japanese internment*. New York: Crown Publishers.

Stuart, J. (1949). *The thread that runs so true*. Carmichael, CA: Touchstone Books.

Stuart, J. (2000). *The best-loved short stories of Jesse Stuart*. Ashland, KY: Jesse Stuart Foundation.

Tajiri, V. (Ed.). (1990). *Through innocent eyes*. Los Angeles: Keiro Services Press.

Takashima, S. (1974). *A child in prison camp*. New York: William Morrow and Company.

Tolan, S. (1992). *Sophie and the sidewalk man*. New York: Four Winds Press.

Tolan, S. (1996). *Welcome to the ark*. New York: Morrow Junior Books.

Tunnell, M., & Chilcoat, G. (1996). *The children of Topaz: The story of a Japanese-American internment camp*. New York: Holiday House.

Uchida, Y. (1971). *Journey to Topaz*. New York: Charles Scribner's Sons.

Uchida, Y. (1978). *Journey home*. New York: Atheneum.

Uchida, Y. (1984). *Desert exile: The uprooting of a Japanese-American family*. Seattle, WA: University of Washington Press.

Uchida, Y. (1987). *Picture bride*. Flagstaff, AZ: Northland Press.

Uchida, Y. (1991). *The invisible thread*. Surrey, England: Beech Tree.

Voigt, C. (1994). *When she hollers*. New York: Scholastic.

Walter, V. (1999). *Making up megaboy*. New York: Delacorte Press.

White, R. (1996). *Belle Prater's boy*. New York: Bantam Doubleday Dell Books.

White, R. (2000). *Memories of summer*. Vancouver, BC, Canada: Douglas and McIntyre, LTD.

Wolff, V. E. (1993). *Make lemonade*. New York: Scholastic.

Wolff, V. E. (1998). *Bat 6: A novel*. New York: Scholastic.

Wolff, V. E. (2002). *True believer*. New York: Scholastic.

Yep, L. (1991). *The star fisher*. New York: Morrow Junior Books.

Yep, L. (1995). *Hiroshima*. New York: Scholastic.

References

Adams, M., Bell, L. A., & Griffin, P. (Ed.). (1997). *Teaching for diversity and social justice: A sourcebook*. New York: Routledge.

Adams, S. (1998). *Appalachian legacy*. Jackson, MS: University Press of Mississippi.

Allen, J. (2003). *Common ground*. Portland, ME: Stenhouse Publishers.

Allen, J. (2002, May). "I am Thorgood, king of the orgies": The reading challenge of content vocabulary. *Voices from the middle, 9*(4), 22–27. Urbana, IL: NCTE.

Anderman, L. H. (1999). Classroom goal orientation, school belonging and social goals as predictors of students' positive and negative effect following the transition to middle school. *Journal of Research and Development in Education, 32,* 131–147.

Anderson, L. H. (1999). *Speak*. New York: Farrar, Straus, & Giroux.

Angelou, M. (1997). *I know why the caged bird sings*. New York: Bantam Books.

Armstrong, T. (2003). *The multiple intelligences of reading and writing*. Alexandria, VA: Association for Supervision and Curriculum Development.

Arter, J., & McTighe, J. (2001). *Scoring rubrics in the classroom*. Thousand Oaks, CA: Corwin Press, Inc.

Ayers, W., Hunt, J. A., & Quinn, T. (Ed.). (1998). *Teaching for social justice*. New York: Teachers College Press.

Barber, S. (1990, October 25). *Adagio for strings*, opus 11. Leonard Slatkin, Conductor. Angel Classics.

Barron, T. A. (2000). *Where is grandpa?* Chris Soentpiet, illustrator; Patricia Gauch, (Ed.). New York: Philomel.

Bartlett, J., & Kaplan, J. (Eds.). (1992). *Familiar quotations: A collection of passages, phrases, and proverbs traced to their sources in ancient and modern literature* (16th ed.). Boston: Little, Brown and Company

Bartoletti, S. C. (1996). *Growing up in coal country*. Boston: Houghton Mifflin Company.

Beers, K. (2001, November 17). *Help struggling secondary readers*. Baltimore: NCTE.

Beers, K. (2003). *When kids can't read, what teachers can do*. Portsmouth, NH: Heinemann.

Bell, I. (1998). *Character building in Zindel's Pigman*. English Online. New Zealand Ministry of Education.

Bott, C. (2002, November). Zines—the ultimate creative writing project. *English Journal, 92*(2), 27–33.

Bridges, R., & Lundell, M. (1999). *Through my eyes.* New York: Scholastic.

Bridges, R. S. (1895). Elegy. In Stedman, E. C., (Ed.), *A Victorian Anthology, 1837–1895.* Cambridge, MA: Riverside Press.

Brownlie, F., & Silver, H. G. (1995, January). *Mind's eye.* Paper presented at the seminar "Responding Thoughtfully to the Challenge of Diversity," Delta School District Conference Center, Delta, British Columbia, Canada.

Brozo, W. G. (1990). Learning how at-risk readers learn best: A case for interactive assessment. *Journal of Reading, 33,* 522–527.

Bullard, S. (1994). *Free at last: A history of the Civil Rights Movement and those who died in the struggle.* New York: Oxford University Press Childrens.

Busching, B., & Slesinger, B. A. (2002). *"It's our world too": Socially responsive learners in middle school language arts.* Urbana, IL: National Council of Teachers of English.

Byers, A. (2000). *Teens and pregnancy: A hot issue.* Berkeley Heights, NJ: Enslow Publishers, Inc.

Campbell, J., Voekl, K., & Donahue, P. (1998). *NAEP 1996 trends in academic progress. Achievement of U.S. students in science, 1969–1996; mathematics, 1973–1996; reading, 1971–1996; writing, 1984–1996.* Washington, DC: ED Publications.

Campbell, L., Campbell, B., & Dickinson, D. (1996). *Teaching & learning through multiple intelligences.* Needham Heights, MA: Simon & Schuster.

Canady, R. L., & Rettig, M. D. (Ed). (1996). *Teaching in the block: Strategies for engaging active learners.* Larchmont, NY: Eye on Education.

Carey-Webb, A. (2001). *Literature and lives.* Urbana, IL: National Council of Teachers of English.

Chapman, T. (Performer). (1988). *Across the lines.* (Compact Disc Recording). New York: Elektra Records.

Christensen, L. (2001). "Where I'm from: Inviting students' lives into the classroom. In: B. Bigelow, B. Harvey, S. Karp, & L. Miller (Eds.), *Rethinking our classrooms: Teaching for equity and justice,* Vol. 2. Milwaukee, WI: Rethinking Schools, Ltd.

Cisneros, S. (1991). *Women hollering creek and other stories.* New York: Random House.

Claggett, F. (1992). *Drawing your own conclusions.* Portsmouth, NH: Heinemann.

Claggett, F. (1996). *A measure of success: From assignments to assessment in English language arts.* Portsmouth, NH: Heinemann Boynton/Cook.

Clark, C. T. (2002, December/2003, January). Unfolding narratives of service learning: Reflections on teaching, literacy, and positioning in service relationships. *Journal of Adolescent and Adult Literacy, 46*(4), 288–297.

Cleveland Clinic Health Information Center. *Rate and Date Rape.* Retrieved on August 21, 2002, from http://www.clevelandclinic.org/health/health-info/docs/0600/0613.asp?index=4538.

Cooney, C. B. (1990). *The face on the milk carton.* New York: Bantam Doubleday Dell.

Cooney, C. B. (1993). *Whatever happened to Janie?* New York: Dell Laurel Leaf.

Cooney, C. B. (1996). *The voice on the radio*. New York: Bantam Doubleday Dell.

Cooney, C. B. (2000). *What Janie found.* New York: Dell Laurel Leaf.

Covey, S. (1988). *The seven habits of highly effective teens.* New York: Fireside.

Cunningham, L. (1996). *Grief and the adolescent.* Newhall, CA: TAG: Teen Age Grief, Inc.

Curtis, C. P. (1995). *The Watsons go to Birmingham—1963: A novel.* New York: Delacorte Press.

Dakos, K. (1998). *Don't read this book, whatever you do: More poems about school.* New York: Aladdin.

Dale, H. (1994). Collaborative writing interactions in one ninth-grade classroom. *Journal of Educational Research, 87*(6), 334–344.

Dale, H. (1997). *Co authoring in the classroom.* Urbana, IL: NCTE.

Daniels, H. (1998). Jotting and sketching: Twenty-three ways to use a notebook. In H. Daniels & M. Bizar's *Methods that matter: Six structures for best practice classrooms.* Portland, ME: Stenhouse Publishers.

Daniels, H. (2002). *Literature circles: Voice and choice in book clubs & reading groups.* Portland, ME: Stenhouse Publishers.

Danks, C., & Rabinsky, L. (Ed.). (1999). *Teaching for a tolerant world: Grades 9–12, essays and resources.* Urbana, IL: National Council of Teachers of English.

Davidson, M. (1994). *I have a dream: The story of Martin Luther King.* New York: Scholastic Press.

Davis, O. (1995). *Just like Martin.* London: Puffin.

Denner, P. R., & McGinley, W. J. (1992). Effects of prereading activities on junior high students' recall. *Journal of Educational Research, 86,* 11–19.

Dewey, J. (1916/1944). *Democracy and education.* New York: Free Press.

Dixon, F. W. (1988). *Cult of crime.* Madison, WI: Demco Media.

Dornfield, M., Clayborn, C., & Hine, D. C. (Eds.). (1995). *The turning tide: From the desegregation of the armed forces to the Montgomery bus boycott (1948–1956).* Broomall, PA: Chelsea House.

Doyle, W. (2001). *An American insurrection: The battle of Oxford, Mississippi, 1962.* New York: Doubleday.

Draper, S. (1994). *Tears of a tiger.* New York: Atheneum Books for Young Readers.

Dresang, E. (1999). *Radical change: Books for youth in a digital age.* New York: The H. W. Wilson Company.

Edelsky, C. (Ed.). (1999). *Making justice our project: Teachers working toward critical whole language practice.* Urbana, IL: National Council of Teachers of English.

Englander, A. (1997). *Dear diary, I'm pregnant.* New York: Annick Press.

Fairweather, R. (1998). *Basic studio directing: Media manual.* Oxford, UK: Focal Press.

FindMissingKids.com. Retrieved on March 3, 2003, from http://findmissingkids.com/shocking.htm.

Fink, D. (2003). *Creating significant learning experiences.* San Francisco: Jossey-Bass.

Fleischman, P. (1988). *Joyful noise: Poems for two voices.* New York: Harper-Collins.

Froomkin, D. (October, 1998). Affirmative action under attack. *The Washington Post company.* Retrieved on July 23, 2003, from http://www.washingtonpost.com/wp-srv/politics/special/affirm/affirm.htm.

Gardner, H. (1983). *Frames of mind: The theory of multiple intelligences.* New York: Basic Books.

Garland, S. (1994). *I never knew your name.* New York: Ticknor & Fields.

Gillet, J., & Kita, M. J. (1979). Words, kids and categories. *The Reading Teacher, 32,* 538–542.

Glasgow, J. (2002). Cyber journaling for justice. In *Standards-based activities with scoring rubrics for middle and high school English.* Vol. 1: Performance-based portfolios. Larchmont, NY: Eye on Education.

Glasgow, J. (2002). *Using young adult literature: Thematic activities based on Gardner's multiple intelligences.* Norwood, MA: Christopher-Gordon Publishers, Inc.

Goodnough, D. (2000). *Cult awareness: A hot issue.* Berkeley Heights, NJ: Enslow.

Guthrie, J. T., & Davis, M. H. (2003). Motivating struggling readers in middle school through an engagement model of classroom practice. *Reading and Writing Quarterly, 19,* 59–85.

Guthrie, J. T., & Wigfield, A. (2000). Engagement and Motivation in Reading. In M. Kamil, R. Barr, P. L. Mosentah,. & P. D. Pearson (Eds.), *Handbook of Reading Research* (Vol 3, pp. 403–425) New York: Longman.

Hamilton, V. (1974). *M. C. Higgins, The great.* New York: Aladdin Paperbacks.

Harmon, B. (1992). *Dead drunk: The Kevin Tunell story.* (Videotape). New York: Ambrose Video.

Haskins, J. (1997). *Bayard Rustin: Behind the scenes of the Civil Rights Movement.* New York: Hyperion.

Haskins, J. (2000) *Jesse Jackson: Civil rights activist (African-American biographies).* Berkeley Heights, NJ: Enslow.

Haskins, J., & Haskins, J. (1999). *The day Martin Luther King, Jr. was shot: A photo history of the Civil Rights Movement.* New York: Bt. Bound.

Holbrook, S. (1996). *The dog ate my homework.* Honesdale, PA: Boyds Mill Press.

Howe, J. (2001). *The misfits.* New York: Atheneum.

Jacobs, H. H. (1989). *Interdisciplinary curriculum: Design and implementation.* Alexandria, VA: Association for Supervision and Curriculum Development.

Keene, E., & Zimmermann, S. (1997). *Mosaic of thought: Teaching comprehension in a reader's workshop.* Portsmouth, NH: Heinemann.

Keslo, M. J. (1988). *Abducted!* New York: Markel.

Kight, S. (2000). *World literature: Opening the door to a 'world' of assessments.* Athens, OH: Southeast Ohio Council of Teachers of English.

King, C., Osborne, L. B., & Brookes, J. (1997). *Oh, freedom! Kids talk about the*

Civil Rights Movement with the people who made it happen. Mississauga, ON, Canada: Alfred A. Knopf.

King, M. L., Shepard, K., (Ed.), & Carson, C. (Ed.). (2002). *A Call to conscience: The landmark speeches of Dr. Martin Luther King, Jr.* New York: Warner.

Kreiner, A. (1997). *In control: Learning to say no to sexual pressure.* New York: The Rosen Publishing Group, Inc.

Langelan, M. (1993). *Back off!: How to confront and stop sexual harassment and harassers.* New York: Simon & Schuster Adult Publishing Group.

Leone, B. (Ed.). (1999). *Poverty: Opposing viewpoints.* San Diego, CA: Greenhaven Press, Inc.

Lerman, E. (1997). *Teen moms: The pain and the promise.* Buena Park, CA: Morning Glory Press.

Levine, E. (2000). *Freedom's children: Young civil rights activists tell their own stories.* London: Puffin.

Long, D. *Kidnapped.* Retrieved on March 3, 2003, from http://duncanlong.com/science-fiction-fantasy-short-stories/kidnap.html.

The Long Walk Home. (1990). (Videotape). New York: Miramax.

Lowry, L. (1993). *The giver.* New York: Bantam Doubleday Dell.

Lyon, G. E. (1994). *Mama is a miner.* Paintings by Peter Catalanotto. New York: Orchard Books.

Lyon, G. E. (1997). *With a hammer for my heart.* New York: Avon Books, Inc.

Lyon, G. E. (1999). Where I'm from. In Lyon's *Where I'm from: Where poems come from.* Photographs by Robert Hoskins. Spring, TX: Absey & Company.

Mackey, M. (2001, September). The survival of engaged reading in the internet age: New media, old media, and the book. *Children's Literature in Education, 32*(3), 167–187.

Mauer, M. (1999, April). The crisis of the young African-American male and the criminal justice system. *The sentencing project.* Retrieved on July 21, 2003, from http://www.sentencingproject.org/pdfs/5022.pdf.

McCaslin, N. (1990). *Creative drama in the classroom* (5th ed.). White Plains, NY: Longman.

McClure, M. F. (1990). Collaborative learning: Teacher's game or students' game? *English Journal, 79*(2), 66–68.

Meek, M. (1983). *Achieving literacy: Longitudinal studies of adolescents learning to read.* London: Kegan Paul.

Me, S. (1987). I am poem. In R. Padgett (Ed.), *The teachers & writers handbook of poetic forms.* New York: Teachers and Writers Collaborative.

Miller, B. (1997). *Teenage pregnancy and poverty: The economic realities.* New York: The Rosen Publishing Group, Inc.

Monseau, V. (1996). *Responding to young adult literature.* Portsmouth, NH: Heinemann Boynton/Cook.

Monte, D. P. (2002). *Trustworthy.* Dayton, OH: Oakwood.

Mullis, I., Campbell, J., & Farstrup, A. (1993). *NAEP 1992: Reading report card for the nations and the states.* Washington, DC: U.S. Department of Education.

Myers, W. D. (1999). *Monster.* Illustrations by Christopher Myers. New York:

HarperCollins Children's Books.

Myers, W. D. (2000). *145th street: Short stories.* New York: Delacorte Press.

Nakajima, C. (1993). *A guide for using journey to topaz in the classroom.* Westminster, CA: Teacher Created Materials, Inc.

Nasaw, J. (1993). *Shakedown street.* New York: Delacorte Press.

National Institute of Mental Health. (2000, September). *Depression.* Retrieved September, 2000, from http://www.nimh.nih.gov/publicat/depression.cfm#intro.

Nixon, J. L. (1999). *The kidnapping of Christina Lattimore.* New York: Bt. Bound.

Noden, H. (1999). *Image grammar: Using grammatical structures to teach writing.* Portsmouth, NH: Heinemann Boynton/Cook.

Ogle, D. M. (1992). KWL in action: Secondary teachers find applications that work. In *Reading in the Content Areas: Improving Classroom Instruction* (3rd ed.). E. K. Kishner, T. W. Bean, J. E. Readence, & D. W. Moore (Eds.). Dubuque, IA: Kendall-Hunt.

Olson, C. B., & Schiesl, S. (1996, Spring). A multiple intelligences approach to teaching multicultural literature. *Language Arts Journal of Michigan, 12*(1), 21–28.

Parks, R., & Reed, G. J. (2000). *Quiet strength.* Grand Rapids, MI: Zondervan.

Parks, R., Haskins, J., & Haskins, J. (1999). *Rosa Parks: My story.* London, England: Puffin.

Pascale, F. (1992). *Kidnapped by the cult (Sweet Valley High, no. 82).* New York: Bantam.

Patneaude, D., Micich, P., & Mathews, J. (1993). *Someone was watching.* Morton Grove, IL: Albert Whitman.

Payne, R. K. (1998). *A framework for understanding poverty.* Highlands, TX: RFT.

Peck, I. (2000). *The life and words of Martin Luther King, Jr.* New York: Scholastic.

Pepler, D., & Craig, W. (2000, April). Making a difference in bullying. Report #60 LaMarsh Centre for Research on Violence and Conflict Resolution. New York: New York University.

Pinkwater, J. (1987). *The disappearance of sister perfect.* New York: E. P. Dutton.

Poetry Alive. Retrieved on August 19, 2003, from http://www.poetryalive.com.

Porterfield, K. M. (1995). *Straight talk about cults.* Retrieved on March 3, 2003, from http://www.FactsonFile.com.

Rasinski, T., & Padak, N. (2004). *Effective reading strategies: Teaching children who find reading difficult* (3rd ed.). Upper Saddle River, NJ: Pearson Education, Inc.

Rennert, R. S. (Ed.). (1993). *Civil rights leaders (profiles of great black Americans).* Broomal, PA: Chelsea House.

Ritchie, N. (2003). *The Civil Rights Movement.* Hauppauge, NY: Barrons Educational.

Robb, L. (2000). *Teaching reading in middle school: A strategic approach to teaching reading that improves comprehension and thinking.* New York: Scholastic.

Robb, L. (2002, May). Multiple texts: Multiple opportunities for teaching and learning. *Voices in the Middle, 9*(4), 28–38.

Rochman, H. (1993). *Against borders: Promoting books for a multicultural world.* Chicago: American Library Association.

Romano, T. (2000). *Blending genre, altering style: Writing multigenre papers.* Portsmouth, NH: Heinemann Boynton/Cook.

Rose, R. (1990). *Twelve angry men.* (Videotape). MGM/UP Home Video, Inc.

Rosenblatt, L. M. (1995). *Literature as exploration.* (5th ed.). New York: Modern Language Association.

Roybal, L. (1994). *Billy.* Boston: Houghton Mifflin Company.

Rozakis, L. (1995). *Homelessness: Can we solve the problem?* New York: Henry Holt and Company, Inc.

Ryder, R. J., & Graves, M. F. (2003). *Reading and learning in content areas* (3rd ed.). New Jersey: John Wiley & Sons.

Salvner, G. M. (2001). Lessons and lives: Why young adult literature matters. *The ALAN Review, 28*(3), 9.

Schmuck, R., & Schmuck, P. (2000). *Group processes in the classroom* (8th ed.). Dubuque, IA: William C. Brown.

Sebestyan, O. (1995). *The girl in the box.* New York: Bantam Starfire.

Seuss, Dr. (1990). *Oh, the places you'll go!* New York: Random House.

Shneidman, E. (1996). *The suicidal mind.* New York: Oxford University Press.

Short, K., & Burke, C. (1991). *Creating curriculum: Teachers and students as community of learners.* Portsmouth, NH: Heinemann.

Short, K. G., Harste, J. C. (with Burke, C.). (1996). *Creating classrooms for authors and inquirers* (2nd ed.). Portsmouth, NH: Heinemann.

Silverstein, S. (1974). *Where the sidewalk ends.* New York: HarperCollins.

Slavin, R.E. (1989). Students at risk of school failure: The problem and its dimensions. In R. E. Slavin, N. L. Karweit, & N. A. Madden (Eds.), *Effective programs for students at risk.* Needham Heights, MA: Allyn & Bacon.

Smagorinsky, P. (2002). *Teaching English through principled practice.* Upper Saddle River, NJ: Pearson Education, Inc.

Snicket, L. (1999). *The bad beginning.* New York: Scholastic.

Snyder, Z. K. (1985). *Famous Stanley kidnapping case.* New York: Yearling.

Sommer, R. L. (1993). *Norman Rockwell: A classic treasury.* Greenwich, CT: Barnes & Noble.

Stover, L. T. (2003, March). Mind the Gap: Building Bridges between Adolescent Readers and Texts. *English Journal, 92*(4) 77–83.

Thesman, J. (1990). *Rachel Chance.* Boston: Houghton Mifflin Company.

Thomas, K., & Moorman, G. (1983). *Designing reading programs.* Dubuque, IA: Kendall Hunt.

Tierney, R. J., Readence, J. E., & Dishner, E. K. (1995). *Reading strategies and practices: A compendium* (4th ed.). Boston: Allyn and Bacon.

Tjaden, P., & Thoennes, N. (1998). *Prevalence, incidence and consequences of violence against women: Findings from the national violence against women survey.* Washington, DC: National Institute of Justice, Office of Justice Programs, U.S. Deptartment of Justice.

Trapani, M. (1997). *Listen up! Teenage mothers speak out.* New York: The Rosen Publishing Group, Inc.

Trapani, M. (1997). *Reality check: Teenage fathers speak out.* New York: The Rosen Publishing Group, Inc.

Turner, T. N. (1997). Engaging social studies book reports. *Social Studies and the Young Learner, 9,* 5–7.

U.C. Berkeley Library. *Evaluating web pages: Techniques to apply and questions to ask.* Retrieved on September 12, 2003, from http://www.lib.berkeley.edu/TeachingLib/Guides/Internet/Evaluate.html.

United States Department of Justice. *An analysis of data on rape and sexual assault.* Washington, DC: U.S. Department of Justice Bureau of Justice Statistics. Retrieved on August 21, 2002, from http://www.ojp.usdoj.gov/bjs/pub/pdf/soo.pdf and http://www.ojp.usdoj.gov/bjs/glance/rape.htm.

Vacca, R., & Vacca, J. (1996). *Content area reading* (5th ed). New York: HarperCollins.

Vacca, R., & Vacca, J. (1999). *Content area reading: Literacy and learning across the curriculum* (6th ed.). New York: Longman.

Vygotsky, L. (1978). *Mind in society: The development of higher psychological processes.* Cambridge, MA: Harvard University Press.

Waddell, M., & James, R. (1997). *Kidnapping of Suzy Q.* London: Chadwick.

Werlin, N. (2001). *Locked inside.* New York: Laurel Leaf.

Wilhelm, J., Baker, T., & Dube, J. (2001). *Strategic reading: Guiding students to lifelong literacy, 6-12.* Portsmouth, NH: Heinemann Boyton/Cook.

Wilkinson, B., Young, A., Jackson, J. L., & Gallin, R. (1990). *Jesse Jackson: Still fighting for the dream (history of the Civil Rights Movement).* New York: Silver Burdett.

Wilson, C. (2001). *Rosa Parks: From the back of the bus to the front of a movement (scholastic biography).* New York: Scholastic.

Wise Brown, M. (1949). *The important book.* New York: HarperCollins.

Wolf, A. (1990). *Something is going to happen: Poetry performance for the classroom.* Canada: Poetry Alive Publications.

Wolff, V. E. (1993). *Make lemonade.* New York: Scholastic.

Wolff, V. E. (2002). *True believer.* New York: Scholastic.

Yarick, S.J. (1995). *The write course: A writing course for community college freshman.* Ottawa, KS: The Writing Conference, Inc.

Index
· · · · · · ·

About the Contributors

Allison Baer is a middle school reading special-ist for Warren City Schools, Warren, Ohio, who is currently a doctoral candidate in middle school literacy at Kent State University, Kent, Ohio. Allison is a past president of OCTELA (Ohio Council of Teachers of English Language Arts), a 1997 Fellow of the National Writing Project at Kent State University, received the Outstanding English Language Arts Educator Award from OCTELA for 2003, and received the Sallie Mae First Year Teacher Award for 1996. She is an active member in OCTELA as well as NCTE and is a frequent presenter at local, state, and national conferences. Allison's research interest is in adolescent readers' engagement in literature. She has also published a chapter in *Using Young Adult Literature: Thematic Activities Based on Gardner's Multiple Intelligences* by Christopher-Gordon in 2002.

Susan Cappetta is a talented middle school teacher of English and social studies at The Fenn School in Concord, Massachusetts. Her B.A. is from Dartmouth College, M.Ed. from Tufts University, and she is cur-rently working on M.A. Children's Literature from Simmons College. Her research interests include multigenre and multi-narratives in Young Adult lit-erature, as well as the intertextual and metafictive com-ponents of Young Adult literature. More specifically, she is interested in creating reading strategies that en-able students to make meaning with these types of

texts. She is an active member in SCBWI (Society of Children's Book Writers and Illustrators), NCTE (National Council of Teachers of English) and ALAN (Assembly of Literature for Adolescents for NCTE).

Linda J. Rice teaches in the Department of English at Ohio University. She earned her Ph.D. (2002) in Curriculum and Instruction from Kent State University, her M.Ed. (1995) in Administration from Westminster College (PA), and her B.A. (1992) in Communication Arts and Literature/Secondary Education from Grove City College (PA). Linda's current classroom based research focuses on performance-based assessments and rubrics with a particular application to young adult literature. Linda's work has been published by Eye on Education (2001) and Christopher Gordon Publishers (2001). In 1998, Linda was named "Outstanding High School Language Arts Educator" by the Ohio Council of Teacher Award from *The Tribune Chronicle*. Linda has ten years of high school teaching experience and earned her National Board Certification in AYA/Language Arts in 2000 before coming to the university to work with pre-service teachers. Linda is an active member of OCTELA and NCTE and routinely presents at their conferences.

Joyce Rowland has been teaching middle and high school English at Bristol High School, Bristolville, Ohio, for twenty-seven years. Joyce holds a M.S. in Educational Administration from Youngstown State University, Youngstown, Ohio. She is a Martha Holden Jennings Scholar and recipient of the Warren *Tribune Chronicle* A+ Teacher Award. Her areas of interest include curriculum development, especially using Gardner's Multiple Intelligences. She was active in developing hands-on English curriculum for the Ohio Tech Prep Consortium in Trumbull County. She is a frequent presenter for the Trumbull County Literacy Conference, OCTELA and NCTE Spring and Fall

Conferences. She also published a chapter in *Using Young Adult Literature: Thematic Activities Based on Gardner's Multiple Intelligences* by Christopher-Gordon in 2002.

Colleen A. Ruggieri teaches American literature, composition, and honors English at Boardman High School in Boardman, Ohio. Ruggieri earned a B.S. in Journalism from Ohio University, a B.S. in Comprehensive Communications Education from Kent State University, and a M.S. in Curriculum and Instruction from Ashland University. She completed post graduate studies at the Bread Loaf School of English campuses in Vermont and Alaska. She has published seven articles in The English Journal, and numerous articles  in other professional magazines and journals. She has been active in writing about ways to implement the state standards into language arts curriculum. Ruggieri's special interests include multigenre writing, multiple intelligences, and adolescent literacy. She is a National Board Certified Teacher, Boardman High School Teacher of the Year, OCTELA High School Teacher of the Year, NCTE Distinguished Teaching Award, Governor's Leadership Award. She is President of the Western Reserve Teachers of English and President-Elect of OCTELA.

 Carolyn Suttles has been teaching English at Bristol High School, Bristolville, Ohio for the last 20 years. She received her BS in Education at Bowling Green State University, Bowling Green, Ohio and her MA in English at Youngstown State University, Youngstown, Ohio. She has distinguished herself by receiving the A+ Teaching Award from *The Tribune Chronicle* and was chosen as a Martha Holden Jennings Scholar. Her special interests include curriculum development using Gardner's Multiple Intelligences. She was a contributor to Trumbull County Tech Prep Communications Curriculum and has published articles in the *Ohio Journal of English Language Arts* and *Inside CEA* (Career Education Association Journal) which reflect her philosophy of teaching. She contributed a chapter in *Using Young Adult Literature: Thematic Activities Based on Gardner's Multiple Intelligences* by Christopher-Gordon in 2002. Currently, she is President of the Ohio Council of Teachers of English. She is a well-known presenter at state and national conferences such as Trumbull Literacy, OCTELA and NCTE.

About the Editor

After having taught English Language Arts in secondary schools for eighteen years, Jacqueline Glasgow earned her Ph.D. in Curriculum and Instruction in Literacy and now teaches in the Department of English at Ohio University, Athens, Ohio. As professor of English education, her courses include: Survey of Young Adult Literature, Readings in Children's Literature, Teaching Language and Composition, and Teaching Literature in Secondary Schools. She was named Outstanding High School Language Arts Educator by OCTELA (Ohio Council of Teachers of English Language Arts) in 1998. She was recipient of the Education Press Association of America Distinguished Award given for Excellence in Educational Journalism to International Reading Association for "Accommodating Learning Styles in Prison Writing Classes" *Journal of Reading*, Learned Article, 1994. She works with secondary teachers in Ohio on implementing state standards and assessment, reading instruction, curriculum development, literature instruction, and teacher research. She is a frequent presenter at OCTELA, NCTE (National Council of Teachers of English, and SIRI (Summer Institute of Reading Intervention) sponsored by the Ohio Department of Education. She is author of numerous articles in state and national English journals and editor of four books: Using *Young Adult Literature: Thematic Activities Based on Gardner's Multiple Intelligences* published by Christopher-Gordon (2002), *Standards-Based Activities with Scoring Rubrics for Middle and High School English*, *Volume 1 Performance-Based Portfolios and Volume 2 Performance-Based Projects* published by Eye on Education (2002), and now this one, *Reading Strategies for Social Issues in Young Adult Literature* by Christopher-Gordon (2004).